HOMILIES FOR WEEKDAYS
OF THE YEAR
Years 1 and 2

HOMILIES
FOR
WEEKDAYS
OF THE
YEAR
Years 1 and 2

MARTIN McNAMARA, M.S.C.
General Editor

Costello Publishing Company, Inc.

COSTELLO PUBLISHING COMPANY, INC.
P. O. Box 9
Northport, New York 11768

Library of Congress Catalog Card Number: 77-91004
International Standard Book Number: 0-918344-04-2

Printed in the United States of America

CONTENTS

FIRST READINGS, YEAR TWO

GOSPEL READINGS, BOTH YEARS

FIRST WEEK OF ADVENT

First Reading (Is. 2:1-5). *God draws all peoples into the eternal peace of his kingdom.* The prophet sees the New Jerusalem as a centre of peace and reconciliation for all peoples. The Church of Christ should similarly be a place where all men can find pardon and peace. Is our Church an effective power for reconciliation between men? Are we ourselves, individually, instruments of peace and not of division, advocates of reconciliation and not of discord and violence?

Alternative First Reading (Is 4:2-6). *God will come to dwell with his people and heal them of their sins and divisions.* God's people will suffer and undergo trials. But chastisement is never his final word; that is always salvation. And so it is that after cleansing trials God will come again to be with his people—the faithful few who continued to believe in his ultimate goodness, and came through purified and pardoned. Out of death comes life! God has come to us in Christ. Do we believe that he is with us always, in good times and bad?

Gospel (Mt 8:5-11). *Christ marvels at the centurion's faith and heals his servant.* Jesus is 'astonished' at the extraordinary faith of this officer of the Roman legion. It was the faith of a good and compassionate man, who cared so much for his servant that he was determined to do all he could to save him. And it was a faith that set no conditions. It is this kind of faith, and not any privileged position, which is the passport to the kingdom of heaven. It is this kind of faith that crosses the barriers that divide people and helps bring about reconciliation and peace.

First Reading (Is 11:1-10). *The Messiah brings reconciliation and peace.* The Spirit-filled Messiah will institute an era of justice and peace for all, and his reign will be characterised by compassion for the weak and the poor. Acknowledgment of God's sovereignty and the living out of his commandments is the surest foundation for peace and harmony among men. We have a duty to work for peace and justice, as we continue to hope for that ultimate future for which in faith the people of Israel hoped too.

Gospel (Lk 10:21-24). *The ways of God are revealed to those with childlike faith.* Jesus rejoiced at seeing the power of God at work in his disciples and in their work. They have, by God's grace, come to see and hear what many prophets and kings have desired to see and hear— namely, that the messianic era was present and a reality in the person of Jesus himself. We should keep ever in mind that the person of Jesus and the meaning of his coming is not grasped by wisdom alone; in fact, it is known only by the revelation of God the Father. Curiously, it is often the unlettered who accept this insight of God; the wise, too reliant on their own powers, fail to see the wood for the trees. All of us need the true wisdom of simplicity of heart to penetrate the secret of Christ.

WEDNESDAY

First Reading (Is 25:6-10). *God offers to all of us a place in his kingdom, where there will be unending joy and happiness.* The prophet uses the image of a heavenly banquet to symbolise eternal happiness and the blessings which will be a part of God's kingdom. There will be universal peace and harmony, intimate friendship with God, and there will be no evils to spoil the idyll. Death, fear and all sorrow will be absent. This 'dream' may appear a long way from realisation. But it is paradoxically a reality. For only God can satisfy our deepest aspirations for peace, happiness and harmony. He has made a start in Christ. That gives us courage as we work towards the full realisation of the 'dream'.

Gospel (Mt 15:29-37). *The kindness of Jesus in the face of human need.* The several cures worked by Jesus and the miracle of the multiplication of the loaves clearly reveal his mercy and compassion. He exercises his messianic power to conquer the evils that hurt people, and he brings people together in the fellowship of a meal. All of this mirrors and is indeed the goodness of God. This is what God is like. God loves man, and he has shown us what that love means in the person and ministry of Jesus. Do we ever say thanks to God for what he is and has done for us?

THURSDAY

First Reading (Is 26:1-6). *If we trust in God we shall not be disappointed.* The prophet expresses great confidence in the Lord, his God. He is utterly dependable, an 'everlasting rock'. He has set aside a 'strong city' —the New Jerusalem—for the God-fearing and upright of heart (the 'poor' and 'lowly'). There they will live in peace and prosperity, protected by the Lord, who will destroy their enemies. Such is the security God brings to those who trust in him rather than in their own power.

Gospel (Mt 7:21, 24-27). *The person who enters the kingdom of heaven is the one who does, not just hears, the will of God.* Jesus here states the criterion of true discipleship. It is not enough to profess allegiance to Christ; the acid test is whether one does the will of God in his daily life or not. The sincerity of a man's conviction is proved not so much by what he says as by the manner in which he lives. 'By their fruits you shall know them'.

FRIDAY

First Reading (Is 29:17-24). *A promise of redemption and better times ahead.* The prophet foretells how the lowly and oppressed will come into their own in the days of the Messiah. A complete upheaval of the order of things will take place. Arrogant oppressors will be brought low; the poor will be exultant and joyful. Pagan nations, seeing the great favours of the Lord towards his people, will be converted. We too need to hope in the face of our own failures and the difficulties of life. We have God as our rock, and we know that if we remain faithful to him, we also will be redeemed and transformed. It is a happy and consoling thought amidst the 'slings and arrows of outrageous fortune' that make their way into the lives of even the most fortunate of us.

Gospel (Mt 9:27-31). *Christ asks each of us to believe in him.* The kernel of this passage is the profession of faith that men are brought to make in answer to the question of Jesus. Their sincerity and earnestness has been proved, and they are cured of their blindness. It is a law of life that each person must learn to stand and walk alone. This is equally true in the spiritual life. Each of us has to face Jesus alone and affirm or refuse his or her own absolute commitment to God. Our faith in him, like that of the blind men, will bring its own transformation in train, and then we too will want to tell everyone what great things God has done for us.

SATURDAY

First Reading (Is 30:19-21, 23-26). *A picture of a restored and redeemed people.* The prophet uses various images to bring home to the people of Israel the happiness that would be theirs when the day of salvation dawned. There will be great prosperity, and a certain transfiguration of nature will take place. All of which will make the days of suffering and distress, that had been theirs, things of the past. What the passage tells us is, that whatever our present sorrows and inadequacies, God will eventually put all things right in a way that will surpass even our wildest

imaginings. Then, like the people of Israel, we too, purified and pardoned, will be able to enter into eternal joy.

Gospel (Mt 9:35; 10:1, 6-8). *Each Christian is a missionary for Christ.*
Jesus, out of compassion for the multitudes (who were spiritually
leaderless and heirs of all the consequences of that—such as bewilder-
ment, doubt, loneliness and error) enlisted the aid of others to further
his mission. He commissions the apostles to preach the Good News; he
would be with them sharing his powers over evil. Each Christian is a
missionary for Christ by definition. And he must fulfill this role not
just in words but in deeds. For 'no man is an island', and nobody goes
to heaven alone!

SECOND WEEK OF ADVENT

MONDAY

First Reading (Is 35:1-10). *God himself will come to save his people.*
God will come to his people in their exile. The sick and unfortunate
will be healed, and he will open a way of salvation through the desert
for all of them. We are a pilgrim people on a journey through life that
sometimes seems like a dangerous desert. We must keep alive our faith
in God and our hope in a future with him, when 'joy and gladness' will
be ours, and 'sorrow and lament will be ended'.

Gospel (Lk 5:17-26). *Christ forgives our sins.* The forgiveness of sins
where we would expect a physical cure clearly indicates that the
struggle of Jesus was against Satan and the kingdom of evil. Suffering,
sorrow, death and evil are the antitheses of the Kingdom of God which
Jesus proclaimed. Above all sin is the barrier to that kingdom. For us, it
should be a great joy that Jesus, out of his true oneness with God,
enables us to rid ourselves of that destructive force. Like those who
witnessed the miraculous cure of the paralytic we should be filled with
awe and full of the praise of God who does 'strange things'.

TUESDAY

First Reading (Is 40:1-11). *God consoles and strengthens his people.*
God consoles and comforts his exiled people in Babylon. He will bring

them safely back to their homeland. And that homecoming will show forth his glory and majestic mercy. Our God is a God of power and majesty; but he is also a God of mercy. He has compassion for us and looks after our every need. And he is trustworthy. In our helplessness we come to know him as our Saviour.

Gospel (Mt 18:12-14). *God loves each and every one of us.* This brief parable does not say that the one lost sheep is equal to the other ninty-nine. It rather insists on the responsibility of the shepherd for every one of the flock. So too God cares for each one of us, even the 'little ones' of this world. It is our task to imitate this Good Shepherd, whose love for us is a seeking, patient and protecting one.

WEDNESDAY

First Reading (Is 40:25-31). *God, who is all-powerful, gives strength to those who are weary.* God created the stars, brings order out of chaos, and watches over all of his creation continually. He does not 'grow tired or weary'. Such a God was a great comfort to his exiled people, whose unhappy lot inevitably made them a prey to discouragement, doubts and fears. He is no less so for us, aware of the limitations and frailty of our nature. If we continue to believe and hope in him we too shall renew our strength and never succumb to spiritual weariness.

Gospel (Mt 11:28-30). *Jesus offers rest and help to anyone in need.* This is an invitation to the poor, the weary and the weak—in short anyone in need—to come to God. There they will find security and peace. For it is the Christian paradox that God's yoke and service—though demanding— is less burdensome than any made by man. This is so because the yoke of God is 'easy' i.e. well-fitting, and so we might say made to measure. And so the burden of God's service is 'light', for it is given and taken in love. Hence the Jewish Rabbis beautifully put it: 'My burden has become my song'.

THURSDAY

First Reading (Is 41:13-20). *God is the loving Redeemer of his people.* God's deliverance of his people from exile in Babylon reveals the strength and tenderness of his love for them. He is with them in all their difficulties, and will bring them safely to peace and prosperity. Such signs of God's favour could not leave his people indifferent to him. The same is true for us. Because God is with us, our difficulties can be over-come and our future is assured.

Gospel (Mt 11:11-15). *Jesus commends John the Baptist.* John the Baptist's function was to herald the coming of the Kingdom of God in the person and work of Jesus Christ. We Christians, who bear the name of Christ, should also be signposts to God. So, like John, we must decrease, that God may increase. Therein lies our true greatness in the kingdom of heaven.

FRIDAY

First Reading (Is 48:17-19). *God laments the waywardness of his people.* This reading lists the blessings God intended for his people were it not for their faithlessness. If they had listened to his voice as revealed in his commandments and observed them, they would not now be in the tragic situation of exile. Yet all hope is not lost, for the God who gently upbraids them is also their redeemer. Salvation and release is just around the corner if they repent and promise to amend their ways.

Gospel (Mt 11:16-19). *Jesus criticises the perversity of his contemporaries.* People rejected the message of John the Baptist because he was too much of an ascetic. Yet they were not satisfied with Jesus because he mixed with sinners and led an ordinary life. Just as the spoiled children refused to play no matter what game was suggested, so too people used any excuse for not accepting the truth Jesus spoke. Similarly, when we do not want to listen to God we find excuses, often by finding fault with those who speak in his name.

SATURDAY

First Reading (Ecclus 48:1-4, 9-11). *The prophet Elijah is praised for his work.* Elijah was a strange, charismatic figure who must have appeared odd, if not mad, to some of his contemporaries. He possessed extraordinary spiritual power, and assumed great importance when the prophets predicted that he would return to inaugurate the messianic era.

Gospel (Mt 17:10-13). *Jesus explains to his disciples that Elijah had 'returned' in the person of John the Baptist but has not been recognised.* John the Baptist came to prepare the way of the Lord and perfect his people in anticipation of the coming of God's kingdom. In this he fulfilled the mission of Elijah predicted by the prophets—a purifying, reforming crusade. But he was cruelly put to death for his trouble, and so too, hints Jesus, would himself. We, like the disciples, need to learn that to follow Christ means suffering and sacrifice. For he is not an all-conquering warrior-king, but the Suffering Servant who died on the cross.

THIRD WEEK OF ADVENT

First Reading (Num 24:2-7, 15-17). *The pagan Balaam prophesies that a royal figure would arise in Israel and come to rule the world.* God's word was spoken through Balaam to his people during their tedious desert journey to the Promised Land. Its ultimate fulfilment would be in Christ. God often speaks to us through the words and deeds of those who are not Christians. We should listen and learn from them something of the mysterious ways of God himself. We live with the reality and not the dream as Balaam and the Israelites did. We ought then to rejoice in the lordship of Christ, while realising that his kingship is not of this world.

Gospel (Mt 21:23-27). *None are so deaf to God's word as those who do not want to hear.* Jesus did not dispute the right of the chief priests— the spiritual leaders of the people—to question him. But he resented their bad faith, as evidenced in their simulated ignorance and insincerity in reply to his own question. 'Principle not expediency' is easier to talk about than to live! Especially in our relationship to God. Once we allow him into our lives we face the choice of living according to his Spirit, or else cultivating a studied deafness to its voice.

TUESDAY

First Reading (Zeph 3:1-2, 9-13). *Salvation is promised to those who are poor in spirit.* There is no hope of salvation for those who tyrannise others and practise or permit all kinds of social injustice. Salvation is for those who are poor in spirit. This kind of poverty is born in a reliance on God's strength and not our own; it calls for an effort to live in truth, sincerity and peace. In short, it demands inner and external renewal of living. We approach it, though ever so gingerly, when we accept the limitations of our humanity and accept the trials of life, trusting in God's mercy.

Gospel (Mt 21:28-32). *Saying 'Yes' to God means doing something about the way we live.* Like the Jewish leaders and the second son in the parable, we often profess to obey God and do not; we promise a great deal and perform little. We have an ideal to aim at—where our words and our deeds meet and match in perfect unison. As we struggle to achieve what appears impossible, let us keep in mind the reaction of the first son. He refused to accede to his father's wishes at first, then 'thought better of it' and did his bidding. This is a good description of repentance, a very necessary disposition for the Christian.

WEDNESDAY

First Reading (Is 45:6-8, 18, 21-26). *The prophet asks God to bring salvation to all men.* God is the creator of the universe and the unrivalled God of all. His word is efficacious and will accomplish its purpose. So the prophet asks him through his creation (the heavens, the clouds, the earth) to bring salvation to all men. Only one thing is necessary for those who wish to be saved—a humble return to God in trust. For us Christians this prophecy is fulfilled in Christ and in the mission of his Church. It remains our task and our privilege to make that 'victory of justice, integrity and righteousness' available to all those who have not heard it.

Gospel (Lk 7:19-23). *We should pray for enough faith to accept God on his own terms.* John the Baptist was no 'reed shaken in the wind'. Yet he was sufficiently surprised at the approach of Jesus to his mission to wonder if he really was the expected Messiah. Jesus invites him to examine his works and draw his own conclusions. There is always something of the unexpected in our dealings with God. 'My thoughts are not you thoughts and my ways are not yours'. We, no less than John the Baptist, will find it so. And we are blessed if we are not scandalised at finding Jesus different from what we expect.

THURSDAY

First Reading (Is 54:1-10). *God's love for man is everlasting and unshakeable.* The prophet speaks of the covenant between God and his people in terms of a marriage relationship. The Exile represented a break in that union, but now it is over. God has taken back Israel; her life will be renewed; she is not to fear any more. For God has given his word that he will never again forsake her. The primary truth of our faith is that God has first loved us, and that his love is everlasting. It is we who flee from him, not knowing that even our sufferings are 'the shadow of his hand outstretched caressingly'.

Gospel (Lk 7:24-30). *Jesus praises and commends John the Baptist and poses a question for us.* The greatness of John the Baptist was that he was God's messenger whose task was to prepare his people for the coming of the Messiah. Yet he belonged to the age of expectation rather than fulfilment. We are privileged to belong to the latter, through historical accident. Do we really appreciate that we are a favoured people? If not, then like the Pharisees who refused the baptism of John, we are in danger of putting ourselves outside God's plan for us.

FRIDAY

First Reading (Is 56:1-3, 6-8). *God's house is open to all those who believe in him.* The prophet speaks of a time after the exile when Jerusalem and the Temple have been rebuilt. There is exhortation to a real conversion of heart; high standards of action are demanded; discrimination towards 'foreigners' is prohibited. And there is invitation to a joyful sharing in liturgical life. It is all summed up in the phrase: 'My house will be called a house of prayer for all the people's'. There in a nutshell is universality, the joy, the right living and the prayerful reverence that should characterise all true followers of Christ.

Gospel (Jn 5:33-36). *The works of Jesus reveal who he is.* John the Baptist was a witness to Jesus, greater than any other human witness. For all that, he was only a 'lamp alight and shining'. And a lamp 'bears a borrowed light'. The works of Jesus are the works of his Father. But Jesus and the Father are one. So his light is not borrowed; it is his own and bears testimony to who he is. The light of our good works—though like John the Baptist's a borrowed one in Christ—should reveal who we are, and be a testimony to our steady effort to adhere to the Father's will.

DECEMBER 17—24

DECEMBER 17

First Reading (Gen 49:2, 8-10). *The Messiah will be a descendant of the tribe of Judah.* This is a prophecy that announces that the messianic king is to come from the line of Judah. Judah was one of the twelve sons of Jacob from whom the people of Israel claimed descent. The expected messiah-king will be a powerful figure, and all the people will obey him.

Gospel (Mt 1:1-17). *The family tree of Jesus Christ, Son of David.* This passage shows how the prophecy in the preceding reading was fulfilled in Mary's son. The list of Christ's ancestors contains some outstanding people, others who were not great followers of Yahweh, and still others who were not even Jews. God's providence watched over all things, and from that line sprung the greatest son of Israel.

DECEMBER 18

First Reading (Jer 23:5-8). *God promises his people an ideal king of the line of David.* Jeremiah, full of the disappointments of the years that saw the downfall of the kingdom of Judah and the Exile, sees hope for the future among those purified by the exile. Through him God promises that he will restore all things in a Messiah who will come from the Davidic line. This Messiah will establish justice and integrity, and in that way will bring his people together again. Only a true sense of justice and integrity will break down the barriers that divide people from one another.

Gospel (Mt 1:18-24). *Jesus is born of Mary, who was betrothed to Joseph, who was of the line of David.* Joseph took Mary as his wife, and so the child conceived in her by the Holy Spirit became a legitimate descendant of the line of David, to which Joseph himself belonged. Thus he could be recognised as the Messiah. He would bring people together in justice, and so save them from the disorder and divisiveness of sin.

DECEMBER 19

First Reading (Jdgs 13:2-7, 24-25). *The birth of Samson is announced by an angel.* The angel of Yahweh announced to the wife of Manoah, who was childless, that she would conceive and bear a son. This son is Samson. He will be consecrated to God, and from God he will receive great strength, which he will use to protect God's people from the Philistines. What is noteworthy here for us is the provident care of God ordering all things to his plan and purpose.

Gospel (Lk 1:5-25). *The birth of John the Baptist is announced by the angel Gabriel.* The angel of the Lord, Gabriel, announces to Zechariah that his wife Elizabeth will conceive and bear a son. This son will be John the Baptist. He, like Samson, will be consecrated to God; he will be great and will be full of the Holy Spirit, and will bring back many of the people of Israel to true worship of the Lord, their God. Zechariah, because of his own advanced age and that of his wife, doubts that the angel's message can come true. And so he is struck dumb, and will remain so until the child is born.

DECEMBER 20

First Reading (Is 7:101-14). *The sign of the Maiden with Child.* Although King Ahaz refuses to ask God for a sign God gives him one. It promises the birth of a child from a maiden. His name will be Immanuel, which means God-is-with-us. Sometimes, like Ahaz, we too are afraid to look at the signs God gives us of his loving concern for us, lest some unwelcome demands be made on us.

Gospel (Lk 1:26-38). *The Annunciation of the angel Gabriel to Mary.* This is the fulfilment of the prophecy made to King Ahaz. The angel Gabriel announces to Mary that, through the power of the Holy Spirit, she is to become the mother of the Messiah. In this child of Mary God is with us. Mary gave her 'Yes' to God's awesome demand. And the Word was made flesh. God asks our 'Yes' too, so that his words may become known and loved in the world today.

DECEMBER 21

First Reading (Cant 2:8-14). *My Beloved comes leaping over the mountains and bounding over the hills.* The lover described here as 'leaping over the mountains' and 'bounding over the hills' to his beloved is clearly an image of the Son of God being carried in Mary's womb over the hill country of Judah as she goes to visit her cousin Elizabeth. Her arrival will be the occasion for her Son's bringing of grace and joy to Elizabeth and her son.

Alternative First Reading (Zeph 3:14-18) describes the joy and exultation of God's people now that their Saviour and King is in their midst.

Gospel (Lk 1:39-45). *The Visitation of Mary to Elizabeth.* A noteworthy characteristic in this well-known account is the great joy shown by Elizabeth at the coming of Mary, the bearer of the Lord. Similar joy should be ours whenever we too are visited by God.

DECEMBER 22

First Reading (1 Sam 1:24-28). *Hannah gives thanks for the birth of her son, Samuel.* Hannah had prayed to God that she might have a son. Her prayer had been answered. Now she returns to give thanks, and 'makes her son over' to the Lord. The *Responsorial Psalm* is the song of thanksgiving attributed to Hannah.

Gospel (Lk 1:46-56). *Mary's Magnificat.* This is Mary's song of thanksgiving for her son, Jesus. It is clearly modelled on Hannah's song. Like it, there is a joyous celebration of God's preference for the humble and the lowly as he works out his plan of salvation for the world of men and women. We belong to God; all we have comes from him. Why are we sometimes so full of our own self-importance that even the God who made us can find no place in our lives for himself?

DECEMBER 23

First Reading (Mal 3:1-4, 23-24). *The preparations for the coming of the Lord.* Everybody will be given the opportunity to prepare for the Lord's coming by a change of heart. The prophet Elijah will be sent to help people in that preparation. And they will need it. For the Lord will come suddenly and with power, and he will test the purity and loyalty of his people. No one can escape or resist his coming.

Gospel (Lk 1:57-66). *The birth and naming of John the Baptist.* John the Baptist is the Elijah foretold in the first reading. He would preach the necessity of repentance and a change of heart in preparation for the Lord's coming. We who are preparing for Christmas in so many ways these days, should not neglect this preparation stressed by John. For repentance is the only preparation for Christmas that really counts in the end.

DECEMBER 24

First Reading (2 Sam 7:1-5, 8-11, 16). *A prophecy made to David that his line would always stand secure before God.* David makes the mistake of thinking that God's continuing presence with his people depends on the building of a Temple. And so he intends to build one. But God, through Nathan, corrects that line of thought, and promises David that his line would always stand secure before him. 'We often think that we have to "house" God within our buildings or our institutions, whereas he wants to live with us on his own terms.'

Gospel (Lk 1:67-69). *Zechariah's song of thanksgiving and hope for his son, John the Baptist.* Zechariah thanks God for the salvation which has already been achieved, and prays in hope for what will be accomplished in the future, through his son. We can truly make this prayer our own as we praise God for what he has done for us down the ages, and we press onwards in the hope of eternal happiness with him.

THE SEASON OF CHRISTMAS

INTRODUCTION TO THE FIRST LETTER OF JOHN

Although the author of this work states frequently that he is 'writing' to his addressees (cf. 1:4; 2:1, 7, 8, 12, 13, 14, 26; 5:13), it is more like a homily or a theological treatise than a letter. The author's main interest seems to be both to encourage his readers in the observance of the one fundamental Christian commandment and to warn them against errors.

The literary characteristics of the work, together with its theological ideas tend to confirm its traditional attribution to the same author who produced 2 and 3 John and the Fourth Gospel. It is thus to be situated towards the end of the first century.

One of John's main intentions is to denounce incipient gnosticism in the community which he is addressing. Such gnosticism tended to dissociate knowledge of God from morality and, therefore, to relegate teaching or doctrine to a mere object of the intellect. Thus John stresses that true knowledge of God is inseparable from the kind of behaviour which God has revealed in Christ. To 'know' in the Bible means to have intimate 'existential' acquaintance with the object of the knowledge. In Christ God has revealed himself as love. Moreover, he has revealed man's vocation to share in that love by loving his fellow men. This he has done through the commandment to love which 'binds' men to Christ and, therefore, to God himself. Thus true Christian knowledge of God is acquired not merely by the mind but by the whole human person, as he follows God in loving. Christian knowledge of God and loving are, therefore, one and the same reality. To claim to know God while hating one's fellow is to live a lie.

Further Reading. Bruce Vawter, The Johannine Epistles, in *Jerome Biblical Commentary, II,* 404-412.

INTRODUCTION TO CHRISTMASTIDE GOSPEL READINGS

The Gospel readings for the weekdays between December 29 and the end of the Epiphany season are taken from all four evangelists. This does not mean that they are chosen at random. A central theme runs through them all in that they all speak of the manifestation of Christ. A progression is also noticeable in the readings. The earlier ones speak of the revelation of Jesus to those who awaited the redemption of Israel (December 29 and 30). Next we hear John the Baptist point out to Israel that the Messiah is already among men (January 2-4). Finally, we read of Jesus revealing himself to men during the course of his public life (January 5-12). These readings, then, form an excellent transition between the Christmas-Epiphany season and the yearly cycle in which the Gospel readings of the public life of Jesus begin. The responsorial psalms and the Alleluia verses follow the same pattern as the Gospel readings and speak of the coming of the kingdom of God and the manifestation of Christ.

DECEMBER 29

First Reading (1 John 2:1-11). *The True Knowledge of God.* John here expresses, in his own way, the message of Jesus concerning the relationship between 'faith' and 'works'. Since God *is* love (cf. 4:8) and his 'word' is his self-communication, the proper reception of this 'word' must involve communion with the love that is God. According to the Christian view, God is known only by loving. If you want to know God, love your neighbour. By this love, God's love is 'perfected'. In other words, men are called to be the instruments or channels of God's love for the world.

Gospel (Lk 2:22-35). *This child will be a light to all the peoples of the earth.* Luke's infancy narrative is flooded with the Old Testament. Today's passage does not speak solely of a post-Christmas event in our Lord's life; it illustrates the effects of his appearance among us. We should note how Luke emphasises the point that Mary and Joseph took the child Jesus to Jerusalem to present him in the temple as was required by the law of Moses; thus saying in his own way what Paul tells the Galatians: when the fulness of time had come God sent his own Son, born of a woman, born under the law, to purchase freedom for the subjects of the law (Gal 4:4-5). But Jesus, Simeon announces, was not only the fulfilment of the promises made to Israel: he was the light to enlighten the pagans.

DECEMBER 30

First Reading (2:12-17). *The Christian and the World.* Although, by faith and baptism, the Christian has already become a child of God and, therefore, conquered evil, he still has to make every effort not to 'love' the 'world'—designating all that is contrary to and at enmity with God. In other words, his behaviour is to flow from a recognition of God's initiative in his life, not from the impulse of his own desire and pride.

Gospel (Lk 3:36-40). *God comes to those who patiently wait for him.* After a prophet, a prophetess—the delicate hand of Luke. Simone Weil, in her writings, stresses the importance of 'waiting on God' in patience. This is a basic christian attitude of enduring constancy in time of affliction, of perseverance with hope. Today it is typified in the figure of Anna, who patiently waited through the trials of a long life, through marriage and widowhood, for eighty-four years, and was eventually rewarded by seeing the Christ. Those who wait on the Lord will not be disappointed.

DECEMBER 31

First Reading (2:18-21). *The Christian's Anointing.* John warns us about the 'lie' that is propagated by the 'antichrist'—the denial that Jesus is the Christ and the denial of Father and Son. For if one accepts that Jesus is the Christ, that is, God's principal agent, one acknowledges that God has 'come' in the 'flesh', in human nature, and implicitly that all men are called to be sons of the Father. Such an acceptance or 'knowledge', is a pure gift of God's choice or election, and is symbolised by the Christian's anointing at his baptism. The Christian is taught interiorly by God and thus has an absolute conviction of the truth.

Gospel (Jn 1:1-18). *The Word was made flesh and dwelt among us full of grace and truth.* This prologue to the fourth gospel is a sublime statement of the central christian truth: the Incarnation. The Word through whom all things were made (Gen 1), the Word of God which remains forever (Is 40:8), this Word became flesh, and flesh will never be the same again—because the divine Word was indeed made flesh and has come to live as man among men and women. He, Son of God, has become a son of man, and he empowers the children of men to become children of God. John wrote both gospel and epistle that we might believe in Christ and find life in him and through him.

JANUARY 2

First Reading (2:22-28). *Staying in the Truth.* If the Christian's possession of the truth is the fruit of God's work within him, it follows that the most important activity for the Christian is to 'stay', 'remain' or 'abide' in it, or alternatively, to allow it to 'stay' in him. Remaining faithful to God's truth as it has been revealed in Christ involves infinitely more than holding on to formulations of Christian doctrine. The truth concerned is a living, growing, active truth, identified ultimately with love. If the Christian has met God only when he has truly loved, so he can be sure that he 'stays' in or with God only if he continues to love.

Gospel (Jn 1:19-28). *Does Jesus stand among us as one whom we do not know?* After his prologue overture, John begins the introduction-proper of his gospel (1:19-51). Before Jesus commences his work of revealing the Father through the signs he does, he gathers the new messianic community around him and attracts to himself many of the Old Testament titles concerning the Coming One of God. In God's plan the Messiah's community comes to him through the witness of John the Baptist. The Baptist here replies to questions about his identity and his mission. His glory is that he bears witness to Christ. This, too, is the great glory of the Christian.

JANUARY 3

First Reading (2:29–3:6). *The Christian's Vocation to be a Child of God.* In revealing himself through his Son Jesus to be Father God has simultaneously revealed that men *are* his children. Nevertheless, since this filiation comes to us in the form of a 'call', in a 'word', it has to be received and acknowledged, and this not merely notionally but really, in terms of a new way of life. 'Like father like son': if God has shown himself to be a loving Father and invited men to be his children, it follows that they will in fact be his children only in so far as they behave like him.

Gospel (Jn 1:29-34). *John the Baptist bears witness.* The Baptist speaks of Jesus as 'the lamb of God', a title evoking the Suffering Servant who 'went like a lamb to slaughter'; and the passover lamb: 'Christ our Passover has been sacrificed' (1 Cor 5:7). Since Jesus permanently possesses the Spirit, he will dispense the Spirit to others (cf. Jn 3:5, 34; 7:38-39; 20:22). The Baptist's calling was to bear witness to Jesus, to point him out as Messiah, and then to recede into the background. Very often, it is other human beings who bring us to Christ, who bear witness to him. Likewise, it is our calling as Christians to bear witness to Christ—to bear witness to him, and then to melt into the background.

JANUARY 4

First Reading (3:7-10). *The Child of God loves his Brothers.* The unique acid test of our divine sonship is our love of our brethren. The true child of God is the one who acts like God by being righteous.. Doing the 'right thing' by brotherly love will achieve the destruction of sin and 'lawlessness'. The Christian has faith or 'knowledge' of God in a conscious and explicit relationship with God not only as creator but also as Father. Yet we cannot call God our Father unless we acknowledge all men as our brothers.

Gospel (Jn 1:35-42). *Because of John's witness the first disciples come to Jesus.* The followers of John the Baptist become followers of Jesus—'to follow' means the dedication of discipleship. Jesus takes the initiative. His first words in the fourth gospel are a question that he addresses to everyone who would follow him: 'What do you seek?' The question touches on the basic needs of man that cause him to turn to God. The disciples reply for us as well as for themselves. We come to Jesus because he is the Christ, and with Peter and the others as our forerunners, we offer Jesus our faith.

JANUARY 5

First Reading (3:11-21). *Love is the Self-giving Service of Others.* The Christian need have no fear of the 'world' ruled by cupidity rather than love. Loving is a share in Christ's death and resurrection. Christ showed that love was a matter of self-giving to the point of death. His death was *for* us, in the sense that it showed us how to give ourselves totally *for* others. It is in such a service that we share in his death and resurrection. Thus for the Christian love has a very precise meaning. It is giving, even self-giving, for others in imitation of Christ.

Gospel (Jn 1:43-51). *The royal, heavenly Son.* In this final passage of chapter one of John, the climax is reached. Already Jesus has been recognised as more than a Rabbi: he is the Christ. Yet, one who typifies Israel reacts incredulously. John's gospel is famous for its irony. This question of Nathanael—'can anything good come from Nazareth?' must be one of the most ironic questions of all time. But Nathanael's response confirms the Messiah title with equivalent ones—'Son of God' and 'King of Israel'. Yet even this confession is insufficient for Jesus. What we have to see is the Heavenly Man revealing his Father, and what such revelation does for us.

JANUARY 7

First Reading (3:22—4:6). *The Efficacy of Prayer.* If we can stand confidently before God because of our love of the brethren, we are bound to have our prayer answered, since we cannot but ask for God's will to be done—a will for the good of his children which is 'perfected' in the love they have for one another. Observation of his commandment is already the answer to our prayer. The only thing worth praying for is thus true human integrity which means being a loving child of a loving

Father. God gives us everything that is necessary to this end, if only we will receive it in prayer. If there is something that we do not receive, we can be sure that it is not useful for our true destiny.

Gospel (Mt 4:12-17, 23-25). *The Manifestation of the Messiah.* To view these verses solely as scene setters would be to miss Matthew's purpose. In his earlier chapters he has presented Jesus as the person in whom Israel will be made new. Now that the Baptist has completed his mission it is time for Jesus to begin his work. For Matthew Galilee is the place of relative tranquility where Jesus can speak to Jew without excluding other nations, the country where holy land and pagan soil are closely joined. Though the Kingdom arises in Israel, it draws in the land of the Gentiles. The light of Jesus shines far and wide; the Good News is about to be proclaimed from the mountain and its effectiveness will be seen in the many miracles he performs. In Galilee the epiphany of Jesus comes to pass.

JANUARY 8

First Reading (4:7-10). *God is Love.* Why Christians must love one another is quite simply because God himself *is* love. God is not just a person *who* loves, he *is* love itself; he is 'giving', 'service', the 'One for others'. This realisation, the climax of the biblical revelation of God, should revolutionise our attitude towards him and towards our fellows. If we are to be children of *this* God, we become 'givers', like him or, more precisely, instruments, channels of his gift.

Gospel (Mk 6:34-44). *He fed them with finest wheat.* This is a story rich in theological overtones. The miracle takes place in a 'desert place', thus evoking the Exodus and the manna, the bread from heaven. Jesus is the good shepherd of Ezekiel 34 who feeds his sheep. He pronounces a blessing over the bread and has it distributed to all present: he is host at a meal—Host at an anticipated Messianic Banquet. Furthermore, he takes. . . blesses. . . breaks. . . gives, as at the Last Supper: he anticipates the eucharistic meal.

JANUARY 9

First Reading (4:11-18). *The Christian has received the Spirit of God.* Believing or the acceptance of God's revelation in Christ is less our work than the work of God within us, through his Spirit. By this Spirit we have a God-given 'connaturality' with God. We share his 'mind'. But God *is* love. This, if we have *his* Spirit, we have his love and, unless we are to be disloyal to his Spirit within us, we must love as he loved us.

Gospel (Mk 6:45-52). *The Lord is my Shepherd.* The story of Jesus walking on the waters helps us to set the feeding of the multitude in the perspective of Jesus revealing himself. To walk upon the waters of the sea is the prerogative of God alone. This story would have had special significance for Christians facing persecution. It must have appeared to them that 'the wind was against them' and they felt worn out. Some may have begun to feel that the Lord had abandoned them to their fate. They are to learn from this story that they are not forsaken, that the Lord watches over them, and that he will come for their salvation.

JANUARY 10

First Reading (4:19—5:4). *We love God in loving one another.* To 'love' God does not involve doing anything *for* God: love is less an upward movement towards God than a downward movement from its origin, God, towards creation, yet elevating creation to the life of God. Thus service or 'worship' of God divorced from the service of one's fellows is the most insidious form of cupidity, because it is tantamount to making God in one's own image. that is, into one who wants to receive. But a man made in God's image, as one who is to love, give and serve has infinite demands made upon himself. The transcendence of God and the resurrection of Christ are the assurance that these demands are worth meeting.

Gospel (Lk 4:14-22). *I am the Good Shepherd.* In contrast to the way Matthew begins the public ministry of Jesus, Luke starts with surprising concreteness. We are constantly reminded in the gospel of Luke that the Holy Spirit is the director of Jesus' ministry. In the power of the Spirit he was born and baptised, and through the same Spirit he begins his preaching with a homily on the prophecy of Isaiah. Jesus tells his audience that the prophetic words of Isaiah have been fulfilled as they listened to them: he himself is the proclaimer of the Lord's year of grace. Above all, his mission will be one of Good News to the 'poor': the needy of all kinds—including sinners, the most needy of all.

JANUARY 11

First Reading (5:5-13). *The Christian's Victory over the World.* Since the way of life John has portrayed is at variance with the way of the 'world', he offers encouragement. The 'world' may stand for the relentless pursuit of self-centred desires and ambitions, but it also falls at death. The Christian, on the other hand, believes in Jesus Christ who, through his resurrection, conquered death. His own death was the expression of his self-giving love, opposed to the 'world', and the example offered to all men. It is by their active faith, that is, by giving themselves in the service of others that all men will conquer the 'world' and, therefore, death. In so far as he 'has' the Son, that is, recognises in Christ his own call to divine sonship, the believer already has eternal life. If we love, we lead God's life and are, therefore, beyond death.

Gospel (Lk 5:12-16). *Cleansing and reconciliation.* Jesus stretches out his hand to touch the leper. This word in action recalls the prophecy with which Luke began Jesus' ministry—the New Exodus through the power of the Holy Spirit: God rescues his people, as of old, with out-stretched hand and gives the Spirit through the imposition of hands. The man, so long excluded from the chosen people because of his leprosy can now rejoin them. God's afflicted people are freed through Jesus who, anointed with the Spirit, remains forever in communion with his Father. In more homely terms, Luke presents Jesus as the friend of the poor and the outcast.

JANUARY 12

First Reading (5:14-21). *Prayer for Sinners.* John repeats his teaching on prayer and proceeds to apply it to the conversion of sinners. Apart from the 'unforgivable' sin of denying God's life-giving 'truth' and ally-ing oneself with 'antichrist', there are other compromises with regard to the 'truth' which are forgivable. John clearly exhorts his readers to pray for a brother involved in such a compromise and states that such a prayer will be effective. But this prayer is not divorced from the good conduct of the brother who is praying. For, as John has already stated, our confidence in prayer is based on our observance of the command-ments. It is because we do his will that our prayer will be answered. Thus, while maintaining the efficacy of prayers for others, John suggests that the faults of others are a challenge to our own integrity.

Gospel (Jn 3:22-30). *He must increase, but I must decrease.* In the prologue to John's gospel we read that the Baptist's role was to bear witness to Jesus, so that men and women might believe in him. In the present reading we have the Baptist's final witness to Jesus in the fourth gospel. Jesus' success in his preaching gave rise to envy among the Baptist's followers. But John himself is full of humble joy at Jesus' success. For him Jesus is the bridegroom come to claim Israel, his people, for himself. The Baptist was the friend of the bridegroom and rejoiced in this honour.

THE SEASON OF LENT

First Reading (Joel 2:12-18). *A Call to Repentance and Prayer.* An invasion of locusts lays Judah waste. The prophet uses this natural calamity as an opportunity for urging the people towards genuine repentance and prayer. Written about 400 B.C., the words of the prophet still ring out in the midst of hearts dulled by routine or made insensitive by backslidings. A fresh beginning is imperative. God is compassionate and understanding, but he requires sincerity. The call to penance and prayer is addressed to all—elders and children, each according to their capacity to respond. Lent is an opporutnity for all.

Second Reading (2 Cor 5:20—6:2). *Now is the favourable time.* Paul, no less than the prophet Deutero-Isaiah whom he quotes (Is 49:8), is very conscious of the grace of the present moment. This moment has its own special urgency, because it is God calling me here and now to be reconciled to him in Christ. The ways in which he calls me are many, but there is one in particular to which Paul is drawing attention here: the minister of the word. In the Christian Church the priest has a special function as an 'ambassador for Christ'.

Gospel (Mt 6:1-6, 16-18). *Good deeds must be done for the right reason.* For the well-intentioned Jew 'good deeds' consisted principally of almsgiving, prayer and fasting. These were deeds which made a man righteous or pleasing before God. When performed sincerely they were a very authentic expression of piety. But all too easily they could be done to attract human attention and praise. The true follower of Christ must do these 'good deeds', but in such a way as to avoid falling into the age-old trap of human flattery and outward show. What matters most is our interior attitude and sincerity before God.

First Reading (Deut 30:15-20). *The Way to Life.* These words of Moses set forth in unequivocal fashion the necessity of personal choice in response to God's love. The Israelites are about to enter the long promised land, the future is in their hands. If they choose wisely, they will live in the love of the Lord. Although Moses is dead, the simplicity and urgency of his parting words remain to challenge other generations. Jesus was adamant that 'a man cannot serve two masters'.

Gospel (Lk 9:22-25). *The Cost of Discipleship.* As a prelude to the journey to Jerusalem, which is about to begin, comes the first prophecy that Jesus gives of his Passion and impending death. It is significant that this prophecy is followed immediately by reference to the requirements for discipleship. Jesus makes no secret of the cost of discipleship; it means dying to self, not once in a while, but daily. The true disciple, like his master, does not save or keep his life for himself, for he has understood that the grain of wheat must die in order to give new life.

FRIDAY AFTER ASH WEDNESDAY

First Reading (Is 58:1-9). *Fasting.* This passage from post-exilic times insists on the inward dispositions that must accompany outward observance. It comes from a time when the need to accentuate outward ritual as a way of preserving national identity had degenerated into something less than desirable. True religion does not consist of empty ritual divorced from genuine concern for those in need. In this respect the passage has a permanent message. It is not unlike Jesus' own teaching about fasting (Mt 6:18) in that he places the emphasis on the motive for fasting rather than on the action itself.

Gospel (Mt 9:14-15). *Jesus's presence among men.* By contrast with John's disciples and the Pharisees who undertook extra fasting in the hopes of hastening the advent of the Messiah, Jesus' disciples appear lax. Jesus' reply to their questioning is simple and direct. They do not fast because his presence with them is cause for celebration. There will be plenty of opportunity later for fasting when he is no longer with them. The Christian experiences, sometimes simultaneously, the call to celebration and to fasting in somewhat the same paradoxical way in which he experiences death and resurrection in the ups and downs of everyday.

SATURDAY AFTER ASH WEDNESDAY

First Reading (Is 58:9-14). *True happiness in the Lord.* Integrity before the Lord is tied up with integrity in human relationships. The prophet reinforces this truth with some illustrations: no more oppression, physical or moral, of one's fellowmen; sharing with those in need; a healthy respect for sabbath observance. This is the true way to be assured of God's guidance and strength in the conflicts of life. The tendency to 'manipulate' God through an impressive array of ritual observances unrelated to one's own moral behaviour is offset by this very practical and direct message of the prophet.

Gospel (Lk 5:27-32). *Responses to Jesus.* The parable of the sower and the seed finds an illustration in this passage. Levi hears the word of Jesus calling him and his response is total. The attraction of Jesus' person was such that he left what he was doing there and then, and hastened to welcome Jesus into his wider circle of family and colleagues in the friendly atmosphere of a meal. The reaction of the Pharisees is like the seed that fell on the edge of the path. They miss the point. Their prejudice gives rise to that oft-quoted and reassuring phrase of Jesus, that he came for all of us who are sick that we might respond to his gentle treatment.

FIRST WEEK IN LENT

MONDAY

First Reading (Lev 19:1-2, 11-18). *Be holy, for I am holy.* This short extract from the Holiness Code (Lev 17—26) is outstanding for its insistence on how to be a good neighbour. It appeals to the holiness of Yahweh as its motivation, and goes on to give what could be termed illustrations of the latter part of the Ten Commandments. While these are expressed in the usual negative formula of the time, 'thou shalt not', the passage is summed up in the positive phrase, 'you must love your neighbour as yourself', which Jesus was to link with the command to love God, making them the two great commandments of the law.

Gospel (Mt 25:31-46). *Brothers in Christ.* The Christian can never be reminded too often that, when he reaches out to another in need, in doing so he is mysteriously but really reaching out to Christ. Even the tiniest gesture performed in this spirit is enhanced and dignified. The parable of the last judgment refers also to a more sobering thought, that in neglecting our brother in need, we are neglecting Christ.

TUESDAY

First Reading (Is 55:10-11). *The Power of the word.* The author of Deutero-Isaiah concludes his work (40—50) with this effective image of the power of God's word. Personified almost as coming down from heaven and returning with mission complete, it was passages such as this that surely inspired St John to choose this image of the Incarnation of Jesus in the prologue of his Gospel. Such passages give us confidence that God's promises will be effective in our lives too.

Gospel (Mt 6:7-15). *Prayer and forgiveness.* The prayer of Christ's followers must be linked with forgiveness. Lest we forget the importance of forgiving others as we hope to be forgiven, a little paraphrase of the fifth petition in the Lord's Prayer is added at the end. It is not easy to forgive, yet Jesus is adamant on this point when Peter thinks that seven times are more than enough.

WEDNESDAY

First Reading (Jon 3:1-10). *His mercy reaches from age to age.* The response of the Ninevites to Jonah's preaching is all the more striking if it is borne in mind that he, a Jew, was preaching to Assyrians, people who had previously caused the downfall of the northern kingdom, Israel. The earlier part of the book shows how Jonah had been reluctant in the first place to undertake this mission and had fled in the opposite direction, had gone to sea. The enduring message of this delightful little book would seem to be that God's mercy will filter through to the most unlikely places and through imperfect instruments. National prejudice and personal inconvenience or reluctance must be overcome.

Gospel (Lk 11:29-32). *The Sign of Jonah.* Jesus refused to work miracles or signs to satisfy popular curiosity and thereby win a following. His miracles are simple and are always linked with the spiritual and symbolic meaning that he attaches to them. When the crowds ask for a sign, they are on a different wavelength. Unless they are able to overcome traditional prejudice and listen to the real message that God is giving them, as the Ninevites did in days of old, they will never recongise who Jesus really is.

THURSDAY

First Reading (Esther 14:1, 3-5, 12-14). *Esther's prayer in distress.* The story of Esther was written at a time when the Jews had just come through a violent persecution. Its purpose was didactic rather than historical. It was understood to be a vehicle for the illustration of the truth that Providence is ever of the side of God's people to save them from the enemy—if they would be faithful. Esther's prayer in distress is a beautiful glimpse of the conviction of the pious Jew that no matter how severe the persecution or pressure, in God alone is there lasting refuge.

Gospel (Mt 7:7-12). *Trust in prayer.* To ask, to seek and to knock are simple actions. Jesus urges his followers to pray with trust, and their petitions will be answered. The powdery desert stone and the snake sufficiently resemble Jewish bread and fish that in shady circumstances they could be passed off as substitutes. Jesus appeals to family experiences to convince us that our heavenly Father cares for us more than we can understand.

FRIDAY

First Reading (Ezek 18:21-28). *Individual Responsibility.* The Jews of Ezekiel's day used to quote a proverb which was a rather bitter caricature of the Semitic sense of solidarity and corporate responsibility: the fathers eat sour grapes and the children's teeth are set on edge (18:2). This fatalist concept of corporate retribution was dangerous. Ezekiel hammers home the truth that ultimately it is each single individual who is responsible for his own actions and for the consequences of those action. From this truth springs hope for a fresh start, with the past forgotten in God's mercy.

Gospel (Mt 5:20-26). *Interior Values.* The virtue of the Scribes and Pharisees consisted in their ability to measure external conformity to to the Law of Moses. It was relatively easy to determine cases of murder from external evidence. Jesus goes to the heart of the man. If the heart is right the external actions will be good. The spirit of reconciliation is quite different from external conformity. Reconciliation is possible if we allow the message of Jesus to penetrate through our anger, violence, bitterness and egoism.

SATURDAY

First Reading (Deut 26:16-19). *A people consecrated to the Lord.* To be chosen or singled out for a purpose implies responsibility. Israel is reminded of the responsibilities which ensue in accepting to become the Lord's consecrated people. She is assured to God's special care if she lives according to his word.

Gospel (Mt 5:43-48). *Perfection.* Perfection for the Hebrew meant wholeness, completeness. The Christian is to be recognised by his unceasing effort to be as open or all-round in his relationships with his fellowmen as his heavenly Father is. For the Father is utterly whole or all-round in his relationships with man. His love is constant and forgiving. It is man who breaks the relationship, and who creates the barriers. The Christian must strive to rise above natural likes and dislikes. To be perfect is to go out to all men in and with the love and friendship of Christ.

SECOND WEEK IN LENT

Monday: *The spiritual well-being of a whole nation reflects the spiritual ideals of its citizens.*

First Reading (Dan 9:4-10). If we are ashamed and humiliated by policies in local and national government, it may be that we have no one but ourselves to blame. The call of the Church in the modern world is not only to protect the family from the intrusion of the State, but to protect the State from grasping and selfish families.

Gospel (Luke 6:36-38). Life offers an opportunity either to withdraw more and more into ourselves or to open our hearts in a spirit of generosity to others. A decision in this matter affects not only the lives of others but our own lives. We either grow in spiritual stature with each act of generosity or diminish with each act of selfishness.

Tuesday: *The wish to place our lives and talents at the service of others should inspire us to a life of complete honesty and sincerity.*

First Reading (Is 1:10, 16-20). A sense of the enormity of sin in our lives can paralyse any attempt to change our ways. Yet there is no sin beyond God's pardon provided we can bring ourselves to express our sorrow.

Gospel (Mt 23:1-12). Our Lord's most devastating words were reserved, not for notorious public sinners, but for the Scribes and Pharisees. In them he condemned hypocrisy and he condemns it in us too.

Wednesday: *Our readiness to suffer especially when we are innocent of any crime can prove a means of bringing us nearer to Christ.*

First Reading (Jer 18:18-20). The final humiliation for Jeremiah was to find his life threatened by the very people whose cause he had championed. This was surely the ultimate in treachery. It is an experience that few can escape.

Gospel (Mt 20:17-28). In the experience of Peter, James and John in Gethsemane we can recognise the beginning of the Church's life of prayer. Close to our Lord when others stay at a distance, the apostles are invited to pray with him for the reconciliation of mankind to God. In baptism we received the same invitation.

Thursday: *Self-denial allows us to die to ourselves and to become alive to Christ.*

First Reading (Jer 17:5-10). The man who has eyes for nothing but the world in which he lives is more dead than alive. He is satisfied with a shallow and insipid existence. The man who turns his mind to spiritual things has a hidden source of strength in God himself.

Gospel (Lk 16:19-31). A life of ease and comfort with no thought for others must lead to a final alienation from God himself. A life of privation can refine the human spirit and bring a man nearer to God.

Friday: *Here comes the man of dreams.*

First Reading (Gen 37:3-4, 12-13a, 17b-28). Joseph's brothers would have murdered him for his delusions of grandeur, his dreams, his fancy coat, had not a better plan come their way. They sold him as a slave. He was a good as dead.

Gospel (Mt 21:33-43, 45-46). The parable of the wicked vinedressers describes the many ways in which the love of God has reached out to men and how finally it came in the person of his Son. As we prepare for Easter we try to penetrate the mystery of the death and resurrection of the Son of God incarnate. A man of dreams indeed. His vision of the destiny of mankind was too much for them and it is frequently too much for us. We are afraid of the demands complete commitment to our faith might make on us.

Saturday: *You are with me always and all I have is yours.*

First Reading (Mic 7:14-15, 18-20). In the role of the Good Shepherd God himself had made a people out of a band of wandering nomads. It required a second miracle of grace to make them worthy of their vocation.

Gospel (Lk 15:1-3, 11-32). The parable of the Prodigal reaches its conclusion with the father's words to his sulking elder son. These words express the totality of the love of God for man. There is no more to be said. You are with me always and all I have is yours.

THIRD WEEK IN LENT

Monday: *Everyone was outraged.*

First Reading (2 Kings 5:1-15). The cure of Naaman the Syrian brought him to recognise the God of Israel. This was something of an exception to the rule. Israel was not particularly interested in the conversion of the pagan world. In theory yes, in practice no.

Gospel (Lk 4:24-30). The narrow-mindedness of Israel was seen at its clearest in Nazareth. The people did not even like to be reminded of God's goodness to Gentiles. Many of us who are outraged by apartheid in distant lands can live with it quite happily at home.

Tuesday: *Unless you each forgive. . .*

First Reading (Dan 3:25, 34-43). The prayer of Azariah comes from a heart deeply saddened by the sight of a nation deprived of sympathetic leadership.

Gospel (Mt 18:21-35). The parable of the unmerciful servant gathers up much of Jesus' teaching on reconciliation. There is one condition placed on God's pardon, namely, man's readiness to pardon others. Our revised Sacrament of Reconciliation tries to capture the spirit of this parable by placing a certain emphasis on our involvement with others. To live at peace with others is an effective sign to the world that we are at peace with God.

Wednesday: *Not to abolish but to complete.*

First Reading (Deut 4:1, 5-9). Moses set out to persuade the people that they would win the respect of the world by their observance of the law of God.

Gospel (Mt 5:17-19). There runs through the Sermon on the Mount a contrast between the Law of Moses and the Law of Christ. A similar tension shows itself in the modern world, especially after Vatican II. Any solution which destroys law in the name of freedom or tradition, in the name of renewal is out of keeping with the mind of the Gospel. The law of Christ is fulfilment not destruction.

Thursday: *Listen to my voice.*

First Reading (Jer 7:23-28). The prophet Jeremiah appeals for a radical change of heart and a readiness to listen to the voice of God.

Gospel (Lk 11:14-23). Jesus' critics did not stop short at any calumny to discredit him. They went so far as to claim he was in league with the devil. There were many who were ready to listen to them. Our listening is of another kind. Strange that a generation that listens to so much should hear so little. Perhaps the prayer of silence should be given priority, especially in our liturgical celebrations. Those few moments of silent reflection which we tend to neglect at Mass are as important as any prayer we might recite.

Friday: *You are not far from the kingdom of God.*

First Reading (Hos 14:2-10). The prophecy of Hosea ends with an act of sorrow and with the promise of pardon.

Gospel (Mk 12:28-34). A discussion of the greatest commandment between Jesus and a scribe leads Jesus to commend the man's good sense. With such a mass of legislation on his mind the scribe might easily have got his priorities confused. This problem remains with us and we must be forever vigilant about our priorities.

Saturday: *Love, not sacrifice*

First Reading (Hos 5:15—6:6). This oracle is a sad comment on the state to which the religion of Israel had fallen. It had become an empty sham, a lie.

Gospel (Lk 18:9-14). Two men went to the temple to pray. The Pharisee prayed to himself. The tax collector prayed to God. Religion, like life itself, is exposed to the danger of self-deception. The impact of this parable, like so many others recorded by Luke alone, lies in the fact that the two men are really the embodiment of two deep sentiments within us all. One would give priority to self and so close our hearts to God. The other would forget about self and so open our hearts to God.

FOURTH WEEK IN LENT

MONDAY

First Reading (Is 65:17-21). *Longing for Security.* The exiles now home from Babylon had their dreams shattered by the harsh realities of life. Isaiah offers them fresh hope. God is going to intervene and bring about a new creation. Joy will replace mourning; man will enjoy a long life and will live in security. His property will no longer be prey for others. God will satisfy his yearning for peace, happiness and security.

Gospel (Jn 4:43-54). *Security in Christ.* The new creation promised by Isaiah begins with Christ. The official's son is saved by the prayer of faith. It is the beginning of new life for both father and son. Contact with Christ brings new life, a new creation (2 Cor 5:17).

In a world full of insecurity man finds his security in Christ. While the world around him may decay, the new life given him by Christ endures. Faith is saying yes to Christ, confident in his power to make us new each day.

TUESDAY

First Reading (Ezek 47:1-9, 12). *The Presence of God.* Sometimes God seems far away and yet he is near. The people of Israel loved to go to Jerusalem, they loved God's dwelling-place. The loss of their Temple and the exile to Babylon brought a crisis of faith. Had God abandoned them? No, says the prophet. God is near and he has new plans; the Temple will be rebuilt and there he will dwell among his people. From his dwelling-place will flow out blessings in abundance. God is full of welcome surprises.

The Gospel (Jn 5:1-3, 5-16). *Presence of God in Christ.* 'Do you want to be well again?' A man must know his need for Christ's help and healing. Here Christ is seen as the source of life and as master of the Sabbath. God is present in him and from him God's blessings flow out to his people (cf. First Reading). Some fail to perceive this: the gap between Jesus and the Jews grows wider.

WEDNESDAY

First Reading (Is 49:8-15). *God's love.* Great is a mother's love for her child but God's love is even greater and it is the key to all that he does. This love of his is about to go into action and bring the exiles home

from Babylon. From that place of spentness God will bring them to a
place of opportunity and there care for them (vv. 9-11). He is ever
involved in the struggles of his people and his love continually creates
new opportunities.

Gospel (Jn 5:17-30). *To love God is to obey him.* The purpose of
Christ's work is to make known the power of the Father's love. That
love enables him to give life, to judge, to do all that the Father asks of
him.

To be loved by someone is to be given a new life, to become capable
of greater achievements. Love can really transform. The love of Christ is
greater. To experience it is to pass from death to life; to let it be effective is to have eternal life already.

THURSDAY

First Reading (Ex 32:7-14). *The power of prayer.* The Bible sees the
desert as a place where man purifies himself of all that is not God. The
temptation to make their own gods proved too much for the Jews and
God threatened to cast them off. Moses pleads on their behalf. It is a
daring prayer reminding God of his promises. Reconciliation is brought
about through prayer and God does not punish his people (v. 14). God
wishes to spare, not to condemn.

Gospel (Jn 5:31-47). *Greater than Moses.* 'The whole earth is a hospi-
tal' (T. S. Eliot). All men are 'paralysed' in some way (Jn 5:5) and
stand in need of healing. Christ's words and his touch bring just that for
the Father is with him; the Baptist and the Scriptures attest to that.
The way he reaches out to people is often through the hands of those
who love. God listened to Moses and spared his people; he listens to
Christ and saves his people.

FRIDAY

First Reading (Wis 2:1, 12-22). *Innocent Suffering.* The faithful Jew
described here took the risk every man of faith takes. His life was a
reproach to others, he put his whole trust in God. The result is mockery,
persecution and death. It's an accurate description of what happened to
Christ. The same Christ carried the burdens of all who suffer for their
trust in God (Is 53:6); sufferings united to his suffering will bring a
share in his victory.

Gospel (Jn 7:1-2, 10, 25-30). *Plotting his destruction.* The Jewish ruling
class wanted Jesus destroyed (7:1) because he was a threat. He not only

put questions to them, he put them in question. Anyway, he seemed too ordinary, 'we know where this man is from' (v. 27). Imprisoned by prejudice they could not see how God was working through Jesus. He despairs of such men (vv. 28-29). He now challenges men to detect God's presence in their own lives and in the lives of their fellow-men.

SATURDAY

First Reading (Jer 11:18-20). *Rejected Prophet.* The fear of rejection frightens most people. Jeremiah's discovery that he has been rejected forces him to reflect on the purpose of his life. He had suffered, preached and worked to lift his people out of their misery. It wasn't appreciated and now he is like a lamb being prepared for slaughter; hence his bitterness (v. 20). In a like situation Christ would pray for forgiveness (Lk 23:34), not for revenge.

Gospel (Jn 7:40-52). *Condemned without a hearing.* Real faith never comes easily. God can be too far away to be seen or too close to noticed. The Jewish leaders could not see him in Christ. They didn't believe and they did not want to believe that Christ could be the source of life (7:37-38) or the source of God's Spirit. The worst kind of sin is the unwillingness to face the truth, it is the closed heart and closed mind.

FIFTH WEEK IN LENT

MONDAY

First Reading (Dan 13:1-9, 15-17, 19-30, 33-62). *God protects the innocent.* The edifying story of Susanna describes how God sees justice done. As the faithful Susanna preferred death to sin so the people are asked to be faithful to their God. With God's help virtue triumphs over vice.

Because of vanity men consider it important how others see them. In reality, it is only God's estimate of them that matters. He alone spares, he alone judges, (Daniel='God judges').

Gospel (Jn 8:1-11). *Greater than Daniel.* Christ shows how out of a shattered life he can recreate something beautiful. The sinner is carried to the feet of Christ and there she is enabled to rise and make a fresh start in life. It echoes the Susanna story. Christ not only protects the innocent, he forgives the sinner. He shows that what matters now is not the outward observance of the law but the response of the heart to love. The sinner before the Sinless is called to repent and 'sin no more'.

TUESDAY

First Reading (Num 21:4-9). *Faith saves sinners.* The grumbling Israelites in the desert are punished by a plague of serpents. Help comes to them in their distress when they repent and when Moses prays on their behalf. Those who look with faith on the bronze serpent are saved. Christ raised up on the Cross (cf. Gospel) brings to mind the serpent lifted up on the standard. To look with faith saves in both cases.

Gospel (Jn 8:21-30). *For or against Christ.* Lifted up on the Cross Jesus will make known fully who he is. There he will reveal the depth of God's love for men. Can men put their faith in a crucified, humbled Christ? Those who truly 'seek him' (v. 21) in faith will find life. Others will remain blind to his identity and die in their sins (v. 24). Men must decide for or against Christ. It is a choice that decides their destiny.

WEDNESDAY

First Reading (Dan 3:14-20, 24-25, 28). *The cost of disciplineship.* The rescue of the three men from the fiery furnace foreshadows the deliverance of Christ from the hands of his enemies. The men were tortured for their faith; they had refused to honour a false god. The pride they had in their faith is echoed in the gospel reading when the Jews claim to be descendents of Abraham and to have God as their father (Jn 8:33, 41). Those who take a stand must have their feet firmly planted.

Gospel (Jn 8:31-42). *Heirs to Faith.* Inherited faith is not enough: each generation has to be reconverted and discover the meaning of faith for its time. Jesus tells the Jews that the truth brings freedom and falsehood imprisons. They must choose. Christ himself is the truth; he frees men from hatred, prejudice and sin. If they 'accept' Jesus (Jn 1:12) and 'remain' in his word by their obedience to him, they become children of God. Without him they remain slaves to sin and his word finds 'no place' (8:37) in them.

THURSDAY

First Reading (Gen 17:3-9). *A Promise is made to Abraham.* God asks something different of each individual. He asked Abraham for unconditional faith and obedience and he got it. Abraham shows us what the essence of faith is; it is to be convinced that God is reliable. Man can lean on God, depend on him, trust in him and he won't be let down. Abraham had such faith and, like all deep faith, it brought blessings to others. Even greater blessings are promised.

Gospel (Jn 8:51-59). *The Promise is fulfilled in Christ.* 'Now we know...' (v. 52). The Jews claim to know for sure that Jesus is possessed. That know-all attitude is the greatest obstacle to faith. Faith means a willingness to learn, to hear and listen to Christ. Where this faith is not present men soon find someone to blame and stones to throw (v. 59). Jesus hides himself from such men. There are many who do not recognise Jesus. Maybe it is because they don't see him in our love.

FRIDAY

First Reading (Jer 20:10-13). *Love costs something.* It is painful to have to rebuke those we love. Jeremiah saw how sin was leading his people to disaster. He pleaded with them, warned them and finally threatened them with judgement. He could not watch in silence as they stumbled towards destruction. They reacted to him with scorn and it hurt him deeply. Small wonder that we find him depressed as he looks back over his life. He remains confident however that God will see him through.

Gospel (Jn 10:31-42). *Sustained by God.* People who throw stones are people who have run out of ideas. For the second time the Jews try to stone Jesus. His work has the stamp of God's approval and he claims that God is his Father. They accuse him of blasphemy. Still, there are some who are well-disposed and they come in faith. Christ does not lose heart for the Father is with him. For Christians too, the power behind them is greater than the task ahead.

SATURDAY

First Reading (Ezek 37:21-28). *United restored.* Divisions between people need not be forever. If God is allowed to be truly present he will create unity and peace. This is the prophet's message. He looks forward to the golden age when the scattered people of his country will be gathered together. God is going to re-establish his people and dwell among them forever. He will give them a prince as ruler and he will bring them into a special relationship with himself. He will give them peace and happiness.

Gospel (Jn 11:45-57). *Unity around Jesus.* At the end of his public ministry Jesus gives the last and the greatest of his signs, the raising of Lazarus. Caiaphas sees in Jesus a threat to political security and calls for his death. But Jesus' death has a deeper meaning. It will unite all nations into one people of God.

Communion with Christ is the beginning of all Christian community. The closer Christians are to Christ the more united they are to one another.

HOLY WEEK

MONDAY

First Reading (Is 42:1-7). *The servant of true justice.* Three of the four Suffering Servant Songs form the first readings for the beginning of Holy Week. This mysterious person, the 'Servant' is an individual, yet he is also the people whom he represents. In the first song (42:1-9) the prophet depicts a chosen one whose mission will be characterised by a quiet and unwavering concern for true justice and by compassion for those in bondage, mental or physical. Five centuries later comes the fullest realisation of this prophecy in Jesus. Succeeding Christian generations find the strength to work for true justice and compassion because of Jesus, the servant of true justice.

Gospel (Jn 12:1-11). *Jesus is anointed.* In a few brief hours' relaxation in a family he loved so well, Jesus accepts in friendship Martha's serving, Lazarus' company at table and Mary's touching gesture of affection. Judas' ill-natured objection to this action highlights again the evangelist's awareness of how men have divided themselves into those who love the Lord and those who reject him. A gesture such as Mary's adds something lovely to life, its scent extends far beyond the present, bringing into being something permanently precious that deserves to be remembered. Jesus understood Mary and accepted her gift and what it stood for.

TUESDAY

First Reading (Is 49:1-6). *The servant has a mission for all peoples.* The chosen servant is reassured that in spite of any momentary feelings of futility, his mission is not only destined for his own people, but will extend to far distant lands. Misgivings, though human, must be firmly put aside, for divine providence is at work at every stage in the difficult journey of life.

Gospel (Jn 13:21-33, 36-38). *Through betrayed, Jesus will be glorified.* The tragedy of the shameful death that Jesus was about to face spills over into this intimate meal. Present among them is one who is to betray him, selfishly, ruthlessly and unrepentingly. Present also is one who will disown Jesus, but impetuously and with immediate remorse and repentance. Jesus knew of Judas' intent much earlier (Jn 6:70-71); he who knew the heart of man so well must have sensed it, but right up to the end allowed him a last chance. While Jesus' message is unfailingly one of God's mercy to all sinners if only they would repent, Judas stands for the grim possibility of total refusal to accept this offer of love.

WEDNESDAY

First Reading (Is 50:4-9). *The servant must suffer.* Although the Lord's servant will champion the cause of justice, liberate the captive and be a light to the nations, he will not escape suffering and insult. The third song explicitly introduces the theme of the suffering which the servant must undergo through being faithful to his mission. This note of suffering is most fully developed in the fourth and final song (52:13–53:12). His strength to endure this unmerited suffering will come from continual listening to and confidence in the Lord.

Gospel (Mt 26:14-25). *The betrayal.* Judas makes final plans for handing Jesus over to the chief priests and receives payment in advance. During supper Jesus indicates his awareness of these plans, allowing Judas a last opportunity. Judas however refuses to the end. His fall was prepared for by a series of petty thefts that ended in uncontrollable avarice. He had missed the central point in Jesus' life and death. To be truly human is to be conscious of human weakness, but confident that, in Christ, it can be overcome.

THE SEASON OF EASTER

EASTER WEEK

MONDAY

First Reading (Acts 2:14-32). *Peter's speech to the people on the day of Pentecost.* The purpose of Peter's words is to explain the charismatic happenings which the assembled Jews have seen, and he does it by means of a speech founded on three texts of the Old Testament. Commentary on the Old Testament was, of course, the ancient Jewish way of preaching, but in Peter's case the special point is that in today's happenings the Old Testament has reached its fulfilment. The three texts he uses are first Joel, to show that the outpouring of the Spirit is a sign of the fulfilment prophesied for the last times; then the Psalms, to show that it was God's plan that his Holy One should be raised from the dead; and lastly Psalm 109, to show that Christ was destined by God to be exalted as Lord to his right hand.

Gospel (Mt 28:8-15). *All of us are witnesses to the resurrection.* The Gospel readings for Easter Week bring together the great traditions of the empty tomb and the appearances of the risen Lord. The Church is destined to be the living witness to death and resurrection, death to sin and resurrection to newness of life. Through her ministry the Paschal Mystery becomes a daily experience for those who learn to deny themselves, take up their cross and follow Christ. Each act of self-denial is death to self and resurrection to life in Christ. Since the Church is Christ in the modern world it could not be otherwise.

TUESDAY

First Reading (Acts 2:36-41). *The reaction of the listeners to Peter's Speech at Pentecost* is repentance and conversion. The reaction to the Word of God must always be repentance, for it judges us and makes for us a standard from which we see that we fail. And, as Peter says, the result of this conversion is the healing advent of the Holy Spirit. The two are inextricably linked, for if we cast out evil, it can only be by it giving place to the Spirit. The two are inextricably linked, for if we cast out evil, it can only be by it giving place to the Spirit.

Gospel (Jn 20:11-18). *She did not recognise him.* Mary Magdalene's anxious search for Jesus reveals the intensity of her love for him and her deep sadness at his loss. She searched for him among the dead only to find that he was alive again. Our encounter with Christ, like hers, may take us completely by surprise, perhaps when we have given up hope of ever finding him. We know that we find Christ wherever there is suffering. We find him where two or three are gathered in his name. We find him in a unique way in the Eucharist.

WEDNESDAY

First Reading (Acts 3:1-10). *Peter heals the cripple in the Temple.* This first miracle of healing done by the apostles makes explicit what is implicit in them all, that they are carrying on the healing work of Christ. Peter heals him in the name of Christ, or in other words by Christ's power, and the miracle is reminiscent of several of Jesus' miracles. The reaction of the healed cripple is characteristic of the whole reaction of all those who receive the message, joy and praise of God.

Gospel (Lk 24:13-35). *Did not our hearts burn within us?* A further vivid tradition of an encounter with the risen Lord is recorded by Luke. The sadness of the two disciples as they left Jerusalem behind and made their way to Emmaus is soon turned to gladness as they recognise Jesus in the breaking of bread. This was a moment of recognition which changed the lives of two men from frustration and failure in their vocation to a burning enthusiasm to share their experience of the nearness of Christ. This can be our experience too. Moments of deep sadness can be changed by the grace of Christ into an experience of the love of God, and we discover the meaning of the Beatitudes.

THURSDAY

First Reading (Acts 3:11-26). *Peter teaches in the temple.* The burden of St Peter's teaching, now and throughout the Acts, is witness to the resurrection. He shows that Christ's resurrection, and—more to the point—even his shameful death, were predestined by God and foretold in the scriptures so that the promises to the Jews might be fulfilled. He and the apostles are the witnesses to the reality of the resurrection, and here he offers as independent proof the healing of the cripple in Jesus' name: if the strength of Jesus can bring healing, then Jesus must be living in power.

Gospel (Lk 24:35-48). *He then opened their minds.* A further appearance of Jesus to his disciples dispels any doubts in their minds about his resurrection from the dead. How could they have missed the meaning of God's plan of redemption? It could not end with death. Left to our own resources our progress in things of the spirit would be little and we would quickly give up the effort. It is the grace of God which opens our minds to discover the unfathomable riches of the love of God revealed to us in Christ. It is a form of pride which moves us to depend entirely on our own efforts when we should place our lives in the hands of God.

FRIDAY

First Reading (Acts 4:1-12). *The Apostles are interrogated by the Jewish leaders.* In accordance with Jesus' promises, the Holy Spirit gives the apostle words to say when he is brought before the courts. He tells them that the name of Jesus is the power in which the apostles act. The early Christians are almost defined in the Acts as those who call upon the name of Jesus, or those over whom the name of Jesus is called. Christians are baptised *into* the name of Jesus, for the name is thought of as a source of power and protection, almost as a magical formula but not in a magical way. It is, then, tantamount to saying that they are those who put all their reliance upon the power of Jesus and enter into his power.

Gospel (Jn 21:1-14). *It is the Lord.* The Apostles, now disillusioned men, return to their former way of life as fishermen. This too was a failure. A further appearance of the risen Lord brings them to life again and a simple meal in his company renews their sense of purpose in life. The words of the Beloved Disciple places him at the head of the Christian tradition of contemplatives. His recognition of the Lord is something between himself and Jesus. Others recognise him in the breaking of bread. He knew instinctively that it was the Lord. We live in a scientific age which must have proof of everything. How do you prove love?

SATURDAY

First Reading (Acts 4:13-21). *Peter and John are cautioned by the court.* It is clear that the authorities are acting in bad faith, for they admit that they can do nothing because the miracle is publicly recognised. Luke is always careful to stress the public recognition and acclaim which is accorded to Christianity; it is no secret religion, nor unknown and held only by unknowns, but all the world knows about it. By their fearless speaking in the teeth of official opposition, the apostles give the first example of that *parrhesia* or free-spoken endurance and perserverance which is such a characteristic of the early community in Acts.

Gospel (Mk 16:9-15). *But they did not believe her.* Mark's record of the appearance of the risen Lord shows how unwilling even his own disciples were to believe. They dismiss the testimony of Mary and of two of their own number. They cannot dismiss the testimony of Jesus standing before their eyes. The time for doubting was over, they must now go out and proclaim the good news to every creature. A strange unwillingness to believe runs through all the records of the resurrection. For some it was occasioned by a stubborn refusal to accept anything that was said about Jesus of Nazareth. For others, who had been nearer to Jesus, the reason is harder to find. There is no escaping the conclusion that faith is the gift of God.

Week Two to Week Seven of Easter

INTRODUCTION TO THE ACTS OF THE APOSTLES

The Acts of the Apostles is aptly chosen for the first readings during Eastertide, since it describes the beginnings of the Church after the resurrection, showing how the Church continues the work of Christ in the world. The motive force in all the important decisions is the Spirit of Christ, directing and guiding the community and its leaders, and the apostles, particularly Peter and Paul, carry on Christ's work not only by preaching his Good News but also by working miracles of healing in imitation of him.

The book was written as a second volume of Luke's gospel, and constantly shows similarities of vocabulary, style and method. As Luke works towards the great climax at Jerusalem, so the Acts works away from there in ever widening circles till the Good News reaches 'the ends of the earth' or Rome. There is little by which to date the book except its relationship to Luke, but this puts it towards the end of the first century. Nevertheless the author shows that, amid his variety of sources, he has clear and exact knowledge of conditions throughout his area in the forties and fifties of the century, often getting right details which only recent archaeological discoveries have enabled us to check. As some stages, when travels are related in the first person, he is relying on diaries of a companion of Paul. At others material of a more legendary character is used. The speeches, as was common in historical writing of the period, do not necessarily represent what was actually said on the occasion, but are more or less elaborated versions of what was appropriate to the occasion, though considerable attention is paid to the particular bent of the speaker; some basic primitive outline may well lie behind them.

One of the most important themes which lurks behind a good deal of the material is the explanation of the movement of Christianity from the Jews to the gentiles. It is stressed again and again that the Christian message is the natural fulfilment of the Jewish hope. Hence the refusal of the Jews to accept it is paradoxical, and can only be ascribed to blindness and ill-will on their parts. This Paul underlines each time he turns from the Jews to the Gentiles. On the other hand it is stressed that the admission of gentiles to Christianity takes place only on the explicit instructions of the Holy Spirit and under heavenly guidance. Another theme related to this is seen in the author's care to show that there is nothing subversive to Rome in the Christian message, that it neither did nor should come into conflict in any way with the Roman authorities.

From other writings of the New Testament and even from glimpses in the Acts itself one may deduce that early Christianity was not free of controversies and even dissensions. The author, however, is careful to insist that these are the merest ripples which do not disturb the profound peace and harmony of the community. Peace is the keynote of the community at Jerusalem, exemplified in community of goods and distribution of them according to need. In the same way Paul is careful to maintain unity between his churches and the mother-community at Jerusalem, and to this end not only observes more of the Law than his principles would demand, but also returns frequently to keep contact with the leaders at Jerusalem and secure their approval, even bringing them gifts from the other new communities as a sort of thank-offering. Over all is the impression of joy, thanksgiving and praise to the Lord for the Good News he has given in the resurrection of Christ to which the apostles are witnesses.

Further Reading: E. M. Blaiklock, *The Acts of the Apostles* (Tyndale New Testament Commentaries, Grand Rapids, 1959). Neal M. Flanagan OSM, in *New Testament Reading Guide,* (Collegeville, 1964). R. P. C. Hanson, *The Acts* (Oxford, Clarendon Press, 1967). Wilfrid J. Harrington OP, *Record of Fulfilment* (Chapman, 1968), chapter 6. Richard J. Dillon and Joseph A. Fitzmyer SJ, in *Jerome Biblical Commentary* (1968). Henry Wansbrough OSB in *New Catholic Commentary* (1969). Ernst Haenchen, *The Acts of the Apostles* (Oxford, 1971).

INTRODUCTION TO THE GOSPEL OF JOHN

A semi-continuous reading of John's gospel accompanies that of Acts during the second to the seventh week of Eastertide. Already during Lent we have had some readings from the gospel of John. These treated of some specifically 'Lenten' topics, for example, the rejection of Jesus, his conflict with those who seek his death and some stories of healing. It seems strange that the whole selection for this period of Eastertide (apart from Jn 21:15-25) is taken from that part of the gospel which deals with the life of Jesus before his death and resurrection. The choice has been well made. It is not determined by a desire merely to present the remainder of the gospel, namely, what has not appeared so far during Lent, Holy Week or the octave of Easter.

All the readings, except an Easter apparition account (ch. 21), are from discourses of Jesus, particularly from his farewell address to an intimate group of disciples before his death and resurrection (13:31–17:26). In these long discourses, which are a distinctive feature of the gospel, certain themes are developed at length, for example, light, life, glory, faith (believing), the Eucharist as our living bread. These have grown out of prolonged reflection on the after-Easter life of Christ and the Christian. The Christ who speaks to us in these discourses often seems to transcend time and space. From chapters 13–17 he is already on his way to the Father. His concern is that he will not abandon those who believe in him and who must remain in the world. Though he speaks here at the Last Supper, he seems to speak from heaven as a risen Lord. The listeners are disciples but his words are directed to Christians of all times, to those who know him as the one who has been 'lifted up' in suffering and in glory. The whole gospel is penetrated by the light of his resurrection. From early on Jesus speaks of his 'hour', the time of his 'glorification', when he passes through death to the presence of his Father from where he sends his Spirit.

This gospel, more than any other, reflects on the meaning of Jesus and Christian life in the light of a highly developed after-Easter understanding, which is a gift of the Spirit. The gospel originates from disciples who 'remember' Jesus (2:17, 22, 12:16) and from the Spirit who 'brings to your remembrance all that I have said to you' (14:26). This remembering is not just a material recall of events and words. It is also a new vision of faith, a reflection within the after-Easter situation in which disciples come to understand the meaning of Jesus' work and teaching. The Christ who speaks and acts in the gospel is the Christ of history as he has been understood over the years by the believing community through the light of the Spirit.

Therefore, when we turn from any other gospel to John we feel we are in a different world. Matthew, Mark and Luke are somehow more concrete. The words of Jesus are interspersed with plenty of action. In John there is less action and longer discourses which develop some favourite themes such as light, truth, faith (believing), love, signs, works. The author demands from us a deeper level of reflection on the meaning of Christ for our lives. That is why some early Christian writers referred to John and to his gospel as 'John the theologian', 'the spiritual gospel'. John gives various levels of meanings to words, events and to the characters of his drama. To 'follow' Jesus, the shepherd means the life of discipleship. Jesus is 'lifted up' on the cross physically in death and also in triumph as a king. The fact that Nicodemus comes to Jesus 'by night' also draws our attention to his lack of faith. The 'beloved disciple' is not only an individual. He also represents all those who are friends of Christ. The Holy Spirit is like a wind. He is a mysterious force which comes from God. We let ourselves go with him. He blows us in the direction God want us to go.

The gospel is about 'signs' (20:30). These are certain events in the life of Jesus which disclose the mystery of his person. They point to the mysterious reality of Jesus as the Son of God. The loaves which Jesus multiplies symbolise that he is the bread of life. He sustains us with his living word and with the gift of his own life in the eucharistic bread. The wealth of imagery in the gospel also discloses the mystery of Jesus and the meaning of his work. The images of the shepherd and the vine unfold his relationships—his relationship with his Father, with the individual disciple and with the community of believers.

These examples illustrate the Christ-centredness of the gospel. Each evangelist forcuses his attention on the mystery of Christ. When Christian artists through the centuries represented John as an eagle, they were acknowledging his deeper penetration into the mystery of the person of Jesus. For them the eagle alone of living creatures could look straight into the sun without being dazzled. Among the gospel writers John has the most penetrating gaze into the mysteries of God made man. For this reason one meets many people who say they find themselves closer to God and to Jesus in John's gospel than in any other book. It is a gospel of personal realtionships. It reflects more profoundly and more explicitly on the quality and consequences of the relationship of Jesus to his Father and to disciples and of disciples to Father, Son and to one another.

The key theme which runs through the whole gospel is: Jesus is the expected one, the Messiah and Son of God. He reveals himself and his Father to us. We are called to respond to him in faith and love. He brings 'light', the self-revelation of God. This evokes a double reaction. Some come into the light. Others reject it and prefer 'darkness'. The gospel is an invitation to reflect on our relationship with the Father and the Son and on the 'fruit' of our communion with them, namely, our fraternal love. It is a call to respond to the Father's life and love which we see in Jesus.

Further reading: W. Grossouw, *Revelation and Redemption*, London: Chapman, 1966. A. M. Hunter, *According to John*, London: SCM, 1968. R. H. Lightfoot, *St John's Gospel* (commentary), Oxford, 1963. R. Russell, 'St John' in *New Catholic Commentary*, pp. 1022-1074.

WEEK TWO OF EASTER

MONDAY

First Reading (Acts 4:23-31). *The Prayer of the Apostles in persecution.* The apostles pray for boldness and endurance in the face of threats, and are duly, in accordance with Jesus' promise, strengthened by the Holy Spirit. Their prayer aptly centres on the theology of Jesus as the Suffering Servant prophesied in the Book of Isaiah; this Servant of the Lord was to suffer and be humiliated, and only so come to be vindicated by God and spread his message to the nations. They see that their way of spreading the Word is to be in imitation of their master's suffering.

Gospel (Jn 3:1-8). *Born of the Spirit.* The readings from the third chapter of John's gospel relate Jesus' dialogue with Nicodemus. The central topic of this dialogue is the meaning and origin of our faith in Jesus. Jesus tries to draw Nicodemus to faith by disclosing the mystery of his own person. Nicodemus comes by night in the darkness of imperfect faith to him who is the light, the revelation of God's life and love. Captivated by Jesus as a great teacher and wonder-worker, he still needs the gift of faith to see the life of God and his Kingdom at work in Jesus. This is the work of the Spirit. In our weakness we need to be constantly open to the vitalising force of the Spirit. He is like the wind. He is not held up by any obstacles, even by those we create ourselves. We can hear his voice when we are alert to the signs of his presence. He will lead us where he wants us to go, not where we want to direct ourselves. He constantly generates new life within us. The sign of growth is when we are led to realise more effectively the message of Jesus in our life with him and with one another.

TUESDAY

First Reading (Acts 4:32-37). *Sharing of possessions in the early Church.* At intervals throughout the first part of Acts we have a picture of the first Christian community at Jerusalem. The present summary concentrates on the unity of mind and heart, expressed materially by community of goods. From the following story of Ananias and Sapphira it appears that members were not obliged to this communion, but that the practice of it was voluntary. It was a proof of their generosity, and a recognition that in the age of Christ's fulfilment the good things of this world have lost their importance.

Gospel (Jn 3:7-15). *Lifted up.* Faith in Jesus is our active response to him who communicates to us his life of intimacy with his Father and our own need for life with God. Jesus knows God; what he speaks to men is God's own truth—the truth about himself and about man's destiny. God's concern for humanity is manifest on the cross in Jesus. There he invites us to believe in his love and to open ourselves to his saving life. In death Jesus is stretched out in pain. He also passes to the glorious presence of his Father from where he still reaches out to draw us to believe in himself and the Father's love.

WEDNESDAY

First Reading (Acts 5:17-26). *The Apostles are imprisoned but miraculously released.* The first of several occasions when the apostles are released from prison by the intervention of God, showing both that God will protect his own, and that nothing may be allowed to prevent the preaching of the message of Christ. When the apostles return to the temple they are to teach about the new life in Christ: as Christ rose to a new kind of life, so the Christian, baptised into Christ, has put his old life behind him and is already transformed into the image of Christ through his Spirit; that is what is meant by 'the new life'.

Gospel (Jn 3:16-21). *God so loved the world.* The breadth of God's love is the whole world of men for whom Jesus died. The depth of his love is his most precious gift, his only and beloved Son whose whole life, especially his death, tells us how much God wishes to share his life with men. To believe in Jesus is to believe that God cares for us and never condemns us. Only man condemns himself if, seeing the light, he deliberately rejects it and conceals himself in darkness. It is told that Alcibiades, who admired his philosopher and friend, Socrates, used to break out now and again: Socrates, I hate you, for every time I meet you, you let me see what I am.

THURSDAY

First Reading (Acts 5:27-33). *Peter speaks out before the Sanhedrin.* What really touched them on the raw and made the Sanhedrin want to execute the apostles was not merely the contrast in Peter's speech between the claims that the leaders of the Jews killed Jesus and the God of the Jews raised him up. Worse, Peter puts Jesus in the honoured position of Moses, for Moses was the 'leader' of the chosen people and their 'saviour' by bringing them out of Egypt. This theme, however, is frequent in the New Testament, that Jesus is the second Moses, bringing to fulfilment what the first Moses began.

Gospel (Jn 3:31-36). *Eternal life.* This passage summarises some of the themes of the dialogue with Nicodemus: Jesus is the revealer of God; through faith in him we come to possess his very life; to reject Jesus is to condemn oneself. Jesus came to tell us what God is like and what we can become. Because he knows God he can give us the truth about God. This truth is the gospel. To listen to him is to hear God. He has the fullness of the Spirit in order to communicate God's word. True life for man is to listen and respond. To refuse to listen is to reject God's offer of love and life. The creative love of the Father through Jesus has changed life for us. God's greatest act of friendship is described in terms of man receiving a share in God's life and becoming a child of God. This new life of sharing in the intimacy and life of God is the life of grace.

FRIDAY

First Reading (Acts 5:34-42). *Gamaliel advises the Sanhedrin to wait and see.* This advice plays, of course, directly into the apostles' hands, and makes the ill-will of the Jews in continuing to refuse credence even more crass. Moreover this advice came from a rabbi—the only one named in the New Testament, being also Paul's teacher—who is known from the Jewish sources to have been one of the most respected teachers of the period. Nevertheless, the confrontation leads the apostles for the first time into physical suffering for the name of Christ, when they are flogged.

Gospel (Jn 6:1-15). *The sign of the bread.* This chapter gives us a 'sign' of Jesus along with its explanation. The bread he multiplies for the crowd is a sign or symbol of the nourishment, of the life we receive through his word and the Eucharist.

The scene reminds us of the Eucharist. Jesus gives this gift out of compassion for the many who are hungry and need his life-giving strength. The bread which Jesus blessed and distributed at the time of the Passover is a sign of the Eucharistic gift of himself. In the Eucharist we celebrate his own passing through death to the life of glory with the Father and the gift of new life which we have received. Fragments are gathered up so that they are not 'lost'. The Eucharist gives us a share in the imperishable life of Jesus. A gift is all the more precious when the giver puts more of himself into it. Christ wants to give himself to us completely. He puts his whole self, his very life into his gift.

SATURDAY

First Reading (Acts 6:1-7). *The appointment of the Seven.* There is a certain amount of dislocation between the cause of this move, namely friction between Jews and Greeks within the community, and the reason given for the appointment, namely to spare the Twelve the cares of administration. In fact the Seven who are appointed seem to undertake the same apostolic work as the Twelve, and probably they are a parallel hierarchy to the Twelve, being the leaders of the Greek-speaking converts, the Twelve performing the same function to those who speak Hebrew. It is the presence of the Spirit and the gifts of the Spirit which are the criterion in their selection.

Gospel (Jn 6:16-21). *I am he.* Jesus shows that he is the one who brings God's strengthing and saving life to his own. Through his word and the Eucharist we receive this power and saving life. Disciples are in darkness because they feel that Jesus is absent. But he 'comes' just as Yahweh came to his people, manifesting his power and consoling them by his presence: it is I. In the Old Testament God often tells people not to be afraid because he is present in their lives. Now Christ assures companions of his presence. He is the Lord of our present who takes away our fears. When the boat rocks and when winds blow strong he speaks to fearful disciples: I am present; you need not fear.

WEEK THREE OF EASTER

MONDAY

First Reading (Acts 6:8-15). *Stephen is arrested.* Stephen, being a hellenistic Jew, makes his apostolate among hellenistic Jews, for all the four groups mentioned, from Cyrene, Alexandria, Cilicia and Asia, would have a primarily Greek culture. One can see that the accusations against him would be insidious distortions of the truth: the 'blasphemies against Moses and against God' would be claims that Jesus takes the place of Moses and shares God's power. And his attack on the temple and its usages is substantiated by Stephen's long speech (not included in these readings) in which his theme is that ritual and temple have in Judaism always been opposed to true service of God.

Gospel (Jn 6:22-29). *Seeking Jesus.* People 'seek' Jesus for the wrong reasons. They were fascinated by what he had done for them. They were caught up by the thrill of unexpected wonders. They are asked to look beyond the bread which man can eat and earn to the mystery and meaning of Jesus. Seeking Jesus means turning towards him as the one who brings to men the ever-sustaining life of the Father. Sometimes we seek a sign, a gift or something from him, not really him at all. True love is to seek the friend himself whom we want to know and love rather than what his friendship can give us.

TUESDAY

First Reading (Acts 7:51–8:1). *The martyrdom of Stephen.* Stephen's martyrdom is the first death in the service of Christ's message, and it clearly shows that Christ's servant is imitating his master's death: there is the same commendation of his spirit (but to the Lord Jesus, whereas Jesus on the cross commends his soul to his Father) and the same forgiveness of his executioners. At the end of his trial, too, he sees the Son of Man as Jesus at his trial had prophesied to the judges that they would see him. The execution scene is also the first glimpse of Saul/Paul.

Gospel (Jn 6:30-35). *The work of God.* People will not believe. Jesus has to 'prove' himself by living up to their expectations of what a Messiah should be and should do for them. Jesus points to himself as the gift of the Father's life which satisfies man's deepest longings. Faith in Jesus is the work of God in us. It is the Father who draws us to Jesus. All that we have, even Jesus himself, is a gift of the Father. He is the initiator and source of all that we have in our life as Christians. All three, Father, Son and Spirit are at work together in the hearts of believers.

WEDNESDAY

First Reading (Acts 8:1-8). *The Christian message spreads to Samaria.*
'The blood of martyrs is the seed of the Church', and the persecution
which starts with Stephen's death is the occasion of the first spread of
the gospel beyond Jerusalem. This is the beginning of the spread of the
Word, first in Palestine, then to Asia Minor, next to Greece, and finally
to Rome, 'the ends of the earth' as Christ had commanded just before
the Ascension. Philip preaches Jesus in Samaria specifically as the
Messiah, because—as we know from non-biblical sources—the Samaritans had a particularly lively expectation of the Messiah.

Gospel (Jn 6:35-40). *The bread of life.* Jesus is the bread of life for
without him real life can neither begin nor go on for us. This real life is
a relationship of trust and intimacy with God, made possible through
Jesus. Once we know and accept Jesus and 'see' in faith who he is and
what he means for us we have come to him and this gives us life. But
our coming to Jesus is a gift. It is the Father's work in us. The Incarnate
Jesus is the one who has been sent by the Father to lead us into a life-
giving communion with God in time and eternity.

THURSDAY

First Reading (Acts 8:26-40). *Philip baptises the official of the queen
of Ethiopia.* The form of this charmingly told story is almost liturgical,
and indeed may well correspond to the earliest baptismal liturgy. The
official is reading from the Bible, or more specifically the Song of the
Suffering Servant of the Lord in Isaiah. It was by means of this text
that the very early Church understood the scandal of the cross, in
which the Chosen of the Lord reaches his glory and the accomplishment of his mission only through suffering and humiliation; this is no
doubt the explanation of the text which Philip gives. After the Word of
God read and explained, comes the sacrament itself. And over the
whole, as always in Acts, presides the Spirit who leads Philip to the
official and takes him away when his work is completed.

Gospel (Jn 6:44-51). *The living bread.* If we are open to God and
willing to be taught by him he will draw us to Jesus. God can and does
draw man but man's resistance can pull against God. To accept God's
offer in Jesus is to discover a life-giving relationship now and in the
world to come. As the 'living' bread Jesus is endowed with the power
to bring us to life. He lay down his own life that we might pass from
the darkness and emptiness of sin into a communion of life and love
with himself and his Father. Because Jesus is living bread, the Eucharist
is a celebration of his life and power.

FRIDAY

First Reading (Acts 9:1-20). *The conversion of Paul.* The conversion of Paul, and so the beginning of the mission to the gentiles, is given special prominence in Acts by being narrated three times. It should perhaps rather be called the vocation of Paul, for it is in the form of the vocation of great Old Testament figures such as Abraham, Samuel and Isaiah. All these, and Paul too, are called to a special task by the Lord, and the emphasis is on the calling rather than the conversion. The salient point of the experience for Paul himself was that Jesus was alive in power, and that he was living in the disciples whom Paul was persecuting. This is the starting point of Paul's theology of the Body of Christ which is the Church.

Gospel (Jn 6:52-59). *Eating my flesh, drinking my blood.* This passage treats directly of the Eucharist. It is the offer of a life-giving relationship with Jesus. He continues his mission to communicate life not only through his living word but also through a sacramental communion in which Jesus and he who believes 'live' in one another. Sacramental union leads to personal union. It is a life shared in common with Christ, a reciprocal indwelling which does not submerge the personality of the other. The Eucharist is the presence of one person to another through self-giving and a communication of life. Throughout this discourse of Jesus faith and Eucharistic communion are closely related. The person of Jesus is the centre of our faith and Eucharistic celebration. Our sacramental communion is an exercise and confirmation of our faith.

SATURDAY

First Reading (Acts 9:31-42). *Peter raises the dead.* We now see that outside Judaea, too, Peter is carrying on the work of Christ, not only in teaching but in bringing healing and life. The story of the raising of Dorcas or Tabitha (it was common in such areas to have alternative names, one Greek and one Hebrew) is especially modelled on the raising of Jairus' daughter by Jesus. Even the words are almost identical 'Get up, talitha' and 'Get up, Tabitha'.

Gospel (Jn 6:60-69). *Words of eternal life.* Jesus' words about his offer of life to men are intolerable for those who are closed to him. To those who accept him for who he is, they are words leading to true life. But man is weak and cannot open himself to Jesus without the help of the Spirit. It is he who makes Jesus' words life-giving and meaningful for us. The Spirit gives enduring power to his words so that they become Spirit-filled and life-giving. They can change our lives provided we recognise in them and welcome the transforming power of the Spirit of Jesus.

WEEK FOUR OF EASTER

First Reading (Acts 11:1-18). *Christ's Message bursts the bonds of Judaism.* Christianity began quite definitely as a movement within Judaism, and the move beyond its boundaries quite certainly needed justifying. It was the leader of the apostles who made the first move, and he is here justifying himself to the community, pointing out that he was merely a passive instrument. It was a vision from heaven which insisted emphatically (the triple repetition) that Jewish dietetic laws were to be abolished, and the Holy Spirit who led him to catechise the first gentile to enter the Church, hardly waiting till the catechesis was finished before taking him into the Church without even the intervention of baptism.

Gospel (Jn 10:1-10). *Called by name.* The Old Testament often describes God's care for his people in images taken from pastoral life. God is the leader and saviour (shepherd) of his people (sheep). He guides them along the right way of life. He cares for them and he accompanies them through their history by his protective presence. Jesus calls himself a shepherd because, if we follow him, he will show us and lead us along the way of true life. He forms a new community in which each person experiences his care and companionship. The Christian does not belong to a vast, impersonal gathering. Jesus calls us personally by name and we recognise the intimate and personal quality of his call. The disciple follows as a faithful companion and realises that Jesus is for him the only way that leads to life.

Alternative Reading *(This gospel may be read when the above gospel, i.e. Jn 10:1-10, is read on the fourth Sunday of Eastertide in Cycle A.)* **Jn 10:11-18:** *A good shepherd.* Jesus is the 'good' shepherd because he cares for and offers a life of companionship to his people. His goodness is realised in various ways. He lays down his life in freedom out of love for men and for his Father. He offers a life of intimacy. He 'knows' us individually. He invites us to experience who he is and what he means to us. To know Jesus is not just an intellectual experience. It is a real experience of a person. It is the life of communion with him. Mankind with all its divisions are invited to become one in him. The image shows what it means to be a 'pastor' and how people can exercise pastoral responsibility. As 'pastor' Jesus cares for those people given to him. He invites them personally, by name, to listen to the call to faith. He knows and allows himself to be known by them in a relationship of understanding and concern. He leads them to true life, to a life of fellowship with one another and with God. He spends himself in dedication, even to the point of giving himself completely on their behalf.

TUESDAY

First Reading (Acts 11:19-26). *The good news begins to spread among the gentiles.* Hard on the reception of the first gentile, Cornelius the centurion, follows the news that a great many gentiles had been admitted to the community at Antioch, which caused a stir in the mother-church of Jerusalem. Barnabas, sent to investiage, not merely makes a favourable judgement but fetches Saul to help.

Gospel (Jn 10:22-30). *In his hand.* All that Jesus does for man is also the Father's doing. The Father cares for and protects all those who listen to Jesus, for in all that he does he is at one with his Father. He, too, listens to his Father in obedience and love. He is one with God because he loves and obeys him perfectly. The Father shares Jesus' concern for disciples. We are asked to believe that even in the most difficult moments we are supported and protected by the strong hands of a Father and our brother, Jesus.

WEDNESDAY

First Reading (Acts 12:24—13:5). *The first missionary journey of Barnabas and Saul.* The next stage of expansion now begins, the first deliberate mission by the Church to win converts, and the first spread of the faith beyond Syria. It is stressed even twice in this short passage that the work is the work of the Holy Spirit, for every successful initiative in the Church comes from the Spirit. It is also interesting to note the structure of the community: they are sent out by a gesture of commissioning—the Jewish gesture for appointing a teacher by imparting the Spirit to him—from the whole community. As yet Barnabas, and not Paul, is the leader.

Gospel (Jn 12:44-50). *Believe in me.* The passage concludes the first half of the gospel (chs 1—12). The meaning of Jesus' life is summarised. He has come to tell us what God is like and what we can become. In him God speaks to us about himself and about the way we find that true life which saves. To believe is to open ourselves to the light, to listen and to see God in Jesus. Believing in Jesus is more than an internal disposition or an external declaration of faith. It is a movement towards a person, Jesus. We attach ourselves and give ourselves to him in trust. In faith we reach out to make his person somehow our own. He becomes our life-principle for he offers us a communion of life and love.

THURSDAY

First Reading (Acts 13:13-25). *Paul preaches to the Jews.* The Acts gives us two examples of Paul teaching, one here to the Jews and one at Athens to the Greeks. Here his theme is that Jesus is the fulfilment of the Jews' own hopes and the accomplishment of the promises made in the scriptures to their ancestors. It is one of Paul's themes, both in the Acts and in his letters, that Jesus was only the logical completion of God's plan within Judaism, and that only their refusal forced the gospel open to the Gentiles.

Gospel (Jn 13:16-20). *Like the Master.* The time is now coming when Jesus passes through death to the life of glory with his Father. He performs a symbolic action to show that self-giving and service mark the quality of his life and death (13:16-20). Then he speaks his farewell message, his last will and testament in the presence of his closest friends (13:21–17:26). The measure of a disciples's greatness is how willing he is to be identified with the fortunes of his Master. Jesus speaks with great sadness when he realises and accepts as part of his Father's plan for him that a specially chosen friend will 'lift his heel' against him, that is, turn informer and hand him over to a violent death. The disciple who serves like Christ makes himself less than others. He understands that he is for others. Self-preoccupation makes the world a place which revolves around ourselves. The pledged Christian who speaks and acts for Jesus will share in his popularity and disrepute.

FRIDAY

First Reading (Acts 13:26-33). *Paul continues his preaching to the Jews in Pisidia.* After his sketch of Old Testament history, showing how God's promises centred on David, Paul goes on to show that the resurrection was their fulfilment, and in particular the fulfilment of the promise in Psalm 2 and of Isaiah. After this reading, Paul went on to apply Psalm 16 'You will not allow your holy one to see corruption' to the resurrection. Thus to the Jews he is using the normal method of Jewish preaching current at the time, a commentary on scripture. This first preaching, as the Acts also informs us further on than the reading, was successful, and Paul was asked to preach again on the next Sabbath. Meanwhile many Jews joined their ranks.

Gospel (Jn 14:1-6). *The way to life.* Jesus assures and consoles his friends. One of the twelve has gone off into the night to give him up. Jesus says he will leave them; they are frightened by the prospect of loneliness. But he will be even more intimately present to them through his Spirit after the resurrection. They will enter into a communion of life with himself and the Father. The Father's love and life which is present in Jesus is so immense that there is room for all in that friendship which he offers. Jesus has made it possible for us to enter into relationship with the Father. In him we see what God is like. He has bridged the infinite space between God and ourselves. The way to God is not a dead, unending road. It is a person and he takes us to our destination.

SATURDAY

First Reading (Acts 13:44-52). *Rejection by the Jews.* Three times in the course of the Acts Paul's preaching of the good news of Christ is solemnly rejected by the Jews and three times Paul solemnly uses the words of scripture to justify his turning from the Jews to the gentiles. This happens once in Asia Minor (here), once in Greece at Corinth and finally at Rome, so once in each of the three main areas of Paul's mission. The triple repetition amounts to a formal rejection of the gospel message, and acts as an explanation of why Christianity failed to spread among the Jews—their ill-will and jealousy—and was forced to turn to non-Jews.

Gospel (Jn 14:7-14). *Going to the Father.* Jesus is the way because he shares his life with the Father and with us. The more we contemplate his life on earth and listen to his words, the deeper our understanding of God. Because he and the Father work together, his words are the Father's voice and his deeds the power of God. He also belongs to our world. Because he is a risen Lord present in our lives we too can do great, 'even greater' things. Jesus now acts more freely in us through his Spirit. The faith and love of Christians make visible the invisible presence of the glorified Lord. The disciple who prays with the Spirit of Christ knows what to ask the Father because he prays out of a life lived in a communion of faith and love with Jesus. He prays trustingly and unselfishly.

WEEK FIVE OF EASTER

First Reading (Acts14:5-18). *Sacrifice offered to the apostles.* There is a definite parallelism in the Acts between Peter and Paul, the apostles respectively of the Jews and of the Gentiles, and one point of comparison is the healing here of a cripple from birth, just as Peter had done in the temple. The contrast of reactions is, however, most marked: on the Jews it had had little effect, whereas the gentiles—more open as well as more credulous—take the apostles to be gods: Barnabas, the leader, is hailed as the leader of the gods, Zeus, and Paul, the spokesman, as his messenger. In his little speech Paul already adumbrates the themes of his great speech to the pagans at Athens.

Gospel (Jn 14:21-26). *To learn and to remember.* Loving Christ means that we respond to his word. As the Father speaks to us in Jesus, such a response brings us into a life of intimacy with himself and his Father. The Holy Spirit enters our lives, too, along with the Father and Son. He is a 'Paraclete' or assistant; he leads us into that life with Father and Son. As he comes in his name, he 'shows' us Jesus. The Spirit is a helper; he teaches us about and helps us remember Jesus. He is a teacher of mind and heart. He deepens our understanding of faith in Jesus and strengthens our response to him. To remember a friend is to bring him from the past and somehow let the memory of his words, his love give meaning to our present. The Holy Spirit confers on Christ and his words present meaning alongside the concrete realities of our experience.

First Reading (Acts 14:19-28). *Return from the first missionary journey.* On their return through the cities they had evangelised, Barnabas and Paul set up a permanent structure in the Christian communities, showing that these had an identity of their own now, apart from the Jewish communities. Nevertheless their structure seems to be modelled on the Jewish communities scattered around the Mediterranean, which were ruled by a council of elders, presided over by a temporary elected leader of the synagogue. There is no sign yet of the later structure of bishops.

Gospel (Jn 14:27-31). *I will come to you.* On his way to death, Jesus asks his disciples to be happy and at peace. They must learn the meaning of his death. He is on the way to the Father, to someone whom he loves and has constantly loved by responding to his will. He will have achieved the purpose for which he came—to bring the life of God among men. They can be at peace for he will continue to be with them through his Spirit. His presence will always remain a source of life and will strengthen them against the power of sin and selfishness. The awareness that Christ is active and present in our lives brings peace. This gift of Jesus is not just absence of trouble or a cosiness which comes from refusing to face reality. It is harmony and union with God and one's fellowmen. It is the experience of being loved by Jesus who has defeated death and who is with the Father.

WEDNESDAY

First Reading (Acts 15:1-6). *Paul and Barnabas go up to Jerusalem.* Peter's vision at Joppe was not in itself sufficient to convince permanently one part of Christians that Jewish Law need no longer be observed, for Christianity was after all only the fulness of Judaism. In fact this so-called 'Judaising' party will continue to appear often in the New Testament and beyond. As late as 300 there were some Christians who wished to observe the Sabbath and some of the dietetic laws. But it is evidence of the early unity within the Christian Church that Paul keeps returning to Jerusalem to check on the agreement of the community there.

Gospel (Jn 15:1-8). *Abide in me and I in you.* The Fourth Gospel is a reflection on our personal relationships. The quality of our relationship with one another, with Jesus and the Father is described in an image. The vine or vineyard was an Old Testament symbol for the people of Israel. Isaiah (5:1-7) describes God's care for his people in terms of a vinedresser who looks after his vineyard with special attention. Jesus speaks of a Father who tends the vine with its branches, who shares his life and love with us, his community, in his Son. The branches abiding in the vine express the intimate relationship offered to us by Jesus. Just as two friends are present to one another in listening, understanding and loving response, so also we are present to Christ—he abides in us and we in him. We become present to one another in a friendship of mutal understanding and response.

THURSDAY

First Reading (Acts 15:7-21). *Controversy at Jerusalem.* The controversy in principle is solved on different levels: the leader of the apostles, Peter, makes it clear that salvation is not by the Law but by the grace of Christ, so that one cannot impose the Law on gentiles. But James, the authoritative leader of the Judaisers, later to be leader of the Jerusalem community, pleads that converts from the gentiles should observe some of the regulations to avoid friction with Jews and to make community between the two more harmonious. Oddly, there seems to be no question yet of Jewish Christians abandoning their Law, which would be the logical consequences of Peter's speech.

Gospel (Jn 15:9-11). *Abide in my love.* Love is a descending gift of the Father. It is also a bond which holds together in an invisible net a series of relationships between Father, Son and ourselves. To love is to be present to another, to share life in concern and understanding. The Father and Son share themselves completely with one another. We are united in a bond of love with Jesus through listening and responding to his word. He, too, listens and responds to his Father's word and will. He remains in that continued presence of familiarity with his Father which always evokes joy. His joy consists in being loved by, in responding out of love to his Father. The message of Jesus about God's care for us brings joy. It tells us about friendship.

FRIDAY

First Reading (Acts 15:22-31). *The Apostolic Letter.* This first Church document, with the classic formulation of decision 'It has been decided by the Holy Spirit and by ourselves', conveys the awkward points in which divergence between Jews and gentiles would make any genuine common life impossible for the Jewish Christians. 'Fornication' probably means marriages forbidden by the laws of Leviticus, and the other matters are table regulations regarding *Kosher* food. The odd thing about the letter is that Paul nowhere seems to show awareness of it or its regulations.

Gospel (Jn 15:12-17). *My commandment.* Jesus speaks about the love of friendship. The friendship he offers comes from his initiative. He has chosen us as his friends; he has given his life on our behalf; he offers us intimacy by sharing with us the secret of his life with the Father. The friendship we return is response to his word and our response of care and concern for our fellowmen. Loving one another is a 'fruit'—it is the visible expression of our friendship with Jesus. This love is a relationship through which heaven and earth, men and God are all bound together. It is a sharing of life together in concern and understanding. Growth in our relationship with Christ is measured by our willingness to forget ourselves in order to enter into the world of others. The size of a person's world is the size of his heart. The measure of our faith in

Christ is the amount of people in whom we are willing to believe and hope.

SATURDAY

First Reading (Acts 16:1-10). *Paul's second missionary journey.* The partnership of Barnabas and Saul splits up through a disagreement about the worthiness of their junior companion John Mark, and now Paul begins to recruit his own team. There is a strange clash between Paul's insistence on having Timothy circumcised and his passing on the Jerusalem instructions that the Law need be observed by Christians only in four particulars. As all other major decisions in the Acts, Paul's decision to carry the faith into Europe is a direct result of the guidance of the Holy Spirit.

Gospel (Jn 15:18-21). *The rejected lover.* Because he loves, the Christian experiences lack of love or hatred. Christ chooses friends who are willing to share in his rejection. The word of Christ which the disciple tries to incarnate in his own life and work sometimes provokes hostility. This hatred is a refusal to be open to God in whose name Jesus speaks to men. A disciple needs to courage to be different. If he cares as Christ cared for his fellowmen, he will stand up and be counted on their behalf. It is dangerous and risky to be different and to practise that higher standard to which Christ calls. The faithful disciple suffers for his choices. He suffers for who and what he is.

WEEK SIX OF EASTER

MONDAY

First Reading (Acts 16:11-15). *Paul arrives at Philippi.* It appears from Paul's own letters that he had a special bond of affection with the community at Philippi; they were the one community which were sufficiently close to him for him to accept gifts of money from them, and when he writes to them he shows an unusual warmth and intimacy. One could not really divine this from the narrative in Acts, for there is little special about their short stay, though Paul has just been joined by the author who now writes in the first person, 'we', and came with Paul from Troas.

Gospel (Jn 15:26–16:4). *You are my witnesses.* When it is difficult to lead the Christian life the Holy Spirit is a helper, a 'Paraclete'. He 'testifies' within us by giving us an inner conviction about the meaning of Jesus in our lives. There can be no effective Christian witness without this inner conviction which comes from intimacy with Christ and which is a gift of the Spirit. A Christian shows that he knows Christ through an external manifestation of faith and love. The way he chooses in not a way of ease because he is a man of fidelity who has to suffer for the decision he takes. He freely chooses to be faithful to that vision of what it mean to be a Christian. Sometimes fidelity to what is deepest in himself means that he is left alone. Friends may depart when he takes a stand in order to be faithful. But he is not alone. In such moments the Spirit is a 'Paraclete'.

TUESDAY

First Reading (Acts 16:22-34). *Paul's miraculous release from prison.* Another parallel between Pater and Paul is here presented, Paul being released from prison by miraculous agency, as Peter was twice in the early part of Acts. Paul shows not only his Christian spirit of forgiveness but also his zeal to spread the gospel in using the opportunity to make converts of the gaoler and his family.

Gospel (Jn 16:5-11). *The convincing Spirit.* The departure of Jesus to his Father through death and resurrection brings about his presence to us in the Spirit. The Spirit strengthens and illumines our faith in Jesus. He gives an understanding of the meaning of Jesus and his work so that we have support of a real assistant or 'Paraclete'. He convinces us that sin is rejection of Christ. He assures us that Jesus has passed to glory from where he continues to help us overcome our sinfulness. This conviction that Jesus is risen, alive and active in our lives is the Spirit's gift. Such Easter faith is as demanding on us as Calvary. It means that we open ourselves to the life and life-giving word of Jesus about love, forgiveness and offering peace to one another.

WEDNESDAY

First Reading (Acts 17:15, 22–18:1). *Paul preaching to the Greeks at Athens.* This second major speech of Paul is an example of his preaching to the gentiles, as his speech at Antioch in Pisidia was an example of his preaching to the Jews. We have no other example of his taking the principles of pagan or natural religion as his starting-point. Perhaps it was simply that there was no occasion for it in his letters; perhaps his failure at Athens warned him not to try it again. The catechesis contains several references to classical literture such as might have been familiar to the audience, and a basis of the Stoic philosophy popular at the time. Most of the earlier part would have been acceptable to his audience, with its emphasis on natural theology, the closeness of God to all of us and the possibility of finding him through nature. But the sudden switch at the end to Jewish eschatology and the introduction of the idea of the resurrection were too bald to escape mockery.

Gospel (Jn 16:12-15). *The Spirit of truth.* The Spirit is also our guide. He leads us along the way towards the truth, to an ever-growing awareness of how Jesus affects our lives. This truth is an ongoing understanding of the meaning of Jesus for a changing world. The deepening of this truth which is God's revelation in Jesus, is not just an intellectual grasp once and for all. It is rather an insight into the present moment in the light of Jesus' person and message. The Holy Spirit is the Spirit of Jesus who is the truth. The sign of the Spirit's presence in our lives is the degree and quality of our following of Jesus in word and action.

THURSDAY

First Reading (Acts 18:1-8). *Paul moves on to Corinth.* This passage provides one of the few indications of date in the Acts: the expulsion of the Jews from Rome took place in 48-50 AD, and Gallio (mentioned in tomorrow's reading) was governor for a few months in 52 AD. Paul's visit to Corinth therefore took place between those dates. Here occurs also the second of the three solemn acts of witness against the Jews, when Paul is compelled to transfer his mission to the gentiles, using the words with which the Jewish crowd called down upon themselves the guild for Christ's condemnation by Pilate.

Gospel (Jn 16:16-20). *The gift of joy.* Jesus assures sad disciples that he will return and that his presence will be a source of joy. There is a joy which is the gift of the Spirit. It does not depend on what people give us or take away from us. At times, in distress and loneliness, there can be strength and peace which arise from the awareness that there is someone in our lives who understands and accepts us fully. This joy is founded on the presence of Christ and realised in us by the Spirit. At the end this presence of Christ will be fully revealed. Only then will the joy of the Christian be complete.

FRIDAY

First Reading (Acts 18:9-18). *Paul brought before Gallio the proconsul.* Gallio perfectly correctly refused to interfere in matters which concern customs of the local population, which were none of his business. In any case the Romans understandably had great difficulty in grasping anything of the intricacies of the Jewish Law. The unfortunate Sosthenes should have expected this result. For the author of Acts it is an important scene, for he is keen to show that Christianity does not clash with or give any offence to loyalty to Rome.

Gospel (Jn 16:20-23). *A new relationship.* Jesus speaks of a time when sorrow yields to joy and perplexity to certain knowledge of faith. The resurrection of Jesus changes his sorrow and ours into joy. It brings us into a new relationship with the Father. A new way to God has been opened up to us by Christ. Though we still walk by faith and not be sight, in Jesus we have a glimpse of God and a new meaning to human existence. It is the Spirit who brings us more and more into contact with Christ and enables us to see the more important things in life. The Father listens to those who are in communion with his Son and who ask him for those important things in prayer.

SATURDAY

First Reading (Acts 18:23-28). *Paul starts his third journey—Apollos at Ephesus.* Paul's first visit to Ephesus on his way back to Antioch had been very short, and so Apollos may fairly be called the founder of the Church there, with the consequence that their knowledge of the faith was very imperfect. It has been suggested that this Apollos, who was obviously a very important figure in the evangelisation, was the author of the Letter to the Hebrews, which has a number of characteristics ascribed to him.

Gospel (Jn 16:23-28). *Ask and you will receive.* A new era has dawned with the resurrection of Jesus. It is the time for man's special intimacy with God. Through his Spirit Jesus helps us understand the Fatherhood of God. He is our brother who prays with us to the Father. Our prayer becomes a prayer shared with him, penetrated by the Spirit and free from egoism. The more our life is penetrated by the teaching of Jesus, the more assured and unselfish does our praying to the Father become. In Christ's presence we discover a love that is absent from our lives. In his presence we think of the way he loved. This helps us to pray with more love in our hearts and in deeper communion with Jesus.

WEEK SEVEN OF EASTER

MONDAY

First Reading (Acts 19:1-8). *Paul arrives at Ephesus.* The disciples at Ephesus had in fact been baptised only into the community of repentance in preparation for the coming of the kingdom, and so formally at least were not yet Christians. The emphasis which this comparatively unimportant incident receives suggests that a polemic against some group of Johannine disciples somewhere in the Church underlies it.

After this Paul stayed at Ephesus well over a year, the longest stay in one place of which we are told, though we know little about his stay until the final riot which led to his leaving Ephesus. At some time during this period Paul was imprisoned for Christ, though the Acts tell us nothing of this.

Gospel (Jn 16:29-33). *I am not alone.* His closest companions will soon abandon him and leave him alone. But that does not diminish Jesus' love for them. He assures them that, though they falter, they will share in the peace and victory which his resurrection brings to humanity. Life will take its toll but the disciple can possess the courage and conquest of the cross. He remembers that Jesus experiences loneliness when disciples have gone and yet is comforted by the awareness that the Father has not gone away. The faithful man gains strength from the cross because he believes that in Jesus' loneliness the Father was present.

TUESDAY

First Reading (Acts 20:17-27). *Paul's summing up of his apostolic activity.* Theoretically this is Paul's farewell to the elders of the Church at Ephesus, but in fact it sums up all Paul's missionary activity, much as did Samuel's final speech sum up his ministry in the Old Testament. There are some memorable Pauline phrases such as come in his own letters, that life is not a thing to waste words on (compare 'Life to me is Christ, but death would bring something more' in Philippians) and that he must 'finish the race'.

Gospel (Jn 17:1-11). *Praying to the Father.* In prayer to the Father Jesus expresses what is deepest in himself. It is a prayer of Jesus the man and divine Son. Out of our world he raises human eyes to 'heaven', that space in which he experiences communion with his Father. His whole life of intimacy is contained in one word: Father. It is an unselfish prayer. His petition for his own glorification is a request that men may come to open themselves to the life and love of the Father which are made flesh in him. The prayer expresses his longings and central pre-occupations—his concern for disciples and for his Father's glory.

WEDNESDAY

First Reading (Acts 20:28-38). *Paul warns of future dangers.* As Jesus in the synoptic gospels just before the Passion warns the disciples of dangers and persecutions to come, so Paul now before his arrest. As Samuel attested his innocence of any motive of gain in his ministry, so does Paul; again this is characteristic, for he more than once in his letters alludes to the fact that he insisted on earning his own keep, so as not to be a burden on anyone. It was only from his beloved Philippians that he would accept money. Less typical of Paul is the quotation of a word of the Lord—in fact it also occurs in popular philosophy of the time—which he does only once in all his letters.

Gospel (Jn 17:11-19). *Keep them in your name.* In prayer we try to get in touch with and express to God the deepest desires and preoccupations of our lives. The prayer of Jesus reveals the nerve-centre of his own life —his life of intimacy and communion with his Father. Besides, people who are an essential part of his life enter into his prayer. Much of his prayer is about his companions of the present and future, so that we are included. His prayer concerns those things which are most important for himself and disciples. He reflects on his own life and mission. He looks forward to his life of glory with the Father. He sees his life and mission as the Father's gift. He reflects on his relationship with his Father and sees his Father's presence in all that he does and is. All that his disciples have received, all that they are—that, too, is the Father's gift. His Father is our Father because he gives us his word, his own life in his Son; he keeps us in communion with himself and with Jesus.

THURSDAY

First Reading (Acts 22:30; 23:6-11). *Paul defends himself before the Sanhedrin.* After Paul's return to Jerusalem he caused a riot in the temple from which he had to be rescued by the Roman guards. When he is brought before the Sanhedrin so that the Romans can discover what the Jews have against him, he again shows his respect for the Law, contempt for which had long been a charge against him. Apart from the clever forensic tactic of confounding his opponents by turning them against each other, the interest of his defence is that he claims to be proclaiming no more than the fulfilment of the hopes of the strictest party of the Jews, and so to be thoroughly orthodox.

Gospel (Jn 17:20-26). *A life of communion.* Jesus has prayed on behalf of disciples for the greatest gift that they may always be kept safe in a life of intimacy and friendship with himself and the Father. Now his prayer takes a sweep into the future to include Christians of all time. His petition again concerns communion—their communion with one another, which is based on their life of faith and love with Jesus and the Father. God's glory, his life and love, is manifested in a Christian life of sonship, faith and concern for one another. Jesus wishes not only that they share life with one another in concern and understanding on earth but also that they come finally to share his own eternal happiness and glory in the presence of the Father. Even though he is departing to his life of glory with the Father he will continue through his Spirit to communicate to us the love and life of God which will bind us together in communion with one another, with Jesus himself and the Father.

FRIDAY

First Reading (Acts 25:13-21). *The governor takes advice on Paul's case.* Paul had been in custody at Caesarea for two years before Festus consulted the neighbouring Jewish ruler, a descendant of the Herod family. The reason for Paul's refusal to stand trial in Jerusalem was no doubt the impossibility of securing a fair judgement there and the danger of being ambushed on the way. As a Roman citizen he had the enviable right of appear to the emperor, though a Roman court would—as Festus realised—hardly be competent to deal with Jewish legal intricacies.

Gospel (Jn 21:15-19). *Pastoral care.* Before the death of Jesus Peter had claimed that he would lay down his life for him (13:37), only to deny him three times shortly afterwards. He trusted in his own enthusiasm and failed. Now, have experienced his own weakness, he is able to assure Jesus three times of his love. He is invited to become, like Jesus himself, a good shepherd who cares for his people and lays down his life for them. Peter is to 'feed' the community of Christ and he will lay down his life for them. Pastoral care includes familiarity with and total concern for the community to the point of giving oneself completely on their behalf. Jesus reminds Peter that they are '*my* sheep.' All those for whom we have pastoral responsibility are not *my* group, *my* parish. St Augustine paraphrases: Tend my sheep as mine, not as yours.

SATURDAY

First Reading (Acts 28:16-20, 30-31). *Paul in Rome.* This is the completion of the programme of Acts, announced as the spread of the message not only in Jerusalem but to Judaea, and Samaria and 'to the ends of the earth', for in Jewish literature Rome is often so called. Paul again protests his fidelity to the Jewish hope, but here too Paul's message is again rejected by the Jews, and he solemnly testifies against them before turning to the gentiles. The way is now open for the spread of the Good News to the whole of the Roman world.

Of the outcome of Paul's case we know no more from the New Testament, nor can anything be deduced from the legal situation. There is only legend to guide us.

Gospel (Jn 21:20-25). *Beyond words.* Each in his own way, Peter and the beloved disciple are called to 'follow' Jesus. Peter follows Jesus to the constraint of the cross. Through the power of the risen Jesus he will realise what he had previously failed to achieve by relying on his own enthusiasm. The beloved disciple 'follows' as a witness to the story of Christ. But no story, not even the most beloved disciple can communicate the infinite and unfathomable riches of Jesus. He is beyond human categories, words and books. He continues to communicate things we do not discover in books. He can make things happen to us which no theologian can teach us.

FIRST WEEK OF THE YEAR

FIRST READINGS, Year 1 (Epistle to the Hebrews)

INTRODUCTION TO THE EPISTLE TO THE HEBREWS

This deeply theological epistle on the saving work of Christ comes to us from the pen of an unknown author. To whom was it written? The addressees are not named in the letter; the title 'To the Hebrews' was added to the text in the second century. The epistle is cited by Clement of Rome (c. 95 AD); hence it cannot be later than that date. It is most likely a document of the second Christian generation and may be reasonably dated in the 80's.

Hebrews is written to a Christian community. At first sight, because of the wide use made of the Old Testament, this would appear to be a predominantly Jewish-Christian church. In fact, this does not necessarily follow—Romans and Galatians, too, presuppose a good knowledge of the Old Testament. The author writes for a community which has grown discouraged and lax. They had been tempted (2:18); their spiritual life had suffered: they had grown sluggish and hard of hearing (5:11; 6:12). Some have lost heart (12:12).

All this explains the tone of the epistle and its repeated exhortations. The readers are first of all called upon to cling to the Word of God as revealed by Christ, lest they should stray from the truth (2:1). They must continue on the way perseveringly, like athletes (12:1). They must not be deceived (13:9), nor overcome by weariness (12:3); they must resist sin (12:4). On the positive side they must look to the joyful certainty of salvation (10:35); they must remain steadfast in hope (10:39). In a word, they must at all times preserve *pistis* ('faith') in its triple sense of docile acceptance of the revealed word, of confidence in Providence, and of persevering fidelity to the divine will (3:7; 4:13; ch. 11).

The central theme of Hebrews is *the priesthood of Christ*, and is formulated by reference to Jewish theological categories: Christ is superior to angels, to Moses, to the levitical priesthood, and Christ's sacrifice is superior even to the high-priestly liturgy of the Day of Atonement. Such Old Testament concepts were well appreciated by some first-century converts, but inevitably lose some of their relevance after twenty centuries. At several points, however, we meet religious truths of perennial validity. The author intended his treatise to be a 'word of exhortation' (13:22); the whole is a magificent statement of the saving work of Christ, and constitutes for us today a moving word of exhortation in a time when we may be tempted to 'fall away from the living God' (3:12).

Monday (Hebrews 1:1-6). *Christ is the expression of God.* The prologue (vv. 1-4) to the epistle announces the great themes to follow: the superiority of the new order of revelation to the old which it perfects; the divinity shared by the Son and manifested to us in him; his place in the cosmos; his role in achieving salvation for us by his Passion and return to the heavenly world; his superiority to the angels. In this prologue Christ has appeared as prophet (1:1), priest (purification from sin) and messianic king (sitting at the right hand of God).

Tuesday (2:5-12). *Jesus achieved his glory through suffering.* The Son became an integral part of our human existence and so leads that existence to the place where he now is at God's right hand. The universe is, in principle, subject to the dominion of Christ; but, in the concrete, it is not yet totally subject. Hebrew's theology sees a thorough correspondence between Saviour and saved, Son and 'sons', Sanctifier and 'sanctified'.

Wednesday (2:14-18). *Christ, our high priest, is like us in all things except sinfulness.* Today's reading introduces the central theme of Hebrews: the priesthood of Christ. Jesus is the perfect mediator because he is true God and true man. Because he shared completely our human nature he can have compassion for us in our sufferings and temptations.

Thursday (3:7-14). *An urgent appeal for attentive listening to the word of God.* Here begins a midrashic exegesis of Ps 95 which continues until 4:13. 'If only you would listen to him today': God speaks to us in many ways; we must learn to recognise and listen to his voice. It is not enough to open our ears to him; we must also open our hearts. If our hearts do not open to God we can be like so many deaf persons, unable to hear his word.

Friday (4:1-5, 11). *Through persevering faith we are called to share in the rest of God.* Under Moses an unfaithful generation was punished by exclusion from the temporal rest of Canaan: their failure was a failure to respond with faith to God's love manifested in his saving deeds. Now the members of the new chosen people are given the promise of a rest which is in heaven, if they remain faithful to an all-knowing God.

Saturday (4:12-16). *Because we have a compassionate high priest we can come with confidence before God.* The demands of God's word spoken through Christ are stringent and there is no escaping from them. We will be judged on how we have responded to God's word. This might seem to impose an impossible task on us but there is no need to be discouraged. We have confidence in knowing that Jesus is our merciful high priest who will give us all the help we need to be faithful to God's word.

FIRST READINGS, Year 2 (1 Samuel)

INTRODUCTION TO BOOKS OF JOSHUA, JUDGES, SAMUEL, KINGS & RUTH

Joshua, Judges, Samuel, Kings. The final edition of the books of Joshua, Judges, Samuel and Kings comes from the Deuteronomic school of writers whose work, begun before the Babylonian Exile, was completed during the exilic period (587/6–538 BC). These writers owe their name to the close affinity between their leading ideas and those of the book of Deuteronomy which they edited too. Most of the material in Josh, Judg, Sam and Kings, however, comes from a more ancient period; the Song of Deborah (Judg 5), for instance, is one of the oldest texts in the Bible. So in many cases one can distinguish several levels of meaning in a given text: that of the old tradition, that of the pre-Deuteronomic collection of traditions, and that of the Deuteronomic editors.

The book of Joshua tells of the Israelites' entry into the Promised Land under the leadership of Moses' successor Joshua (ch. 1–12: mostly old traditions from the territory and sanctuaries of Benjamin). The apportioning of the land among the Twelve Tribes is then described (ch. 13–22). Chapter 23 (see also ch. 1) is a major Deuteronomic interpretation of these events: the land is the Lord's gift to his people and will remain theirs if they faithfully observe the Law of Moses, keeping the Lord's covenant and avoiding contamination with foreign gods; but if the people transgress, the Lord will remove them from the good land he has given them (an explanation of the Exile). Chapter 24 then tells of the covenant-making ceremony at Shechem.

The book of Judges describes the unsettled times after Joshua's death, when the Israelites were often subjected to foreign oppression from which they were saved by the 'Judges' (in fact, charismatic military leaders). The Deuteronomists interpreted the old traditions especi-

ally in the passage 2:6—3:6: a cycle repeated itself in those days—
infidelity to the Lord, enemy oppression, cry for help and rescue by a
'Judge', relapse into infidelity after the Judge's death.

The books of Samuel are centred on three personages: Samuel, the
last Judge (1 Sam 1—15), Saul the first king (1 Sam 9—31), and David
his successor (1 Sam 16—2 Sam 24). Deuteronomic editing, less prominent in Sam than in Judg or Kings, is clear in 1 Sam 12: though the
people's call for a king was wrong, the Lord will not abandon them for
that, provided they and their king will follow the Lord's commandment; if not, disaster will surely come. One of the most important texts
for the understanding of royal messianism in the Bible is 2 Sam 7,
Nathan's promise to David.

The books of Kings begin with Solomon, and then tell of the
separated kingdoms of Israel and Judah which came to an end in 721 BC
and 587/6 BC respectively. The Deuteronomic editors draw a sombre
lesson all through: disaster came to Israel and Judah because of the
kings' infidelity to the law of Yahwah; with few exceptions (in Judah,
Hezekiah and Josiah) the kings allowed idolatry to contaminate the
purity of Yahwism (see especially 1 Kings 11:1-13; 2 Kings 17:7-23;
21:2-16). But the Exile is not the Lord's last word; the promise to David
(2 Sam 7) remains, and a glimmer of hope is held out to a shattered
people (see 2 Kings 25:27-30) if only they repent and turn back to
Yahweh (see 1 Kings 8:33, 35, 46-53; and already Deut 4:29-31).

Ruth. The message of this delightful short story, dating probably to
the monarchical period (1000-587 BC), is that God's control of events,
though hidden, is complete. He watches over all that happens to Ruth
the Moabitess and her mother-in-law Naomi. Ruth is to be an ancestress
of David, a link in the Lord's plan of salvation for his people; simple
events in rural Bethlehem take on a depth of meaning unknown to the
protagonists.

Monday (1 Sam 1:1-18). *The pilgrimage of a barren wife.* The many
traditions about Samuel point to his importance in early Israel. The last
of the Judges (see 1 Sam 7), Samuel was instrumental in establishing a
monarchical system of government in Israel—a much debated change, as
the constant tension between kings and prophets down through the
centuries of Israel's history was to show.

Today's reading tells of the barrenness of Hannah who was to
become Samuel's mother. For a similar motif see the instances of Isaac
(Gen 11:30; 16:1; 18), Esau and Jacob (Gen 25:21), Samson (Judg 13:
2), and John the Baptist (Lk 1:7).

Tuesday (1:9-20). *Heartfelt prayer is answered.* Hannah prays for a son and promises to dedicate him in a special way to Yahweh. The title Yahweh Sabaoth seems to have been especially associated with the Ark at the sanctuary of Shiloh (and later at Jerusalem); its meaning is uncertain—Lord of Israel's armies, Lord of the heavenly armies (stars? angels?), or All-powerful Lord. Hannah's earnest prayer is granted and the story of Samuel begins.

Wednesday (3:1-10, 19-20). *Samuel called to be a prophet.* As Hannah had promised, Samuel was dedicated to Yahweh's service at Shiloh. After Samuel had been awakened three times by a mysterious voice, the old priest Eli understands that it is Yahweh who is calling and he instructs Samuel to answer 'Speak, Yahweh' your servant is listening'. With this docile openness to the Lord's word Samuel's prophetic activity begins.

Thursday (4:1-11). *The Ark is captured by the Philistines.* 1 Sam 4—6 (and 2 Sam 6) tell of the vicissitudes of the Ark, a portable sanctuary regarded here as a powerful protector of Israel in time of war. The Philistines, an Indo-European people who had settle along the Mediterranean coast of Palestine about the same time as Israelite groups entered from the east, were Israel's great rivals during the time of Samuel and Saul and were finally subdued only in David's time (2 Sam 5; 8). The disastrous defeat suffered by the Israelites at Aphek served as a lesson that possession of Yahweh's Ark was no magical guarantee of victory; the texts suggests that it was the wickeness of the two sons of Eli the priest that made Yahweh turn against his own people.

Friday (8:4-7,10-22). *A king like the other nations.* A stronger centralised form of government, a monarchy, seemed necessary to coordinate Israel's resistance to the growing Philistine threat. But monarchy was always a sign of contradiction in Israel. While some favoured it and saw it as part of God's plan, others regarded it as abandonment of the Lord who was Israel's only king in order to seek security, as other nations did, in a human king. Today's reading belongs to the more negative current of thought; it looks back on the origins of the monarchy in Israel and notes its disadvantages, religious and practical.

Saturday (9:1-4, 10, 17-19; 10:1). *Saul is anointed prince over Israel.* In contrast to yesterday's reading, the present texts shows a more enthusiastic attitude towards the origins of monarchy in Israel. Saul, a noble and handsome man, is chosen by Yahweh to rule his people. As often in the Bible, the call comes in very ordinary circumstances: looking for his father's lost she-asses, Saul finds a kingdom. Samuel, here called a seer, anoints Saul prince, and the Anointed One (Messiah) is commissioned to save Yahweh's people from their enemies.

GOSPEL READINGS (Mark)

INTRODUCTION TO THE GOSPEL ACCORDING TO MARK

Mark is the first known Christian writer to have compiled a gospel out of traditional narrative and discourse materials, and to have fashioned it into a vehicle of his own theological interpretation of Jesus' person and mission. For that reason the real interest of Mark lies in seeing it as a whole, relating individual passages to the gospel's overall structure and outlook, and comparing Mark's treatment with Matthew's and Luke's later versions of the same synoptic materials. Since the fragmentation of the gospel into brief liturgical readings can obscure the broader theological message of Mark, it is essential to keep this overall message clearly in mind.

Mark wrote between 65 and 70 for a community of Christians converted from paganism. He incorporated into his Gospel earlier narratives which portrayed Jesus as a miracle worker, but counterbalanced this potentially misleading portrait with one that emphasises Jesus' suffering and death as the essential element of his messiahship. Although Mark sees this as the central message of Jesus' ministry, he portrays it as a secret which Jesus disclosed very cautiously and explained only to his closest disciples who, as it turned out, were still unprepared for the jolting events of his arrest, trial and crucifixion. Historically, of course, Jesus' ministry was not concerned directly with his own person, but with the proclamation that God's eschatological Rule (or Kingdom) was close at hand. In Christian preaching it is the crucified and risen Lord who is now proclaimed, but Mark projects this post-resurrection kerygma into Jesus' ministry. Throughout the gospel the reader should be aware of this dual outlook: the underlying historical tradition and Mark's superimposed reinterpretation of it in the light of Christ's resurrection.

Mark was undoubtedly motivated by the needs of his Christian community who themselves faced persecution and death under the Emperor Nero. Apart from its historical conditioning, however, Mark will always confront the reader with the inscrutable mystery of Jesus' suffering and death, and challenge him to accept a messiah who, though he was the Son of God (1:1; 15:39), came 'not to be served by to serve, and to give his life as a ransom for many' (10:45).

Monday (Mk 1:14-20). *Jesus begins his public ministry.* Jesus' ministry historically grew out of John the Baptist's, but in Mark John is a prefiguration of Jesus (6:14-29), and thus John's being handed over foreshadows Jesus' fate (9:31; 10:35; 14:10). The scene of Jesus' ministry is Galilee, but it is also the place where the risen Christ is encountered (16:7), and this suggests the final outcome of Jesus' ministry. Jesus preaches God's Good News: see Is 40:9; 52:7; 61:1 where the term denotes the proclamation of eschatological salvation. Old Testament allusions of this sort stress the fulfillment aspect of Jesus' mission and message. Finally, Jesus' preaching contains both a proclamation and an exhortation. In Mark the accent is on the former: the final inbreaking of God's saving power (or Kingly Rule). Thus, Mark compresses into these two vv. not only the historical details of Jesus' early preaching, but also some suggestion of the meaning of this inaugural event as perceived after Christ's resurrection.

The call of the disciples is a lesson in Jesus' authority: he calls and they immediately respond. Discipleship, which Mark describes as following Jesus, involves renunciation of livelihood and family ties, the same kinds of sacrifice which Mark's Roman readers were sometimes called upon to make. Only later (8:34ff) will Jesus reveal the supreme demand of discipleship: following him to martyrdom.

Tuesday (1:21-28). *Jesus taught with authority.* In Mark Jesus' teaching is a revelation of himself rather than of a doctrine. Notice throughout Mark how people are amazed at Jesus' teaching and how there is a mysterious quality especially in his parabolic teaching (4:10-12, 33-34). In this passage Jesus' teaching, healing, and self-revelation are closely intertwined.

In Jesus' world grievous sickness was attributed to demons. By curing sickness Jesus was symbolically displacing Satan's power with God's Rule. It is typical in Mark that Jesus' true identiy is not fully recognised by humans until his death. For men to recognise him for who he really is, miracles can be misleading; they need to be confronted by the necessity of his suffering and death, and that can only be disclosed gradually. This Marcan device is often called the Messianic secret.

Wednesday (1:29-39). *Jesus cures the sick.* The symbolism of Jesus' cure of Simon's mother-in-law is contained in the phrase, *he raised her* *up.* a suggestion that Jesus communicates the effects of his resurrection. The sequel shows that Jesus' miracles revealed something of his identity even if only the demons understood. Jesus' retirement to a lonely place suggests that he wished to escape from the crowd's misdirected enthusiasm. This is not the only occasion when Peter will wish Jesus to capitalise on the popularity caused by his miracles, or when Jesus will refuse to encourage the crowds in this sentiment (see 8:27-33). Notice how central in Mark is the thought that Jesus' miracles are an ambiguous disclosure of his messiahship unless complemented by the knowledge of his passion and death.

Thursday (1:40-45). *Jesus cures a leper.* By Mosaic Law lepers were segregated from God's people. By healing this disease Jesus displays a power superior to the Law and sets the stage for the conflicts in chapter two about his orthodoxy. The miracle conveys a paradoxical Christological point: Jesus upholds the Law, but his authority is superior to the Law's. The latter could deal with evil only by keeping it at a safe distance; Jesus deals with it by uprooting it and replacing it with God's gifts.

Friday (2:1-12). *The Son of Man has authority to forgive sin.* The symbolism of Jesus' miracle is explained in verses 6-10 which lead to the pronouncement about his authority to forgive sins. This forgiveness is linked to faith. Like the Old Testament prophets, Jesus called for faith, i.e. a trusting self-commitment to God. In addition Jesus called for acceptance of his proclamation of God's Rule. To Mark's readers faith means belief in the risen Christ, and is the prerequisite of sharing in his eschatological gifts. Verses 6-10 also introduce a hostility between Jesus and his critics which will continue in this chapter and lead to the plot in 3:6. Mark never allows his reader to forget the forces in Jesus' ministry which led to the cross.

Saturday (2:13-17). *Jesus came to call sinners to repentance.* Jesus' call of Levi, and especially his companionship with sinners, was a challenging symbol of God's healing power. Mark hints that this kind of action, which defied the religious sensibilities of Jesus' critics, was responsible for his death. The narrative and the saying in verse 17 contain an important soteriological point which Paul develops in Gal 5:21, that Jesus exercised God's saving power by identifying with the sinners he was sent to save.

SECOND WEEK OF THE YEAR

FIRST READINGS, Year 1 (Hebrews)

Monday (Heb 5:1-10). *Christ, the ideal high priest, is sympathetic to human weakness, appointed by God, and eternal.* This passage shows that Christ has perfectly fulfilled the requirements of priesthood. It falls naturally into two parts: (1) the qualities necessary for the priestly office (1-4); (2) Christ possesses these qualities (5-10). A high priest is a man officially instituted as a mediator between God and men, who defends the cause of men before God, and who offers the gifts of men to God, especially sacrifice for sin. But, a true high priest must be compassionate, showing great benevolence and indulgence to sinners, and he must be chosen and called by God. Christ was called by God and, through his obedience, gained an enriching psychological experience, a practical comprehension and appreciation of suffering which would enable him fully to sympathise with his brethren. As a result, he is consummated in perfection, author of eternal salvation, a high priest according to the order of Melchizedek.

Tuesday (6:10-20). *An exhortation to faith and perseverance.* The author reminds his readers of the promises attaching to their good deeds and encourages them to persevere in the faith, ending, as always, on a note of hope. God's unfailing promise gives the firmest ground for Christian hope. The anchor of faith keeps the Christian moored to his goal, the heavenly sanctuary into which Jesus has gone before.

Wednesday (7:1-3, 15-17). *Christ is priest forever 'like Melchizedek of old'.* The author intends to prove the superiority of Christ over the levitical priests. He begins by showing the excellence of the type of this priesthood, that of Melchizedek, although he soon concentrates completely on the antitype, Christ. Melchizedek, who appears in the Bible like a meteor (Gen 14:17-20) interests the author only as a type of Christ. Three circumstances impress him: the etymology of the names; the conduct of Abraham in regard to the priest-king of Salem; and the silence of Scripture concerning his origin. Melchizedek 'continues a priest forever' because his priesthood, being personal, not subject to the laws of human heredity, and scripturally without beginning or end, enjoys a 'negative' eternity. The Priesthood of Melchizedek and Christ is distinguished from all other priesthoods in that it has no human origin nor any human succession. The transitory nature of the levitical priesthood is marked by its suppression; the new priesthood according to the order of Melchizedek is eternal.

Thursday (7:25—8:6). *Shadow and substance.* Verse 25 forms a transition: it concludes the argument of verses 20-24 and introduces the peroration, verses 26-28. It is an excellent definition of the priestly office of Christ. In heaven he continues to offer himself to the Father that we may receive the redemption which he won for us on Calvary. Verses 26-28—a hymn to the High Priest whose holiness and perfection place him above all priests, even Melchizedek himself. In contrast is the old order and cult: earthly and figurative (8:1-6).

Friday (8:6-13). *Christ is the mediator of a new covenant.* At Sinai God chose Israel to be his people; he entered into a special relationship with them: 'I will be your God and you shall be my people'. But Israel failed to live up to the demands of this covenant. Six centuries after Sinai the prophet Jeremiah speaks of a *new* covenant which God will make with his people. This was fulfilled in Christ and sealed with his blood.

Saturday (9:2-3, 11-14). *Christ has fulfilled the Old Testament worship by offering his own life to the Father on the Cross.* On the Day of Atonement the Jewish high priest entered the Holy of Holies. Within he sprinkled the blood of animals and on emerging he sprinkled the people. The people were thus 'purified' and a bond established between themselves and God. But that was only a pale reflection of the reality: Christ, by his death has entered the Father's presence and from there he sends forth his Spirit, to cleanse us, to renew us and to create a bond between ourselves and God.

FIRST READINGS, Year 2 (1 & 2 Samuel)

Monday (1 Sam 15:16-23). *Obedience is better than sacrifice.* Instructed by Samuel in Yahweh's name to wage a holy war of annihiliation on the Amalekites who had been Israel's enemies during the Exodus, King Saul wins a crushing victory but does not kill the Amalekite king Agag. He also holds back the best of the captured sheep and oxen in order to sacrifice them to Yahweh. This well-meant gesture was however direct disobedience to Yahweh's command, and brings about Saul's rejection as king. For all the primitive cruelty of the 'ban' concept (found among Israel's neighbours too), the text teaches that liturgical actions can never replace plain obedience to God's commands (see Is 1:10-20; Mt 12:7).

Tuesday (16:1-13). *David is chosen to replace Saul.* Today's reading draws religious lessons from Yahweh's choice of a shepherd boy from Bethlehem to replace Saul. Saul will continue to reign for some years yet but the Lord's favour is no longer with him. As often in the Bible, the Lord's choice falls on the most disadvantaged, here the youngest of eight sons (compare Gen 25:23; 1 Cor 1:27-28). Royal anointing brings an abiding gift of the spirit of Yahweh.

Wednesday (17:32-33, 37, 40-51). *The Lord puts down the mighty and raises up the lowly.* The present chapter tells how David was sent by his old father Jesse to visit three of his brothers who are fighting in King Saul's army against the Philistines. Goliath, a redoubtable Philistine champion, has terrified the Israelite forces, so the young shepherd boy's offer to take up the Philistine's challenge seems foolhardy. But the most sophisticated armaments are of no avail if Yahweh is on the other side. Human boasting is laid low, 'so that all the earth may know that there is a God in Israel'.

Thursday (18:6-9; 19:1-7). *Saul's jealousy, Jonathan's friendship.* David's rise towards the throne and Saul's rejection have been decreed by Yahweh (see 1 Sam 15; 16). On the human level Saul began to feel ill-disposed towards the successful young hero when David was seen to enjoy more popularity than the king. Saul will make several attempts on David's life (1 Sam 18:10-11, 20-27), but Jonathan, Saul's son, brings about a temporary reconciliation. Jonathan's friendship for David will appear several times in subsequent chapters (1 Sam 20; 23: 15-18).

Friday (24:3-21). *David spares Saul.* Saul's jealous hatred forces David to flee from the court and live as an outlaw. Several campaigns were organised by Saul to hunt down and kill David.

Cutting off the hem of a garment was a symbolic action of grave import, for the hem represented a man's personality, freedom, and rights. David's action in fact suggested that Saul had lost his authority and kingship. However the text insists more on David's forbearance. He does not take matters into his own hands; the Lord will give him the kingdom in due time; meanwhile, in spite of the attempts on David's own life, Saul as the Lord's anointed one is to be spared.

Saturday (2 Sam 1:1-4, 11-12, 17, 19, 23-27). *David's lament over Saul and Jonathan.* King Saul and his son both died in battle against the

Philistines at Mount Gilboa. The way to the throne now seemed open for David, but his reaction is not one of joyful satisfaction. The death of Saul and Jonathan moved him deeply and a splendid elegy (part of which is given in today's reading) bears witness to David's nobility of spirit not only towards Jonathan but also towards Saul who had sought his life.

GOSPEL READINGS (Mark)

Monday (Mk 2:18-22). *A new age has dawned with Jesus.* Jesus' views on fasting, as recorded in Mt 6:16-18, show that he placed no value on mere externals. Jesus answers his critics with a parable comparing his ministry to a wedding, a time of rejoicing which fasting ill befits. The incompatibility between Jesus' proclamation of God's Rule and the Mosaic economy by which his critics (and even the Baptist) were living, is described in the two parabolic sayings in verses 21-22 which play on the contrast old-new.

Tuesday (2:23-28). *The sabbath is made for man.* Charged with violating the sabbath, Jesus appeals to the Old Testament where David's circumstances excused him from the Law. But Jesus goes on to say that man is ultimately the measure of the binding force of the Law, a thought which may have been added to Jesus' own saying, but which is consistent with his attitudes. By the time Mark was written, Paul had formulated a solution to the problem of the force of the Mosaic Law under the Gospel.

Wednesday (3:1-6). *Jesus came to bring life.* According to the parallel in Mt 12:9-14, Jesus cites common practice and then argues *a fortiori*: it is no violation of the Law to rescue an animal on the sabbath; how much more valuable is a human life! But in Mark's version Jesus appeals to a more universal principle: saving a life takes precedence over the sabbath observance. The lesson of all these controversies is related to Jesus' display of authority in his miracles: he deals with physical evil not by taking restrictive measures (as the Law prescribed), but by healing it from within. On the other hand, the Law properly interpreted cannot stand in the way of God's benefits. Jesus' activities constituted just such an interpretation, and the upshot of this first confrontation is a plot against Jesus.

Thursday (3:7-12). *The nature of Jesus and his mission is intimated.* A preview of coming events. The presence of the disciples looks to Jesus' choice of the Twelve (3:13-19), his explaining the parables to them (4: 10-20), and the miracles performed in their presence (4:35—5:43). The gathering of the crowds from all regions of Palestine is a prelude to his creating a new Israel in the choice of the Twelve. The Phoenician towns of Tyre and Sidon call attention to Jesus' interest in the pagans (5:1-20; 6:31—8:10). The boat previews events on or near the Lake (4:1—5:21; 6:32-50). The desire of the healed to touch Jesus foreshadows miracles in which Jesus heals by a touch (5:28, 41). And the demons' recognition of him as the Son of God is a reminder that Jesus is the hidden Messiah who restrains the 'strong man' Satan (3:24-27).

Friday (3:13-19). *Jesus chooses his twelve apostles.* Jesus' choice of the Twelve is a symbolic act which Mark sees as leading to the creation of a new People of God (like Israel of twelve tribes). The function of the Twelve is to be with him and to be sent out to preach and have authority over demons. The incident looks ahead to 6:7-13 where Jesus sends them out to exercise the messianic powers he has shared with them.

Saturday (3:20-21). *Jesus' relatives believe he is mad.* Jesus returns to Capernaum and is surrounded by an enthusiastic crowd. His relatives go out to draw him away from the crowds into the privacy of the family household, since his activity was becoming a source of embarrassment. Mark includes this obscure episode as a prelude to Jesus' saying in 3:31-35 about his true family, and to his townspeople's rejection of him in 6:1-6.

THIRD WEEK OF THE YEAR

FIRST READINGS, Year 1 (Hebrews)

Monday (Heb 9:15, 24-28). *The one sacrifice of Christ is all-sufficient.* The Redeemer is a Mediator. What he mediates is the new covenant of friendship between God and mankind, a covenant sealed in his own blood. He does not offer himself again to effect a periodical expiation, like the annual expiation made by the Israelite high priest; now, once and once only, he has appeared for the destruction, through the sacrifice of himself, of sin and the power of hell. According to the law common to all men, Christ could sacrifice himself and die only once. When he will appear a second time (the first time, by the incarnation, he came to redeem mankind), he will have nothing to do with sin, for it has been radically abolished by the unique offering on Calvary—through the redemptive blood presented to God by his Son. Then the salvation of the faithful will be total and definitive.

Tuesday (10:1-10). *Cause of eternal salvation.* 'Behold, I come to do your will, O my God': the response today sums up Christ's whole attitude during his life on earth. His death on the cross was the expression of the surrender of his being to the will of the Father: 'Father, into your hands I commit my spirit' (Lk 23:46). Jesus, having poured out his blood for the remission of sins and having entered into heaven to intercede for men (ch. 9) is the author of a real sanctification and of eternal salvation. This peerless sacrifice is set in contrast to the sacrifices of the Old Law.

Wednesday (10:11-18). *No other sacrifices for sin.* The multiplicity of the futile actions of the levitical priests is contrasted with the single, permanently effective action of Christ. The sacrifice of Christ has been made once for all, and the forgiveness it achieved has been achieved once for all. There is no more sacrifice to be made for sin. There remains only to apply the sacrifice of Christ through the sacramental order.

Thursday (10:19-25). *From exposition to exhortation.* One of the features of the letter to the Hebrews is that every so often, after contemplating some aspect of the mystery of Christ's priestly sacrifice, the author comes down to earth with a practical application. The passage is a call to confidence in the High Priest: the way to God is Christ himself (cf. Jn 14:6). The great truths we believe ought to flow into our daily lives, our relationships with our fellow-Christians. The author shares the expectation, which was general in the early Church, of an early return of Christ ('the Day').

Friday (10:32-39). *The generosity of times past.* The readers must recall their earlier steadfastness in face of persectuion; now again there is need of that patient endurance and a firm faith. Their fidelity in the past is the best ground of confidence for the future.

Saturday (11:1-2, 8-19). *The faith of men of old.* The passage 11:1-40 deals with the faith of the great men and women of the Old Testament, with the reminder that faith is necessary for those who move onward to draw near to God. Faith is the firm assurance of the fulfilment of our hope. For, faith is oriented to the future and reaches out to the invisible. Grounded on the word of God, it is a guarantee of the possession of heavenly blessedness; it persuades us of the reality of what is not seen as yet and enables us to act upon it.

FIRST READINGS, Year 2 (2 Samuel)

Monday (2 Sam 5:1-7, 10). *Jerusalem the political centre.* Shortly after Saul's death David had been chosen as king of the southern region, Judah (2 Sam 2:1-4). After the murder of Ishbaal, a son of Saul, who had been set up as king of the rest of Israel (2 Sam 4), the elders of Israel accept David who now reigns over the united kingdoms of Israel and Judah. The capture of Jerusalem, the supposedly impregnable city of the pre-Israelite Jebusites, gave David a capital strategically situated in neutral territory between the two parts of his kingdom.

Tuesday (6:12-15, 17-19). *Jerusalem the religious centre.* The Ark had been housed in various temporary sanctuaries after its recovery from the Philistines (1 Sam 6; 2 Sam 6:1-11). David now brings it from the last of these to his newly-won capital city. In this way he binds the northern tribes of Israel, whose cultic object the Ark had been, to himself and to Jerusalem all the more closely. David, though not a priest, offers sacrifice; the anointed king could act as the religious head of the people in exceptional circumstances.

Wednesday (7:4-17). *The prophecy of Nathan.* David's proposal to build a house (= temple) for the Ark is countered by Yahweh's promise through the prophet Nathan to give David a House (= dynasty). It is David's son Solomon who will build the temple.

This text is the basic theological statement of the perpetuity of David's line and provided grounds for the expectation of a royal messiah. Centuries later, the Son of David whose risen body is the new temple will give access to the ultimate place of rest for God's people.

Thursday (7:18-19, 24-29). *David's prayer of thanksgiving.* Seated before the Ark of Yahweh, David thanks the Lord for the promises made to him. First an act of humility: neither David nor his House are worthy of such great favours. Then repeated expressions of praise of the Lord's greatness and fidelity, and acknowledgement of the fact that all the Lord's benefits will lead men to confess that Yahweh is God over Israel. There is much to be learned from the spontaneity and God-centredness of this prayer.

Friday (11:1-10, 13-17). *David's sin.* There is an abrupt descent from
the heights of 2 Samuel 7 to this account of David's sins of adultery
and murder—a reminder that the treasure of God's promises is indeed
carried about in vessels of clay (see 2 Cor 4:7), a reminder too that
Biblical narratives are not merely edifying examples but convey all the
light and shade of real life, for it is there that God's word comes to
meet man.

Uriah's refusal to go to his own home reflects the religious obligation
of sexual continence laid on Israel's warriors during a military campaign
(see 1 Sam 21:5). Uriah paid for his fidelity with his life.

Saturday (12:1-7, 10-17). *You are that man!* Nathan, who had brought
the word of promise (2 Sam 7), now brings Yahweh's word of judgement of David's sins of adultery and murder (2 Sam 11). Nathan makes
David judge himself by means of the parable of the poor man's ewe-
lamb. With admirable frankness David admits his guilt and Yahweh
releases him from the sentence of death he deserves. But the child born
of the union with Bathsheba falls ill and dies, in spite of David's fasting
and prayers; and the future sorrows of David's reign, in particular of his
son Absalom's revolt (see especially 2 Sam 16:20-22), are seen as
punishment for David's sin.

GOSPEL READINGS (Mark)

Monday (Mk 3:22-30). *The end of Satan's power.* Jesus denies the
accusation that his powers are from the devil, and explains his true
relation to Satan. Satan is like the owner of a house who must first be
overcome if his possessions are to be taken from him. Jesus implies that
by curing the sick he is breaking Satan's grip on man and allowing
God's Rule to have sway. Mark probably understood Jesus' saying
about the unforgivable sin to mean that there is no hope for one who
does not see that Jesus is God's prophet possessed by his Holy Spirit.

Tuesday (3:31-35). *The true family of Jesus.* The point of this narrative
is in Jesus' pronouncement that his true family includes all who do
God's will. Many New Testament writers stress the unity which we have
in Christ, a unity based on faith, transcending flesh and blood ties, and
making us his brothers and friends.

Wednesday (4:1-20). *The parable of the sower.* Jesus' sower parable
contrasts the farmer's sowing to the bountiful crop that inevitably

grows from the good soil. Similarly, though much of Jesus' ministry seems like wasted effort, it is the first act of the drama that will usher in God's Rule (the harvest). Jesus intended the parable to counteract the disappointment which many felt about the uneventful appearances of his ministry.

Mark then shifts the scene and has Jesus alone with his disciples. What concerns Mark is not the meaning of the sower parable but the reason why Jesus spoke in parables at all. The quotation from Is 6:9-10 says equivalently that Jesus used parables to conceal the truth from the crowds lest they turn to God and be forgiven. This harsh thought reflects Mark's view of why Jesus' people, even down to Mark's time, did not accept Christ.

Jesus's explanation of his parable is quite different from the meaning explained above. Here the accent is on the unproductive soil and the farmer's wasted efforts. Unlike the parable which is kerygmatic, the explanation is moralistic, warning against the wrong way to receive the word. The style and vocabulary of the explanation indicate that it was made up by a Christian catechist and came to be joined with the sower parable as a unit of gospel tradition. Although the explanation misses the main point of Jesus' parable, it stresses a valid secondary point, that Jesus' proclamation of God's Rule challenges the hearer to act decisively and productively in the face of adversity.

Thursday (4:21-25). *Jesus is the light of the world.* Mark brings together several sayings of Jesus into a double parable on concealing and revealing. The lamp is an image of Jesus' proclamation: if its meaning is hidden from some, it can only be temporarily, for light must shine! *The measure you give. . . :* Those who hear and accept Jesus' message (like the good soil) will be rewarded.

Friday (4:26-34). *Parables on the nature of the kingdom of God.* Jesus' parable contrasts the farmer's sowing to the crop that eventually spings up, and implies that the same organic relationship holds between Jesus' ministry and God's Rule. The timing of the latter is less important than the fact that Jesus gets the process under way. The mustard seed parable makes a similar point: from a tiny seed springs a full-grown bush; from the unpretentious event of Jesus' ministry God's Rule will inexorably break out. Mark concludes this parable discourse with two verses that again reflect this view about the purpose of Jesus' parables. In Mark Jesus' true identity is a secret that he reveals only to those he chooses; it is also the central message of his preaching. In reality, Jesus' message was concerned with God's Rule and only secondarily with his own place in the eschatological drama. In Christian preaching it is the risen Lord who is now proclaimed, but the evangelists read this post-resurrectional kerygma back into Jesus' ministry. In John Jesus' self-proclamation is public and solemn; in Mark it is enigmatic and private.

Saturday (4:35-41). *By calming the storm at sea Jesus reveals his power.* In the Old Testament God's creative power is described as a conquest of the sea or sea monster (Gen 1:2; Ps 89:10) and is paralleled by his deliverance of Israel through the Reed Sea (Is 51:9-10). Thus for Mark Jesus' miracle reveals him as the one in whom God's creative and redemptive power is now exercised.

FOURTH WEEK OF THE YEAR

FIRST READINGS, Year 1 (Hebrews)

Monday (Heb 11:32-40). *Heroes of faith.* The author breaks off his detailed series of particular individuals and actions and continues with a more general picture of the exploits and hardships of the Israelites from the time of the Judges onwards. Now that 'these last days' (1:2) have arrived with Christ, the believers who persevered during the days of the old covenant have their hopes fulfilled along with Christians.

Tuesday (12:1-4). *Look to the example of the life of Christ and take courage.* The realisation that the saints of the Old Testament, their noble ancestors in the faith, are witness of the great race which Christians must run, will give them heart and encourage them to persevere. But the example that is best calculated to sustain the patience and courage of Christians is that of their Lord who was humiliated and crucified only to rise again and enter into his glory. Jesus is the 'pioneer' —that is, 'chief', 'leader'—offering the example of a faith strong enough to enable him to endure the sufferings of his whole life. 'Looking to Jesus': here is the kernel of the letter. The author wrote to people who had grown lukewarm in the faith, who needed to be brought back to their first fervour.

Wednesday (12:4-7, 11-15). *Our trials and troubles are the proof of God's love for us.* Suffering is part of the Christian life, a factor of the divine pedagogy. When God punishes his children, he does it as a Father, for their good. This is a training which will help them towards that holiness of life which will bring them to 'the peaceful fruit of righteousness' (12:11). The Christian life consists in striving for peace with our fellowmen and for a share in God's own holiness.

Thursday (12:18-19, 21-24). *Sinai and Zion, symbols of two orders of salvation.* The heavenly city, goal of the Christian's pilgrimage, at last appears in detail. At the same time the contrast of the two covenants is made with the symbolism of two mountains—Sinai, the mountain where the old covenant was made, and Zion, the mountain of the heavenly Jerusalem. The author bids his readers: you no longer belong to the old covenant, but to the new. Look no more to Sinai but to the heavenly Jerusalem and its atmosphere of assurance and hope. More than hope, for you already possess the good things of the new economy; you are already citizens of the heavenly Jerusalem. The 'sprinkled blood' of Christ has realised the reconciliation between God and sinful people.

Friday (13:1-8). *Unselfish love and concern for others are to be the marks of the true disciples of Christ.* An exhortation to fraternal charity, in the practice of hospitality and in generosity to prisoners and those suffering ill-treatment. Marriage is worthy of special respect. We, today, live in a time of great and rapid change. We are sometimes tempted to ask if there is anything, even within the Church, that will not change. Here we have the answer. Jesus Christ is the same yesterday, today and forever: the same love that led him to die for us on the cross, the same truth that he committed to his Church to teach.

Saturday (13:15-17, 20-21). *Concluding exhortations and prayer.* Christians have something of their own to bring to their celebration of the mystery of the sacrifice of Christ: a liturgy of praise. Unlike the single and unique sacrifice of Christ, this liturgy of praise continues throughout the age of redemption. Obedience to the community leaders is inculcated and the author asks for the prayers of the community. A wish for peace and for progress in virtue reminds the readers that they are in the care of 'our Lord Jesus Christ, the great Shepherd'.

FIRST READINGS, Year 2 (2 Samuel, 1 Kings)

Monday (2 Sam 15:13-14, 30; 16:5-13). *David flees from his son Absalom.* Absalom was embittered by two years of exile and then banishment from the court imposed on him by David for the murder of Amnon, his half-brother and David's eldest son (2 Sam 13—14). Resolved to seize the throne Absalom has won over many of David's subjects, and now his forces are approaching Jerusalem.

David's flight leads him up the Mount of Olives (near the Garden of Gethsemane) and on towards the Jordan. He bears admirably with the savage insults of Shimei, a member of Saul's clan, and refuses to take vengeance on his enemy (compare 1 Sam 24).

Tuesday (18:9-10, 14, 24-25; 18:30—19:3). *Absalom's death and David's grief.* Absalom made the fatal mistake of allowing David time to gather his forces (2 Sam 17:1-23), so when battle was joined east of the Jordan David's professional soldiers easily had the better of Absalom's volunteers. Though David had ordered his general Joab to spare Absalom's life (18:5), Joab puts the security of the state before the feelings of the father and has Absalom killed. News is brought to David whose fatherly anguish is portrayed in an unforgettable scene. The depth of a father's love for a son who has sinned against him opens horizons towards Lk 15 and 1 Jn 4:9-10.

Wednesday (24:2, 9-17). *A sinful census and David's repentance.* Why was this military census regarded as sinful? In general there was an old taboo against counting heads (attested outside Israel too, and see Ex 30:11-16); furthermore in the present case strict Yahwists considered that a census of the available warriors was an infringement on Yahweh's prerogatives. Since strength and victory really came from Yahweh and not from human might (see Judg 7:1-8; 1 Sam 14:6), a military census made with a view to general conscription was seen as sinful reliance on one's own strength. Here, as in 2 Sam 12, David's sincere repentance and generous assumption of responsibility are admirable.

Thursday (1 Kings 2:1-4, 10-12). *David's last testament.* Solomon has already been installed as David's successor (1 Kings 1), and the Deuteronomic writer spells out in his characteristic language the conditions Solomon will have to observe if Yahweh's promise to David (2 Sam 7) is to be fulfilled. Since however history was to show that Solomon and most of his successors would not live up to the required fidelity to Yahweh, these last words of David convey an implicit explanation of future disasters (the Exile).

Friday (Sir 47:2-11). *Praise of a mighty and holy king.* Looking back from the second century BC, Ben Sira praises the Lord's greatness displayed in the illustrious men of his nation's past (Sir 44–50). Today's reading presents his panegyric of David; he extols David's bravery and military successes, insists on his organisation of Israel's worship (dealt with at length in the post-exilic 1 Chron 15–16; 22–29), and makes only passive reference to David's sins.

Saturday (1 Kings 3:4-13). *Solomon's prayer for wisdom.* Solomon's unselfish prayer for practical wisdom in his task of judging and governing the Lord's people is answered, and David's successor is also granted what he had not asked for—riches and glory beyond that of any other king.

A later Deuteronomic writer, with his absorbing interest in Jerusalem as the only legitimate place of worship, notes a shadow in this bright picture of the new king. Solomon offered sacrifices (to Yahweh, no doubt) in the high places, the local sanctuaries often of Canaanite origin scattered throughout the land.

GOSPEL READINGS (Mark)

Monday (Mk 5:1-20). *Jesus cures a man suffering violent convulsions.* In an unusually detailed narrative, Mark recounts the cure of a man suffering violent convulsions. Cast as an exorcism, the miracle reveals Jesus' power to rescue from all that separates us from God. His defeat of the demons is so complete that even the swine cannot abide their presence. The fact that this takes place in non-Jewish territory means that Jesus' mission is not unrelated to the gentiles.

Tuesday (5:21-43). *The raising of the daughter of Jairus.* Both the woman and Jairus are examples of faith; the woman especially shows that while Jesus' powers may seem magical (it is enough to touch his robe), faith is necessary if one is to benefit from the deeper saving power which his cures embody. This symbolism is powerfully expressed in the next miracle which shows that death itself is subject to Jesus' authority.

Wednesday (6:1-6). *Jesus is rejected by his own townspeople.* Jesus' rejection by his own townspeople foreshadows the final rejection in Jerusalem. The Nazarenes' offence (*skandalon*) at Jesus and their unbelief recall Paul's description of Christ's death as a *skandalon* (stumbling block) for Israel, and Israel's unbelief (1 Cor 1:23; Rom 3:3).

Coming as the conclusion of a large section of Mark, this episode signals the beginning of a new phase of Jesus' ministry in which the Twelve will be more prominent, and in which Mark will show Jesus' interest in the pagans.

Thursday (6:7-13). *How Christian missionaries should travel.* Mark has modified Jesus' instructions to reflect the practice of later missionaries who carried a staff, wore sandals, and owned several tunics (see Mt 10: 9-10 where these are forbidden). The command 'no bread' is emphatic, for Jesus himself will soon feed the crowds with bread. Jesus also highlights the reception given or denied the Twelve rather than (as in Mt 10:12) the punishment for rejecting them. They share Jesus' healing powers and preach repentance, but only Jesus proclaims God's Rule.

Friday (6:14-19). *An account of the martyrdom of John the Baptist.* Jesus is viewed as the successor of John the Baptist and as a prophet, especially Elijah whose return to earth was to be a sign of the eschaton (Mal 4:5). The mention of John's 'resurrection' shows that his is a prefigurement of Jesus. Herod's awe for John parallels the awe felt for Jesus by his disciples, the people, the healed, the high priests, and scribes. Like Jesus John was upright and holy (Acts 3:14), gladly listened to (12:37), and buried by his disciples (15:45-46). Thus, John's story should be read as a foreshadowing of Jesus' death and resurrection.

Saturday (6:30-34). *Jesus has pity on the multitudes.* This passage introduces the feeding of the 5,000. Jesus' being alone with the Twelve in a desert place prepares for this self-revelation to them as a new Moses with a new form of manna. In Matthew Jesus retires to be safe from Herod who has just killed the Baptist; in Mark the reason is theological: to rest, an Old Testament theme for the Israelites' occupation of the Promised Land, often connected with the escatological shepherd (Ps 23). In Mark Jesus pities the crowd not because of their sick (Mt 14:14) but because they are shepherdless. Their needs are fulfilled by Jesus' teaching them, a Marcan theme suggesting a self-revelation of Jesus.

FIFTH WEEK OF THE YEAR

FIRST READINGS, Year 1 (Genesis 1–3)

INTRODUCTION TO THE PENTATEUCH

The first five books of the Bible–Genesis, Exodus, Leviticus, Numbers and Deuteronomy–are commonly known by the collective title the *Pentateuch*, a Greek word that can be roughly translated as 'the five scrolls'. Originally these five books formed one whole, a consecutive narrative that recorded Israel's understanding of the great events that took place between the creation of the world and the settlement of the Israelite people in Canaan.

The Hebrew designation for these books is the *Torah*. Although this word is often translated as *The Law* it's meaning is much wider. We might take the word Torah to mean 'instruction', and we could understand the group of books called 'The Torah' as the body of literature that contains the instruction in legal, historical and cultic matters which every Israelite might be expected to make his own.

The Pentateuch or Torah tells of the origin of the world and of mankind; it tells the story of the Patriarchs and of Moses; it describes the making of the Sinai covenant which marked the establishment of Israel as a people; it records the laws that regulated the social and religious life of the people; it describes the sojourn in the wilderness, and, having recorded the death of Moses, it leaves us with the Israelites within sight of the land that had been the goal of all their journeying.

However, we read these narratives not merely as historical documents. Their message for us is primarily religious. They point to God as the creator of all things, as the One who controls all history, who guides man's destiny, and enters into a personal relationship with him.

A Blending of Sources. All modern scholars agree that the Pentateuch as it has come down to us is the result of the work of several editors who combined many independent sources into one composition. There is no general agreement about the place and date of origin of each of these sources, or of their exact extent; But we can safely say that four principal sources–known as J, E, D and P–can be distinguished in the Pentateuch. Differences in vocabulary, literary style, theological points of view etc., help authors to distinguish one source from another.

The J, or Yahwist source gets its name from the fact that it refers to God as Jahweh, usually written Yahweh in our modern English Bibles.

It dates from about 950 BC, and its author (or authors) seem to have been the first to arrange the traditions of Israel into a continuous account. It begins with the story of the creation of man and animals (Gen 2) and follows the course of events that led to Israel's settlement in Palestine.

The name E or Elohist for the second source comes from the fact that in it God is known as Elohim. This source seems to date from about 850 BC and is seen as a record of the traditions that were known in northern Palestine. It begins with the story of Abraham (Gen 15), and runs parallel with the J narrative as it traces the story of Israel from the time of the Patriarchs to the occupation of Canaan. The two sources, J and E, seem to have been combined sometime after 700 BC.

Unlike J and E, D is not a strand of tradition that runs right through the Pentateuch, but a whole book (Deuteronomy) which is inserted into the Pentateuch narrative. It is believed to be the 'Book of Law' that was found in the temple in 621 BC during the reform of King Josiah (cf. 2 Kings 22:8-10). Its contents are mainly legal, and it establishes regulations for the religious, social, administrative, commercial and family life of the people.

The P or Priestly source is so designated because of the priestly interest of its authors. We owe this source to Babylonian exiles who continued to record the traditions of Israel after their return to Palestine in the fifth century BC. These writers were interested in setting forth the priestly law that governed the ritual of the temple and the celebration of religious festivals, and they paid special attention to genealogies (cf. e.g. Gen 5:1-32). Although the P source contains some inspiring and poetic passages (e.g. Gen 1–2:4a) it is generally dull and uninteresting, and of little value to the modern reader. The irrelevance of much of the P material is reflected in the fact that from the long section from Ex 35:1, through Leviticus, to Num 10:11 which comes from this source, only a few passages have a place in the lectionary.

The Priestly source was soon combined with the earlier traditions, and the Pentateuch as we know it had taken shape by about 400 BC.

Selecting the best. Anyone who has attempted to discover the riches of the Pentateuch for himself will readily admit that this extensive body of literature is not always easy to understand or appreciate. It does indeed contain gems of literature and inspiring religious passages, like Gen 22 and Ex 15. But these are balanced by texts that are sometimes of little or no interest to Christians today (see e.g. the census recorded in Num 26:1-51, or the war described in Gen 14:1-6), sometimes shocking to our moral sensibilities (see e.g. Gen 12:10-20), and sometimes disconcerting in their treacherous and violent tone (see e.g. Gen 34).

The compilers of the lectionary have enabled us to discover the riches of the first books of the Bible by offering us what one might call 'The Best of the Pentateuch'. In their choice of readings Genesis is well represented because of the importance of the theology of the primeval history (Gen 1–11), and because of the significance of the Patriarchal history in Israel's later life (Gen 12–50). As one would expect the story of Moses, the Exodus and the Sinai covenant (Ex 1–24) is recalled at length in the new series of readings. On the other hand, only a few texts from the legalistic and ritualistic material which we owe to P (see above) have found their way into the new lectionary. Since Deuteronomy contains many beautiful exhortations which clarify Israel's obligations to the covenant God who chose her it is not surprising that this book is generously represented in the compiler's choice.

Genesis 1–11. In 1948 the Biblical Commission asserted that the aim of the first eleven chapters of Genesis was to 'relate in simple and figurative language, adapted to the understanding of a less developed people, the fundamental truths underlying the divine plan of salvation, as well as the popular descriptions of the origin of the human race and of the chosen people.' What we look for, then, in these chapters is not a scientific explanation of the creation of the world and of man's position in it, but an expression of the fundamental truths of Israel's faith. Using popular narratives, mythological themes, and imaginative language the authors teach us that God is creator of all things, and that man who was destined to enjoy the friendship of God rebelled against his creator and incurred his anger. Yet wilful man was never abandoned by the God who continued to love his creature even when he had to punish his waywardness.

Monday (Gen 1:1-19). *The creation of the world.* Here we have a majestic affirmation of Israel's belief that all things owe their existence to God and that the whole created universe is good and beautiful. We hear nothing of sin, or pain, or death. We are told only of a world that was created in an orderly fashion, and in which each element had its own role to play. The recurring refrain 'God saw that it was good' asserts the belief that the world conforms to a divine plan, reflects the divine wisdom, and invites man to praise the architect of our wonderful universe.

Tuesday (1:20–2:4). *The creation of man.* Yesterday's reading recounted the story of the creation of the inanimate world. Today's passage brings us into the domain of life. Having created fishes of the sea, the birds of the air, and the animals that inhabit the earth, the Lord blessed them and gave each species its role to play in his universe.

On the sixth and final day of his creative activity God created man, the noblest of his creatures. The statement that man and woman are made in God's image (v. 27) means that, as creatures endowed with intellect and will, they share in God's lordship over all created things. Theirs is the task of developing the rich resources of the world and of placing them at the disposal of all men.

Wednesday (2:4-9, 15-17). *The origins of man.* There are few today who would take this imaginative account of creation literally. We know, for example, that the statement that 'God formed man of dust of the earth' (v. 7) is meant to convey the idea of man's creatureliness and his total dependence on God. God's breathing the breath of life into man's nostrils graphically expresses the conviction that human life is a gift from God. Man's happiness in a delightful garden (vv. 8-9) symbolises the blessed fellowship with God which he enjoyed. The 'tree of the knowledge of good and evil' from which man was forbidden to eat (v. 17) is a symbol of the limits which the Lord placed to man's freedom.

Thursday (2:18-25). *Man and wife.* The statement that 'It is not good that man should be alone' (v. 18) declares that man would be incomplete without the companionship of woman. Man's dominion over all living things is insinuated in the story of his giving their names to all animals (vv. 19-20). But this dominion does not bring happiness. Man needs 'a helper fit for him' (v. 18). That woman is such a helper or companion is the message of the strange story of the rib-operation (vv. 21-22). This teaches that woman is of the same nature and dignity as man and that she is therefore worthy to share his life with him. Indeed, it is the creator's will that one man and one woman should form a partnership that would be lifelong and exclusive (v. 24; cf. Mark 10:2-9).

Friday (3:1-8). *The Fall.* Today's reading answers the questions 'How did sin gain a foothold in God's good world? Why did man lose the state of intimate fellowship with God which he once enjoyed?' The author's answer is that all evil in the world is the result of man's refusal to obey the Creator's will.

But he gives this answer in symbolic and imaginative language. He introduces the serpent (v. 1) as the personification of temptation. The serpent is the evil force that led man into sin (compare Wis 2:24; Rom 5:12). He persuaded the woman that God's command not to eat of the forbidden tree was motivated by a selfish desire to retain the divine privileges for God himself. He assured her that if she disobeyed the divine command she would be like God 'knowing good and evil' (v. 6), that is, able to decide for herself what is good and what is evil. The woman took the bait and induced Adam to join her in disobedience. But the rebels immediately felt guilty. 'They knew that they were naked' (v. 7), that is, they experienced a sense of embarrassment before God and in each other's presence.

Saturday (3:9-24). *The punishment of sin.* Overcome by a sense of remorse and shame the disobedient man and woman tried to shift the blame from themselves (vv. 12-13). But the guilty accomplices cannot escape punishment. For his part in the rebellious episode the serpent must crawl upon the ground (v. 14). The woman must bear the pains of childbirth (v. 16), and man must work painfully to win a living from the earth (vv. 17-19a). Death is also a punishment for sin (v. 19b; cf. 1 Cor 15:22; Rom 5:12). Expulsion from the garden symbolises fallen man's hopelessness, and his inability to restore the happy relationship with God which he had forfeited.

But the outlook is not totally black. For in the divine promise 'he shall bruise your head' (v. 15) we see a prophecy of Christ's victory over Satan. Referring to this promise the Vatican II *Constitution on Divine Revelation* (n. 3) remarks that after the Fall God's promise aroused in our first parents the hope of being saved.

FIRST READINGS, Year 2 (1 Kings)

Monday (1 Kings 8:1-7, 9-13). *The Ark is brought into Solomon's temple.* The temple of Jerusalem which David had wanted to build (1 Sam 7) was in fact erected and furnished by Solomon (1 Kings 6—7). Today's reading describes the ceremony of dedication of the temple. When the Ark had been placed in the Holy of Holies, a cloud (symbol of the Lord's presence: see Ex 13:21) fills the temple to signify Yahweh's acceptance of this special meeting place with his people. The verses which conclude the reading come from an ancient poetic collection.

Tuesday (8:22-23, 27-30). *Solomon's prayer during the dedication of the temple.* This reading is an extract from the long prayer (vv. 22-61) made by Solomon after the Ark had been brought into the temple. The Deuteronomic writer who is responsible in large measure for the present text stresses Yahweh's covenant fidelity which demands a faithful response from the people. While imploring Yahweh's blessings on the Jerusalem temple he insists that Yahweh's presence is not limited to a temple built with hands—a truth of great importance for the Jewish exiles in Babylon and one which will reappear in the New Testament (see Acts 7:46-50).

Wednesday (10:1-10). *Solomon and the Queen of Sheba.* Sheba was a kingdom in the Arabian peninsula noted for its trading activities. The queen's visit to Solomon may well have been primarily a business affair (see vv. 2 and 10), but the author uses the account to praise Solomon's wisdom, riches and glory (see 1 Kings 3:5-14). Non-Israelites praise Yahweh also at Ex 18:9-11 and 2 Kings 5:15-19.

Thursday (11:4-13). *Consequences of Solomon's infidelity.* For reasons of state Solomon had contracted numerous marriage alliances with foreign princesses and had built sanctuaries to enable his wives to continue worship of their various gods. These sanctuaries are seen by the Deuteronomic writer as abominable occasions of Solomon's falling away from exclusive service of Yahweh. The punishment was to be the break-up of Solomon's kingdom after his death. All the northern tribes would secede under Solomon's minister Jeroboam; only Judah was to remain with Solomon's son Rehoboam.

Friday (11:29-32; 12:19). *Political schism.* Popular discontent against the House of David mounted in northern Israel because of the burdens of taxation and forced labour laid on the population by Solomon's centralised administration. Jeroboam who had been in charge of the forced labour projects in the north was called by a prophet to be the instrument to punish Solomon for his infidelity to Yahweh. Solomon forced Jeroboam to flee to Egypt (11:40), but the division of the kingdoms became a reality after Solomon's death. From then on (ca. 931 BC) Biblical history deals with the independent and often hostile kingdoms of Israel and Judah.

Saturday (12:26-32; 13:33-34). *Religious schism.* The Deuteronomic writer explains the original sin of the northern kingdom—the establishment outside Jerusalem of official places of worship, where moreover genuine Yahwism was corrupted by Canaanite cults. Jeroboam's own intention was doubtless a political one: unless he broke his subjects' religious attachment to Jerusalem, they would eventually be won back to political allegiance to the Davidic line.

Though the golden calves were probably meant to represent the throne or pedestal of the invisible Yahweh, not his own image, the danger of contamination with Canaanite religion, where the bull was a prominent symbol, explains the severity of the text's condemnations.

GOSPEL READINGS (Mark)

Monday (Mk 6:53-56). *A summary of Jesus' activities, emphasising the enthusiasm of the crowds after the feeding of the 5,000.* The narrative portrays Jesus in an almost passive role, suggesting that he was uncomfortable with the crowds and anxious to evade them. The true sequel is in 8:14-33.

Tuesday (7:1-13). This passage contains *two pronouncements of Jesus on ceremonial handwashing and on ritual gifts.* In the first Jesus exposes his critics' hypocrisy as preferring a man-made tradition to God's commandment of love. In the second he indicts those who observe the custom of Qorban to evade the duty of supporting their parents. Under the guise of dedicating money for sacred purposes, they would retain ownership and spend it on themselves.

Wednesday (7:14-23). *Blessed are the pure of heart.* Jesus' saying on defilement is unparalleled by any known rabbinical sayings. Its implications were only gradually realised, for there was some debate in the apostolic church whether pagan converts should observe Jewish dietary laws, and the issue was only resolved c. 49 AD (Acts 10:14ff; 15:28-29; Gal 2:11-17).

Thursday (7:24-30). *Cure of a pagan woman's daughter.* Another sign of Jesus' interest in pagans. The contrast 'children, dogs' = 'Jews, gentiles', but the woman retorts that the dogs have every right to the food which the children reject. The passage reflects the later tension between the apostolic church and the Jewish people.

Friday (7:31-37). *Jesus cures a deaf and dumb man.* Jesus' actions are familiar sacramental gestures symbolising the restoration of hearing and speech. The miracle may be an Old Testament fulfillment (Is 35:5-6; Ez 24:27), but equally important for Mark is its value as a revelation of Jesus.

Saturday (8:1-10). *The feeding of the 4,000* is a variant of 6:34-44; it emanated from a gentile Christian community which interpreted Jesus' miracle as a sign foreshadowing the mission to the pagans. The context (7:31; 8:10) shows Jesus to be in pagan territory, and the com-

ment, *Some have come from afar*, recalls an Old Testament expression
for the gentiles (Is 49:12; 43:6). Jesus' actions recall his eucharistic
gestures (1 Cor 11:24). The numbers (7 loaves, 7 baskets, 4,000 people)
evidently have meaning for Mark, for they are emphatically repeated in
8:19-20, but there is no satisfactory explanation of them.

SIXTH WEEK OF THE YEAR

FIRST READINGS, Year 1 (Genesis 4—11)

Monday (Gen 4:1-15, 25). *The first murder.* Today we begin the story
of the consequences of the Fall. Gen 4:1—11:9 describe how sin, once
it had gained entry into the world, spread like a contagion until the
whole of humanity was totally corrupt.

Today's story of Cain's murder of his brother shows that strife
among men was an immediate conseqence of sin against God. The
murderer's insolent response ('am I my brother's keeper?', v. 9) to
God's question shows that the shame and remorse which Adam and Eve
felt (cf. Gen 3:7-13) find no place in Cain's heart. Sin has gained control
of him.

Tuesday (6:5-8; 7:1-5, 10). *The flood.* Sin gradually increased in the
world until the heart of man was totally corrupt and incorrigibly
inclined to evil (cf. 6:5) so that God decided to destroy the world by a
flood. Only the just Noah (6:9) was destined to be saved. He was to
become the father of a purified humanity.

The story of the flood is an adaptation of a similar Babylonian narrative. But the biblical author has given the story a purely religious
interpretation. It shows how God manifested his *justice* by punishing
sinful mankind. But it also shows that in saving Noah God revealed his
mercy and his unwillingness to destroy man completely.

Wednesday (8:6-13, 20-22). *A new beginning.* When the flood had
abated and Noah emerged from the ark his first reaction was to offer a
sacrifice to God (v. 20). The Lord who had been compelled to punish
guilty man now accepts this gesture of worship and reverence. His
assurance that he will never again destroy every living thing, and that

the order of nature will never again be disrupted (vv. 21-22) is a source of security and hope for man.

Thursday (9:1-13). *A blessing and a covenant.* As God blessed Adam and Eve the parents of the whole human race (cf. 1:28), so also did he bless Noah and his sons in whom the human race received a new beginning.

God's blessing is, as it were, confirmed by a covenant (vv. 8, 13). As he was later to make a covenant or pact with Abraham (Gen 15) and with the Israelites on Sinai (Ex 19—24), so now does he enter into a covenant with Noah. Without imposing any conditions on Noah he assures him that he will never again destroy the world by a flood.

Friday (11:1-9). *The Tower of Babel.* Even after the purification brought about by the flood mankind returned to sin. In spite of God's blessing, and in spite of his covenant with Noah, restored humanity followed the rebellious ways of its ancestors. Sin was deeply engrained in human nature. The story of the Tower of Babel is an illustration of man's ambition and of his refusal to submit to God's will. His plan to build a tower with its top in the heavens (v. 4) is an expression of his desire to enter by his own power into God's domain. His longing to make a name for himself stems from a pride that ignores the rights of the Creator. But his inordinate designs were frustrated by God and only succeeded in shattering the unity of the human race (vv. 7-10), a unity that would be restored only at Pentecost (cf. Acts 2:1-11).

Saturday (Heb 11:1-7). *The just ancestors.* Hebrews 11 recalls the great cloud of Old Testament witnesses (cf. 12:1) whose faith and perseverance are a model for us Christians. Today's reading from that chapter praises the faith of the just men, Abel (Gen 4:4), Enoch (5:21-24) and Noah (6:9), who lived in the period between Adam and Abraham. This reading then offers a kind of summary of the readings from Gen 1—11 that have occupied us over the past two weeks.

FIRST READINGS, Year 2 (The Epistle of James)

INTRODUCTION TO JAMES

Apart from its brief address and greeting (1:1), this work does not have the semblance of a letter. It is more like a series of rather loosely connected exhortations, doubtless originating in the liturgical preaching of early Christian communities, which are presented in letter form to a wider audience. Nevertheless, the celebration of the liturgy remains the most likely setting of the work in its present shape. It would have been read to a community engaged in worship. This liturgical background puts the various exhortations in sharp relief. It also makes its reading in the course of our liturgy particularly appropriate.

Tradition has ascribed the work to James, 'the brother of the Lord' and head of the Jerusalem church. This is to take the address (1:1) at its face value. Modern opinion is generally inclined, however, to consider it as an example of 'pseudepigraphy', a procedure whereby an anonymous author attributes his work to a well known, authoritative personage, in order to give it more appeal. This was a comon and accepted practice in the ancient world, attested particularly in Jewish literature, and its occurrence in the literature of the New Testament in no way impairs the authority of any given work.

Because of its clear reflection of Old Testament themes, especially those associated with the wisdom literature, and its kinship with other Jewish literature, the 'letter of James' appears to be addressed to Judaeo-Christians, that is, Christians of Jewish origin and background. It is remarkable that the only specifically Christian characteristics are found in 1:1 and 2:1. Without these, it could easily pass as a work of Jewish literature. This fact, along with the traditional ascription to James, 'the brother of the Lord', might suggest an early date for the work, that is, before 62 (the accepted year of James' death). But many scholars would still place it later, towards the end of the first century.

Monday (James 1:1-11). *Joy in trial and poverty.* Having presented his credentials and suggested that his readers are the New Israel, by referring to them as 'the twelve tribes of the Diaspora', the author spotlights his readers' paradoxical situation: in the abnormal and troublesome condition of 'Dispersion' they should rejoice. These 'trials' are the providential means by which they will achieve true Christian maturity. Such an attitude towards the adverse experiences of life is true 'wisdom', given to the man who asks God for it with complete confidence. Because God's wisdom turns the world upside-down, wealth is ephemeral, and 'poverty'—an attitude of mind and heart according to which a man is totally dependent on God—is permanent, like the Lord's word on which it is based (cf. Is 40:6-8).

Tuesday (1:12-18). *Man's cupidity and God's gift.* Man's experience of 'evil' is of his own making, in the sense that it springs from his selfishness, according to which he desires to have everything his own way.

Were he totally integrated, open-minded and well disposed towards his Maker, as towards a loving Father, he would not experience anything as 'evil' or, even, as a 'trial'. He would instinctively integrate even the adverse circumstances of his life into a 'catholic' view of creation in which everything is good. Because Christians have not yet achieved this mature view they continue to be tried. In this sense their trial will cease only when they acquire by God's gift the right attitude towards suffering.

Wednesday (1:19-27). *Active faith.* Since man's regeneration as a child of God is 'by the word', he must 'be quick to hear'. Conversion is a matter of humbly receiving God's implanted word, that is, allowing God to take the initiative. Yet this is not a mere passive reception. If a man hears it properly he must allow it to produce its effects in his own life.. Such religious integrity—the conformity of life with belief—is a major concern of James, and possibly the best known of all religious themes.

Thursday (2:1-9). *Impartiality.* Since Christians have been reborn as God's children by the word of truth, they must behave as such and imitate God's impartiality; God has shown himself to be generous to *all* men, *without reproach.* The reprehensible behaviour of showing respect to wealthy members of the community, while reglecting the poor is contrary both to God's revealed behaviour and to the readers' own experience. Partiality or prejudice is a contravention of the 'royal' law of the love of one's neighbour.

Friday (2:14-24, 26). *Faith and works.* If faith is essentially active, it follows that a faith without works is sterile and useless. Such 'works' are the consequence of 'the faith of our Lord Jesus Christ'. James' insistence on the 'royal law' of love shows how close he is to St Paul's stress on faith *working* through love. A notional acceptance of truth divorced from a behaviour in accordance with that truth is a monstrosity. Both James and Paul are champions of religious integrity.

Saturday (3:1-10). *The power of the human tongue.* Because he is reborn by God's word, man's task is, quite simply, to listen to God, albeit actively. Speaking, on the other hand, symbolises the human initiative which is inspired by selfishness and desire. For this reason James warns would-be teachers in the community.

His own strong language on the subject of the tongue can be understood only against the background of the biblical idea of the word. Not unlike God's own creative word, man's word is both self expressive and effective. A man asserts himself, for good or evil, in his words, which reveal and establish his relationship with the world and his fellows. Thus a man is as good as his word.

GOSPEL READINGS (Mark)

Monday (Mk 8:11-13). *Jesus refuses to work a miracle.* The sign from heaven which the Pharisees seek is interpreted by Mark as a test, just as the untrusting Israelites tested God during the exodus (Ex 17:7). Based on Dt 32:5; Ps 95:10, *this generation* becomes a New Testament designation for those who do not believe Jesus on the basis of his miracles, but seek further unmistakable proof (Mt 12:39-45).

Tuesday (8:14-21). *Jesus puts his disciples on their guard.* Originally designating Pharaoh's obduracy (Ex 10:1), the *hardened heart* becomes a New Testament expression for Jewish resistance to Jesus (3:5), and here, of the disciples' unperceptiveness. In the Old Testament remembering God's mercies is a vehicle of revelation and the basis of fidelity to his covenant. Thus, Jesus' questions are meant to lead the disciples to reflect on the Christological revelation implied in Jesus' breadbreaking miracle. Yeast symbolises a corruptive force, and Jesus' caution against the yeast of the Pharisees and of Herod refers to their view of a national political messiah, a view capable of infecting Jesus' disciples as well and preventing them from seeing the true messianic import of his miracle.

Wednesday (8:22-26). *Jesus cures a blind man.* This cure parallels that of the deaf and dumb man in 7:31-36. In both cases Jesus takes the man aside and uses symbolic gestures in the healing. Mark's pairing of the miracle may intend an allusion to Is 35:5-6 which mentions the restoration of both sight and hearing. Even more striking is the fact that the man's sight is only gradually restored, just as in the next passage (8:27-33) the disciples only gradually see, first, that Jesus is the Messiah, and then that this entails suffering and death. This miracle, therefore, should be seen as a prophetic gesture preparing for Jesus' enlightenment of his disciples.

Thursday (8:27-33). *Peter confesses that Jesus is the Messiah.* The incident at Caesarea Philippi is the turning point of Mark, for it summarises the message of Jesus' Galilean ministry ('You are the Messiah') and gives Jesus' remaining ministry a new direction ('The Son of Man must suffer'). *Messiah:* Israel's religious hopes were essentially interwoven with hopes of political restoration by God's Anointed (the Davidic king; 1 Sam 2:10; 10:1; 2 Sam 23:1). This title and its Greek counterpart *christos* were later applied to the risen Christ, but the gospels show him as rejecting the title, or at best accepting it with such strong qualification as to give it a new, non-political meaning. Here the qualification takes the form of Jesus' first prediction of his passion. Peter's designation of Jesus as Messiah evokes only a noncommittal order to tell no one about him, for it would have struck Mark's readers as odd that Jesus refused the very title (*christos*) which was to become almost like his second name. His real reaction is expressed in his rebuke of Peter: it is diabolical to think that Jesus is a political messiah; could they not perceive that he was on a collision course with the religious authorities that would eventually lead to his death?

Friday (8:34–9:1). *Only by dying to ourselves can we live to God.* Mark joins several sayings of Jesus into an instruction on the ultimate demands of discipleship. All emphasise that the good at stake is life itself, and all seem relevant to Mark's readers, faced with martyrdom. Although Jesus' preaching focused directly on God's demands, it also implied that commitment to God involves acceptance of Jesus' proclamation of God's Rule. Thus, Jesus says, whoever is ashamed of me now will be the object of God's judgment at the end. The gospel tradition has elaborated this thought into a saying which portrays Christ as himself returning as Son of Man to judge those who rejected him.

Saturday (9:1-13). *The transfiguration of Jesus.* The momentary revelation of Christ's paschal glory complements that of his suffering and death. Certain elements (the cloud, mountain, Moses, tent) are patterned on the Sinai theophany (Ex 24:15-18), while others (the vision, Elijah, the fear, dazzling clothes, secrecy motif) are inspired by apocalyptic descriptions of the Son of Man (Dn 7; 8; 9; extrabiblical writings). Essentially, the transfiguration is a Christian commentary on the mystery of Christ: he is a new Moses, bathed in the radiance of God's glory on a new Sinai, the fulfillment of the Law (Moses) and the prophets (Elijah), and the beloved son (= prophet-servant, Is 42:1) of Yahweh.

According to Mal 4:5-6, Elijah's return was expected to signal the Day of the Lord (Yahweh) and the general resurrection. Thus, the dialogue between Jesus and his disciples revolves about two conflicting views of Jesus: (1) the popular view that he is Elijah, sent to inaugurate the great purification, and (2) his own assertion that he is the Son of Man sent to suffer and die. Jesus resolves the problem: Scripture is

correct; Elijah *has* come (as John the Baptist) to prepare the Day of
the Lord (Jesus). Fittingly, therefore, his murder points to Jesus'
impending fate. This bit of scriptural reasoning apparently originated
in the primitive church, perhaps with Mark himself.

SEVENTH WEEK OF THE YEAR

FIRST READINGS, Year 1 (Ecclesiasticus)

INTRODUCTION TO ECCLESIASTICUS

'The life-time scrap-book of a lecturer or teacher always contains a
variety of material–so too this book.' This is how J. G. Snaith in his
recent commentary has described the Book of Ecclesiasticus or of Ben
Sirach. Ecclesiasticus was originally written in Hebrew about 190 BC by
Jesus ben Sirach, a Jewish teacher who lived in Palestine. This original
work was translated into Greek by the grandson of the author and it is
the Greek translation that the Church has recognised as belonging to
the canon of Scripture. The author is in the wisdom tradition of Israel
but his pursuit of wisdom is joined to the total tradition of the Hebrew
religion with its special emphasis on the Law. Therefore, for Ben Sirach,
wisdom is practically identified with the Law of Moses, but certainly
not in a manner which is mutally exclusive.

Because the book was composed at a time when the upper classes in
Palestine were adopting the customs and manners of the pagan Greek
civilisation, the author is at pains to instruct his co-religionists on the
value of their own traditions. Thus the book strikes an apologetic and
polemic note in places. Ben Sirach stresses all the values of Israel's
inheritance–its Law, its temple worship, its priestly office, its sacred
books. He accepts too the wisdom of Israel which is contained in works
like Proverbs but his treatment of the conduct and moral life of men is
more elaborate than that of the collection of maxims found in Proverbs.
This is only to be expected in a work coming from the pen of a single
author.

The material in the book is vast, ranging from instructions as to how
to behave at banquets to meditation on the mind of God in giving true
wisdom to Israel in the form of the Law. Apart from the psalms, Eccle-

siasticus has been the most quoted work of the Old Testament in the liturgy of the Church. This is not surprising as various life situations are dealt with, which factor makes it a good reference work for choosing readings for Masses used on various occasions with groups, for instance, in schools or factories. Readings from Ben Sirach occur in Weeks 7 & 8 of Year 1.

Further Reading: Laurence Bright (ed.), *Psalms and Wisdom*, Scripture Discussion Commentary, 6, London, 1972, Introduction to Sirach, pp. 184-196. B. Vawter, *The Book of Sirach*, Paulist Bible Pamphlet Series, New York, 1962. John G. Snaith, *Ecclesiasticus*, The Cambridge Bible Commentary, Cambridge, 1974.

Monday (Eccles 1:1-10). *God's wisdom is poured out on creation and given to religious people.* The author appreciates the limits of human wisdom. Hence God is the only Wise One. His wisdom cannot be fully grasped but its marks can be seen in creation as a gift from God and this by all mankind. It is found especially by those who love God.

Tuesday (2:1-11). *True service of God involves an ordeal.* Experience and tradition show that those who sincerely serve God have to suffer. The continuous practice of the virtues and the patient waiting for God's saving action are always called for.

Wednesday (4:11-19). *Those who follow the ways of the Wisdom of God receive their rewards.* In this passage, the concept of God's wisdom is personified. The passage urges people to keep to the ways of God's wisdom, God's will, I think we would say. Despite the setbacks and ordeals of this manner of living, man will reach true contentment.

Thursday (5:1-8). *Advice—do not be independent of God.* In the tradition of Israel's wisdom teachers, Ben Sirach exhorts his listeners not to put their complete trust in creature comforts like riches or the pursuit of passion. The fear of God is always to be a guideline to human life.

Friday (6:5-17). *Advice on friendship.* Again, in the wisdom tradition, this passage offers the fruit of experience and human insight regarding man and his choice of friends.

Saturday (17:1-15). *God made man in his image and gave him power over creation.* People are the highest point of God's creative work. While they have authority from God over creation and the ability to praise him, they also have the responsibility of using the things of life according to God's designs.

FIRST READINGS, Year 2 (James)

Monday (3:13-18). *True and false wisdom.* Continuing his insistence on the opposition between a behaviour which comes from God and that which originates within man, James here contrasts God's wisdom with that of the world. The hallmark of God's wisdom is meekness, whereas earthly wisdom is characterised by selfishness and pride. The 'seed' of God's word brings a harvest of 'righteousness' received in peace and humilty. Man's works are in the final analysis the good fruits of divine wisdom—the work of God within man.

Tuesday (4:1-10). *God and the world.* Conflicts have their origin not in God but in human passions which are at war within man. Thus the 'world' in the sense of selfish cupidity is at enmity with God. Yet by virtue of the spirit placed within man, he is not simply left by God to his own devices. God constantly appeals to him to turn away from the 'world' and become his child—a conversion only possible through humility.

Wednesday (4:13-17). *Against presumption.* One aspect of the openness to God's word which James repeatedly recommends is complete trust in God's providence. Man's whole future, as well as his present, is in God's hands. Thus it is presumptious to make plans for the future, without reference to God's will. It is abundantly clear that James' readers are proud and arrogant, shown by their refusal to do what they know to be right. James strikes at their consciences by presenting them with examples of right behaviour.

Thursday (5:1-6). *Against the rich.* From the beginning of his work James has shown his antagonism towards the rich. A 'rich' man is one who has gained his wealth at the poor man's expense and is arrogant because of his possessions. He is typically 'evil' because he places his confidence in the world and not in God. He has reason to weep and howl in view of the judgement which James foresees in the immediate future. The unjust man has signed his own death warrant. In the end he will reap the fruits of his own sowing.

Friday (5:9-12). *Patience in view of the parousia.* Unlike the rich, the 'poor', that is, those who are being 'tried' should be patient because their vindication is at hand. James' repeated exhortation not to judge one's fellow is now based on the assurance that 'the Judge is standing at the doors'. This Judge, that is, Christ will reverse the present unjust situation, but only on the condition that men themselves 'work

God's righteousness' by their good behaviour according to his word. The 'just' man too pronounces his own judgement by his attitude to God's word.

Saturday (5:13-20). *The power of prayer.* By prayer a man expresses his total dependance on God. It is only the prayer of the man living in complete openness to God that produces its effects, an effectiveness due to the permanent presence of God as loving Father. Just as prayer *to* God is openness to him, so prayer *for* others is an expression of concern for them and a realisation of the selflessness necessary for right relationship with God.

GOSPEL READINGS (Mark)

Monday (Mk 9:14-29). *Jesus cures an epileptic.* Jesus' cure of the epileptic is portrayed (1) as a public display of Jesus' power over the demon (see 1:21-25; 3:22-30), (2) as an invitation to faith in Jesus (see 2:1-12), and (3) as a symbol of his own death and resurrection (note that the boy is *like a corpse, . . . dead, . . .* until Jesus *raised him up*; see 1:31; 5:38-41).

Tuesday (9:3-37). *Jesus' second passion prediction* is a variant of 8:31. The disciples' lack of understanding is followed by an instruction which equates greatness with humble service. *Whoever receives one such child:* varients of this saying (Mt 10:40; Lk 10:16; Jn 13:20) refer to the welcome shown Jesus' disciples. Mark has transformed it into a lesson on how they are to welcome even the lowliest.

Wednesday (9:38-40). *Anyone who is not against Jesus is for him.* This passage reflects a problem in the apostolic church: what to do when non-disciples exorcise demons in Jesus' name (Acts 19:13)? Jesus' tolerant answer goes counter to the later practice attested in Acts 8:18-24; 13:6-12; 19:13-20, although the latter may have been a reaction to elements of sorcery. Jesus' final saying is remarkable because its implications are just the opposite of Mt 12:30 = Lk 11:23.

Thursday (9:41-50). *We should be ready to sacrifice everything for Jesus.* A composite of many independent sayings especially meaningful to Mark's readers during the Neronian persecutions. The hyperbole of Jesus' words is meant to underscore the urgency of his warnings. *Gehenna:* a ravine near Jerusalem used as a dump for burning garbage. In Jesus' time its fires were considered a symbol of hell. *Salted with* *fire:* Jesus suggests that persecution will cleanse the disciples, purifying as both salt and fire. They in turn must be a purifying agent (salt) and not be contaminated by evil.

Friday (10:1-12). *Divorce is forbidden.* Jesus' teaching on marriage goes beyond the Mosaic regulation of divorce (Dt 24:1-4) and appeals to the state originally intended by God (Gn 1:27; 2:24) where marriage was indissoluble. *Whoever puts away. . . :* Jesus' saying is an absolute prohibition of divorce, unlike Mt 19:9 which envisages an exception for 'unchastity'. It is difficult to decide which version is closer to Jesus' own pronouncement, but even the Matthean saying with the exceptive clause may refer to concubinage or betrothal rather than marriage. An important aspect of this scene is Jesus' authoritative interpretation of the Law (see 1:40-45; 2:36–3:6).

Saturday (10:13-16). *The kingdom of heaven is for the humble.* This pronouncement story continues the theme of Jesus' instruction on humble service (9:33-37). Children typify the lowliness and insignificane necessary to accept the paradox of Jesus' rejection and death.

EIGHTH WEEK OF THE YEAR

FIRST READINGS, Year 1 (Ecclesiasticus)

Monday (Eccles. 17:24-29). *Reform your lives to experience God's mercy.* An exhortation to people to 'leave sin behind' and turn to God. The passage shows that the New Testament understanding of Resurrection and the future life is not yet present to the mind of Ben Sirach.

Tuesday (35:1-12). *Worship and virtuous living are due to God.* The mind of Ben Sirach is clearly manifest in this passage. Worship, keeping the commandments and the traditional Jewish good works like almsgiving all lead to happiness and communion with God, especially when coming from a generous and cheerful heart.

Wednesday (36:1, 4-5, 10-17). *A prayer for mercy.* The author prays that God will show compassion to his people. This showering of favours on them will, to his mind, bring about the turning of all nations to acknowledge the God of Israel as the Lord.

Thursday (42:15-25). *The splendour of God's wisdom in creation.* The unfathomable mysteries observed in the created world are all known to God. Man can admire the universe but its deepest secrets remain with God.

Friday (44:1, 9-13). *Praise for the great men of the past.* The history of Israel portrays great individual characters. Today's reading encourages a look at their lives while granting that some have been forgotten. (The Lectionary does not mention the list which is found in Chapters 44—50 of the book.)

Saturday (51:12-20). *Thanksgiving for the gift of Wisdom.* Ben Sirach concludes his long work with a prayer of thanksgiving. He can declare that his prayers and search for wisdom have been worthwhile. His teaching, which we have shared, is thus the fruit of his experience.

FIRST READINGS, Year 2 (1 Peter, Jude)

INTRODUCTION TO FIRST LETTER OF PETER

Because of the mention of him made in the address (1:1), this work has been traditionally ascribed to Peter, the Apostle, at least as his dictation (cf. 5:12); if this traditional view is accepted, it is a comparatively early work, appearing before the traditional date of his death—64 AD.

It is addressed to several churches in Asia Minor and thus appears as a kind of encyclical letter. Apart from its introduction and conclusion, it does not seem to be a letter. It is more like a homily or sermon, delivered now as a reminder of the meaning of the Christian life given at baptism, now as an exhortation to constancy in the face of suffering, especially the suffering caused by persecution. The best explanation of this rather complex literary phenomenon is that 1 Peter, in its present form, is a letter addressed to Christians in the face of persecution but drawing on material which had its original setting in the baptismal liturgy of the early Church, celebrated at Easter. This would account for both its baptismal and paschal overtones and its insistence on the indissoluble connection between Christian existence and suffering.

INTRODUCTION TO THE LETTER OF JUDE

Apart from its address and greeting, this work appears more like a sermon or a homily than a letter. It is addressed to a community or communities as a warning against certain errors, which appear as an incipient form of gnosticism. The existence of these errors within the

community suggests a fairly late date for the work but prior to any
systematic gnosticism and to 2 Peter, which clearly uses it. Most scholars
would place it about 80 AD.

Given this background, it could have been written by Jude, the
brother of James, with the assistance of a secretary. In any case, it is
improbable that an author would have chosen such an obscure pseudo-
nym to give authority to his work.

Monday (1 Peter 1:3-9). *The Christian hope.* This passage is in the form
of a 'blessing' or thanksgiving to God for the salvation which he has
achieved through Jesus Christ. It is the sort of prayer which would have
been voiced by a bishop in the celebration of baptism. The newly-
baptised still look forward to maturity which, in their case, is the completion of their salvation. In the meanwhile Christians must undergo
various trials. But these, rather than being the cause of sadness, are the
motive of great joy, because through them the genuineness of Christian
faith is tested.

Tuesday (1:10-16). *The Christian life is a share in the sufferings and
glory of Christ.* Peter has already intimated that the Christian view of
salvation is based on Christ's own career. He now confirms this by
stressing that the prophets foretold the Christian 'grace' or 'salvation' in
the guise of the sufferings and subsequent glory of Christ. In other
words, the 'salvation' of Christ, that is, his resurrection from the dead
and the 'salvation' of Christians are one and the same. Christ's suffering
and resurrection are *for* all men, not merely in the sense that he suffered
and rose in their place, but in the sense that he is the type or exemplar
which all men should follow.

Wednesday (1:18-25). *Christian behaviour and God's initiative.* Peter
exhorts his readers to lead the lives of God's children, in the sure knowledge that their confidence is based not on their own efforts but on
God's redeeming initiative. Thus the tension of the Christian towards
his future is finely poised between God's initiative and his own behaviour. What the divine initiative has achieved in Christ is communicated to men in the word of God, that is, in the reality of God as it is
acceptable and assimilable by man, by an 'obedience to the truth' which
is nothing less than complete conformity with God's revealed love.

Thursday (2:2-5, 9-12). *The Church is a royal priesthood.* Just as the
baptised share in Christ's death and resurrection, so they share in his
priesthood. Christ's death and resurrection are here expressed in the

metaphor of the rejected stone which becomes the cornerstone. By their new moral behaviour Christians are to form a 'spiritual house' and become a 'royal priesthood', thus accomplishing the promise made to Israel of old (cf. Ex 19:6). The 'spiritual sacrifices' which the baptised are to offer are indeed the new moral life, but also the declaration of the work of salvation. Their priesthood is therefore prophetical, consisting in the publication of the good news which they have received by their faith.

Friday (4:7-13). *Mutual service within the community.* The essence of the Church's life is service. It 'serves' God, that is, offers glory to him, through Jesus Christ, by fulfilling the role of the Suffering Servant and sharing in Christ's sufferings. It serves the world by being a kind of pilot light through its good behaviour. And individual members serve one another by putting their God-given talents at the disposal of their fellows.

Saturday (Jude 17, 20-25). *Loyalty to Tradition.* Jude's concern in his short sermon is to encourage his readers 'to struggle for the faith which was once for all delivered to the saints'. Here 'faith' is used in the 'objective' sense of that which is believed. Clearly this faith is being jeopardised by false teachers, whose errors in doctrine are accompanied by dissolute morals. The advent of these heretics should cause no alarm, since it is pre-figured, together with their downfall, in the Old Testament and Jewish apocryphal literature. Moreover the apostles themselves predicted their arrival. As opposed to these heretics, the faithful should not merely 'hold on to' their faith, they should 'build themselves up' on it. This involves prayer, remaining in God's love and waiting for Christ's mercy. It is less a harking back to the past than a movement towards the future, on the basis of the past. Likewise, this loyalty to tradition is not merely defensive. It involves too the conviction and the salvation of others. Finally, in a magnificent doxology, Jude stresses that fidelity to God's revelation is really the work of God himself within the beliver.

GOSPEL READINGS (Mark)

Monday (Mk 10:18-27). *Jesus invites a rich man to sell everything and follow him.* Jesus endorses the Mosaic commandments, but with God's Rule imminent, these are not enough; one must also be a disciple of Jesus. During his ministry Jesus required that his disciples renounce their possessions, in keeping with the proclamation that God's Rule was close at hand. In the early church this radical demand was relaxed, but by adding to the story of the rich man a group of sayings, Mark brings out other lessons: (1) that wealth stands in the way of commitment to Christ; (2) that even Jesus' disciples found this difficult to understand (Jesus must repeat the lesson for them); and (3) that only God can give one the force to do what is necessary to follow Christ.

Tuesday (10:28-31). These *sayings on the rewards of discipleship* counterbalance the previous sayings on its difficulties. Mark has edited them somewhat so as to make them more applicable to his readers. Thus, rewards come *with persecutions*, and only *in the age to come* will the present status (first, last) be reversed.

Wednesday (10:32-45). This passage is dominated by *Jesus' last prediction of his suffering and death.* Jesus undoubtedly sensed that his conflict with the temple authorities would result in his death, but the predictions in Mark are Christian formulations in the light of the events. In late Judaism, *Son of Man* designated an apocalyptic figure on whom God had conferred sovereignty, and who was to appear as judge (Dn 7: 13-14). Mark underscores the irony of Jesus' suffering and death by using this title in the passion predictions, implying that Jesus' authority as the risen Lord was inseparable from his suffering and death. This is the lesson with which Jesus rebuts the misguided request of James and John. The mention of the cup foreshadows the Eucharist (14:23) and the cup of Jesus' suffering (14:36). Jesus' instruction on greatness reverses the secular norm of authority and is based on Jesus' own mission to *serve and give his life as a ransom for many.* This saying, based on Is 53:10-12, identifies Jesus as the atoning servant of God.

Thursday (10:46-52). *Jesus heals a blind man at Jericho.* Just as the gradual healing of the blind man in 8:22-26 introduces the gradual revelation of Jesus' messiahship to the disciples (8:27-33), so Bartimaeus' spontaneous hailing of Jesus as Son of David prepares for Jesus' triumphal ride into Jerusalem amid the acclamations of the crowd. The accent is less on the cure (no healing gesture is mentioned) than on Bartimaeus' faith and his use of the messianic title Son of David.

Friday (11:11-25). *Jesus drives money changers from the temple.* Jesus is now in Jerusalem where he performs two prophetic gestures. The cursing of the fig tree dramatises God's judgment on a barren Israel, and the driving of the buyers and sellers from the temple, which follows naturally on Jesus' messianic entry into the city, symbolises God's judgment against the temple abuses. The concluding verses about the withered tree bring together several disparate sayings about faith and prayer.

Saturday (11:27-33). *Jesus' authority challenged by the scribes and elders.* These final readings from Mark portray Jesus in controversy with the religious leaders. In context, their challenge concerns Jesus' messianic entry into Jerusalem and cleansing of the temple; historically it may have referred to his teaching and baptising. Jesus refuses to answer their challenge, but implicit in his pronouncement is the same dilemma (from heaven or from man?) as he posed them concerning the Baptist.

NINTH WEEK OF THE YEAR

FIRST READINGS, Year 1 (Tobit)

INTRODUCTION TO THE BOOK OF TOBIT

Most commentators now see the Book of Tobit (Tobias) as an edifying story loosely set in a discernible historical situation. It is not possible to name either the author or the date and place of composition, but it was probably composed around 200 B.C. Again we are not certain whether it was originally for the Jews of the Diaspora or for those in Palestine. The purpose of writing however is reasonably clear. The basic aim of the unknown author is to proclaim that God is still with his faithful ones despite all appearances to the contrary. The providential care of the Lord is a reality in the lives of his people who are trying to live virtuously. Various other themes come to the surface throughout the book: the efficaciousness of prayer, mutual support in family life, the value of the traditional work of almsgiving, the witness of God's servants in a pagan society, even the anticipation of the Christian concept of marriage appear as an example to all the readers of this work. Each passage that is read in the lectionary will bring one or other of these themes before us.

The Story. At Nineveh there dwelt a pious but now blind man, Tobit, exiled with his tribe of Napthali after the fall of the Northern Kingdom, Israel. Tobit's kinsman, Raguel, has a daughter called Sarah, who had lost seven husbands one after another. In fact, one was killed on their wedding night by the demon Asmodeus. Tobit's son, Tobias, starts out to find a spouse from his own tribe, guided by Raphael, an angel of God. Under the angel's guidance, Tobias arrives safely at Raguel's home, is married to Sarah without any ensuing misfortune, and even finds a cure for his father's blindness. The prayers and almsgiving of Tobit are thus answered by God in his own providential and mysterious manner.

Further Reading: D. R. Dumm, *Tobit* in Jerome Biblical Commentary, London, 1976.

Monday (Tobit 1:1; 2:1-8). *The good works of Tobit.* On the feast of Weeks (Pentecost) Tobit invites the poor to share his table, but circumstances compel him to leave his feasting in order to bury his fellow-Israelite. Certainly an edifying opening to an edifying story.

Tuesday (2:9-14). *The suffering of Tobit.* An accident causes Tobit to lose his sight—in God's providence, even the just suffer. The stricken Tobit is supported faithfully by his wife, but scrupulously, Tobit keeps himself from even the appearance of infidelity. His religion, although presented somewhat in an exaggerated manner is distinterested—he does not seek immediate repayment or reward for his almsgiving.

Wednesday (3:1-11, 16-17). *The prayer of Tobit.* Tobit prays for God to relieve his from his sufferings by requesting death. Sarah finds herself in a similar position and makes a similar request. But the prayers of both are to be answered in God's own manner. No prayer is useless before God!

Thursday (6:11; 7:1, 9-14; 8:4-8). *The prayer of husband and wife.* The son, Tobias, accepts Sarah as his bride, and knowing the need for God's protection, they pray with the best of intentions.

Friday (11:5-15). *Prayer of thanksgiving.* 'He has scourged me and now has had pity on me.' The return of Tobias and the healing of his father's blindness draw out the prayer of praise and thanks from the old man Tobit.

Saturday (12:1, 5-15, 20). *God answers and responds to good works.* The end of the edifying story. Raphael explains how prayer with fasting and almsgiving is always efficacious. God responds to man's efforts at good living in his own way, but can always be trusted to do so.

FIRST READINGS, Year 2 (2 Peter, 2 Timothy)

INTRODUCTION TO THE SECOND LETTER OF PETER

Like the other so-called 'catholic' letters (James, 1 Peter, Jude), 2 Peter has the semblance more of a sermon than of a letter. It is addressed to Christians both as a warning against error and as an encourgement in view of the apparent delay of the parousia. Both of these points indicate a fairly late date for the work, as does its manifest dependence on Jude. It is generally recognised as 'pseudepigraphy' and as originating towards the end of the first century or at the beginning of the second.

INTRODUCTION TO THE PASTORAL LETTERS

The two epistles to Timothy, and the one to Titus, are well named the Pastorals (PE) because of their sustained instructions on the fulfilment of the pastoral ministry in the local church. Inevitably, however, this focus upon the ministry also involves many references to Christian principles and practice which are useful for every member of the community. Indeed, considering the brevity of these three letters they contain a wealth of material upon such themes as faith, fidelity to the apostolic message, practical charity, prayer, responsibility and moderation.

Whereas the PE explicitly claim to come from Paul the apostle, recent scholarship has serious doubt as the the genuineness of this claim. Elements both of content and of style (vocabulary and syntax) tend to distinguish these letters from the early Pauline writings, to such an extent that some would opt firmly for the 'pseudonymous' authorship of the PE: they would be the work of some anonymous Christian official, writing around the end of the first century, but claiming the authority of St Paul to lend greater weight and significance to his reflections upon the organisation of the church. Other scholars, however, continue to maintain the traditional attribution of these letters to Paul; they could explain the differences in style and content as due to new circumstances towards the end of the apostle's lifetime, and to his having given greater latitude of expression to the 'secretary' through whom he wrote the PE than to the 'scribes' of his earlier letters.

Whether pseudonymous or authentic, the PE certainly convey some of Paul's dominant ideas: Justification by grace, through baptism and the Holy Spirit (Tit 3:4ff); God's eternal plan of salvation (2 Tim 1:9; Tit 1:2); apostolate as gift and task, for the salvation of others (1 Tim 1:12ff; 2 Tim 1:11; Tit 1:3); suffering, as inescapably bound up with apostolic ministry (1 Tim 6:12ff; 2 Tim *passim*); joyful confidence in the reward God has in store, at the day of Christ's return (1 Time 6:15; 2 Tim 4:8; Tit 3:7). On the other hand, they seem to differ from Paul's earlier portrayal of the Church, by emphasising structured and formal authority (linked with ordination), and paying special attention to the human and social virtues of moderation, sobriety, obedience and hard work, rather than to the specifically Christian ideal of total conformity to Christ (whose early return was expected in, say 1 Thess 4:15; 1 Cor 7:26).

The recipients to whom the PE are addressed were well-known Christian leaders mentioned elsewhere in the New Testament. Timothy, son of a pagan father and a Jewish-Christian mother, was a young man when invited to join in Paul's second missionary journey, in 49 AD (cf. Acts 16:1). Later texts show him an esteemed and faithful assistant (Acts 19:22; 1 Cor 4:17 etc). In the two letters addressed to him he is addressed as though still youthful—a fact which must not inhibit him from firmly leading the church at Ephesus. His task consists in propagating the faith, as received from Paul—himself appointed by direct divine decree. He is to establish doctrinal, ethical and liturgical discipline, and to appoint other ministers capable of guiding their local communities in faith and good order. Titus is also mentioned as a co-worker with Paul, in the undoubted Pauline letters (Gal 2:1; 2 Cor 7:6; 8:23 etc). According to the letter addressed to him, he was left behind on the island of Crete to perform a task similar to that of Timothy at Ephesus. Both recipients of the PE are shown as delegates of the great apostle. Paul remains in charge of the churches he has founded, even if he must exercise his guidance at a distance, by letter. Basis for this apostolic authority is the express will of God, whose choice is as mysterious as it is merciful (cf. 1 Tim 1:18; 3:15; 4:6; 2 Tim 1:11; Tit 1:3; 2:11f).

The substance of these three letters appear in the weekday lectionary, although one might wonder at the omission of texts such as 1 Tim 4:6-11; 5:1-8; 6:17-21. Other passages have been left out, for obvious reasons of quaintness or irrelevance (1 Tim 2:9-11; 4:1-5; Tit 1:10-16). In the brief commentary in this book, we concern ourselves only with the material found in the lectionary. Much fuller explanation of the text can be read in the commentaries on the PE by Conzelmann, Barrett, Easton, Falconer, Kelly, Jeremias or Spicq.

Monday (2 Peter 1:2-7). *The Christian's call to share in the divine nature.* The author begins by stressing God's initiative in the Christian life. It is God who has 'called' men to his own glory and excellence. Thus man's true destiny is beyond himself, that is, away from self-seeking 'passion'. Positively it is to participate in the very nature of God. This 'nature' is the essence of the biblical God, namely, love. But this divine initiative in man's destiny does not dispense man himself from responsibility. On the contrary, he must make every effort to become what he is called to be. Because God's nature is love, the summit of the Christian's life is love.

Tuesday (3:11-15, 17-18). *Waiting for the new creation.* Though the major part of 2 Peter warns against the dangers of heresy and offers the means to combat it, an important concern is the apparent delay in the arrival of the day of the Lord. He fixes his readers' attention rather on man's *spiritual* end. For the effect of reflection on the future is a new life of piety led in the present. Moreover, it is by such a life that the believer not only waits for the day of the Lord but actually 'hastens' it. In other words, the new creation will replace the old only when men have learnt to live in 'righteousness'.

Wednesday (2 Tim 1:1-12). *The plea of a Christian prisoner.* This letter claims to come from Paul, an accredited apostle of Christ, to Timothy, a young Christian minister, and shares the general ecclesial concerns as the first letter to Timothy. Its special characteristic, however, is the writer's awareness of being a prisoner for Christ's sake, destined for execution, and the consequent vibrant plea he makes to his young disciple to carry on the work of preaching the gospel. True to this context, the tone of the letter is warm, personal, even emotional. Paul recalls how Timothy has come from a Christian family, and hopes that he will remain loyal to this heritage. He then mentions the ministerial heritage he himself has passed on to the younger man by ordination, and urges him to persevere courageously in pastoral work, even at the cost of personal suffering. All of this will come to a glorious conclusion; God may be trusted absolutely to fulfil his promises 'on that Day'.

Thursday (2:8-15). *Remembering.* A leader in the local church is responsible for reminding the congregation of the core of faith: in order to share in Christ's glory, we must share also in his passion (–this message appears in verse-form in vv. 11ff). First, however, he must remind himself! Hence the exhortation to Timothy: 'Remember Jesus Christ, risen from the dead'. Once again Paul mentions his own imprisonment, as an instance of what it means to 'die with Christ', and adds that he offers this 'for the sake of the elect'. Thus, the appeal of verse 15 (to work hard at assimilating and spreading the word) is abundantly motivated.

Friday (3:1-17). *Be true to your training.* Still upon the theme of personal witness and example, Paul exhorts his disciple to 'continue in what you have learned'—not simply in the sense of book-learning (for Timothy has studied the Scriptures since childhood), but also what he has learned by observing the conduct of the apostle. He emphasises the very full training Timothy has received, encouraging him simply to continue on the path he has entered.

Saturday (4:1-8). *A man for all seasons.* This final extract from 2 Tim is most aptly designated an 'Apostolic Testament', being a call for heroic service issued by one whose own apostolate is now drawing to its glorious conclusion. Following in Paul's footsteps, the Christian minister must urge, convince and rebuke, preaching God's word in settings both favourable and hostile—he must, in short, be a Man for All Seaons, capable of steady endurance. A vibrant urgency is given to this call by the apostle's imminent martyrdom. His ministry (the 'race', the 'good fight') faithfully completed, it simply remains for him to receive from Christ the crown of his labours. He hastens to add, however, that the same reward awaits everyone who looks forward eagerly to the Lord's return.

GOSPEL READINGS (Mark)

Monday (Mk 12:1-12). *The parable of the owner of the vineyard.* This parable is based on Is 5 where the vineyard stands for Israel, condemned to destruction for producing only wild grapes. The fate of the servants suggests the treatment suffered by the prophets, and is climaxed in the murder of the beloved son (Jesus). For this the owner destroys the guilty tenant farmers and devises the vineyard to others. In its gospel context this refers to the passage of responsibility for God's people from the temple priesthood to the Christian leaders, but the parable has been edited in the transmission, and it is difficult to say how much was part of Jesus' original story. The citation of Ps 118:22-23 is a clear Christian addition: it is cited elsewhere in the New Testament as a foreshadowing of Jesus' being rejected in his passion and of his becoming the foundation of a new edifice through his resurrection. The parable and its sequel, the attempt to arrest Jesus, are clear harbingers of his impending passion. Remember that in Mark this takes place just several days before Jesus' trial and death.

Tuesday (12:13-17). *Render their due to Caesar and to God.* Between 6–70 AD Palestinians paid a poll tax to the Emperor. It was bitterly opposed both as a token of subjection to Rome and as a violation of the use of graven images (the silver coins of tribute). The fact that Jesus' questioners possessed and used imperial coinage was tantamount to their recognising the Emperor's sovereignty. Thus Jesus could tell them to 'Give the Emperor what is his due. . .' meaning that the Emperor's claim on their loyalty was insignificant compared to God's, particularly in view of the imminence of God's Rule. By the late 60's, however, when Mark was written and when Roman Christians were subject to persecution, Jesus' answer was reinterpreted to mean that one's civic responsibilities need not conflict with one's religious loyalties.

Wednesday (12:18-27). *Jesus says that the dead shall rise again.* The belief in individual resurrection was an out-growth of the Old Testament belief in Israel's collective survival, and only emerged ca. 165 BC in Dn 12. The Sadducees did not accept the belief because it was not explicitly stated in the Pentateuch. Jesus answers (1) by rejecting their argument about levirate marriage as irrelevant (resurrection involves a wholly new life, not a resumption of natural human relations), and (2) by showing that belief in resurrection is implicit in the Pentateuchal title 'God of Abraham, Isaac, and Jacob' (Ex 3:6). Since 'He is not God of the dead, but of the living', these patriarchs must have been raised from the dead. Jesus' reasoning is tortuous, but it touches the well-spring of the belief in resurrection: Israel's experience of God as intervening to give life to his people.

Thursday (12:28b-34). *The Great Commandment—Love of God and the neighbour.* Rabbinical writings attest an interest in the first or parent commandment which encompassed all 613 individual commandments of the Torah. Jesus fittingly cites Dt 6:5, the beginning of the Shema (hear) which Jews recite daily and which contains the fundamental covenant commandment, 'You shall love Yahweh your God'. The originality of Jesus' answer lies in his placing Lev 19:18 (love of neighbour) on equal footing with love of God to form a single commandment.

Friday (12:35-37). *Jesus is more than a mere son of David.* In the preceding controversies Jesus was challenged or questioned; now it is Jesus who challenges the authority of the scribes by raising a question to which they had no answer: How can they say that the Messiah is David's son? Jesus' proof text is Ps 110:1 where the author (David) writes, 'The Lord [Yahweh] said to my lord [the Messiah]...' Jesus' argument assumes that David wrote the psalm and that 'my lord' was David's designation for the Messiah. Given these commonly held rabbinical assumptions, Jesus' question is unanswerable, for David would not call the Messiah 'my lord' if the latter were his son. (Modern biblical scholarship has no such problem, for David was not the author of the psalm, and the person addressed as 'my lord' is the newly enthroned king.) Historically this incident had nothing to do with Jesus' being (or not being) the Messiah or David's son. It was an academic discussion designed to show that Jesus' adversaries could hardly challenge his interpretation of scripture when they themselves were unable to deal with certain scriptural passages.

Saturday (12:38-44). *A condemnation of the scribes. The widow's mite.* Jesus' controversies with the temple authorities are climaxed in a sweeping condemnation of the scribes for their pride, exaction, and hypocrisy. In contrast to that Mark closes this section with an incident illustrating Jesus' view of true piety. The widow was so poor that she could donate only two copper coins (less than 2% of a labourer's daily way), but the value of her offering was to be measured in terms of the self-giving it represented. Thus, the liturgical reading of Mark ends on a note of hope and piety which contrasts strongly with the obduracy and conflict which Jesus encountered in Jerusalem and which would shortly lead to his arrest, trial, and crucifixion.

TENTH WEEK OF THE YEAR

FIRST READINGS, Year 1 (2 Corinthians)

INTRODUCTION TO SECOND LETTER TO THE CORINTHIANS

This letter was written by Paul probably in the autumn of 57 AD. According to 2 Cor (7:5-7; 8:1-16; 9:2), it was written in Macedonia after Paul had left Ephesus. 2 Cor is the expression of very strong emotions. Paul appears in it as a highly sensitive man, affectionate, but hurt by much of what went on in the Corinthian church. In Corinth, as in Galatia, he had his adversaries, only, in Corinth, they were not 'Judaisers' but missionaries from Palestine who regarded themselves as 'divine men' with the power to make others 'divine' like themselves. Christ is seen by them as the supreme example of the divine man, and consequently, his humanity is played down. Against this enthusiatic unrealism, Paul emphasises the death of Jesus and the role which weakness and suffering has to play in our lives as Christians.

Monday (2 Cor 1:1-7). *God conforts us so that we can offer others consolation in their sorrows.* The key word here is *comfort.* It recurs nine times in five verses. Comfort is need in affliction (*thlipsis*), that which burdens man's spirit and tempts him to lose heart. The comfort Paul has in mind is 'the comfort which brings courage, which enables a man to cope with all that life can do to him.' (W. Barclay, *The Letters to the Corinthians*, p. 190.)

Tuesday 1:18-22). *Paul tells the Corinthians that there was no vacillation in his behaviour, just as there was nothing vacillating about Christ.* The background to this strange passage will throw some light on it. Paul had promised to visit Corinth, but the situation there had become so bitter that he postponed his visit (v. 23). For this he was accused by his enemies of saying 'yes' and 'no' at the same time. He was, they said, untrustworthy. Perhaps, therefore, his message is equally not to be trusted. Paul responds by proclaiming that Christ, who *is* his message, is the affirmative answer to all of God's promises. All the hopes and aspirations of Israel were fulfilled in him. Believing in a God who carries out his promises thus, could Paul be anything but sincere?

Wednesday (3:4-11). *The new covenant contrasted with the old.* Paul here contrasts, as he frequently does, the old covenant with the new. God's sufficiency, not Paul's, made Paul a minister of this new covenant. It is a covenant not of written letters but of the Spirit. Written letters bring death, but the Spirit brings life. A legal religion (the old covenant) imposes rules from outside; a religion inspired by the Spirit imposes rules within. The legal one passes a verdict of guilty on the despondent sinner; the spiritual one gives him life and hope. Moses' face admittedly shone after he had received the old covenant from God. But it was a transitory thing. Now that Christ has come, the radiance of his Spirit causes the radiance on the face of Moses to pale indeed. And the new radiance is something permanent.

Thursday (3:15–4:1, 3-6). *The Spirit of God brings life and liberty.*
That which once radiated, namely the Law of Moses, has now become a
veil preventing those who refuse to see beyond it from coming fully
alive. Such people, tied down by yesterday's legalities, are not free.
Only when freedom becomes a reality can man truly see, only then will
the very light be free to shine for him. Surely a call to man to free himself from the tyranny of the past and live with vision in the vibrant
present.

Friday (4:7-15; cf. 6:1-10). *Divine power triumphs through human
weakness.* We meet in these passages once more with Pauline paradox:
'We are in difficulties on all sides, but never cornered. . . while we are
still alive, we are consigned to our death every day. . . so that in our
mortal flesh, the life of Jesus may be openly shown.' What is of supreme
importance here is that Paul presents the saving action of God as taking
place not in spite of human weakness and contradictions, but because
of them. The 'treasure' we carry about in earthen vessels, and it is
precisely *in* our mortal flesh that the life of Jesus becomes incarnate
and is openly shown. In these readings, the mind is prepared for the
development of this idea of Paul's which we find in 2 Cor 12; see Saturday of Week 11.

Saturday (5:14-21). *God reconciled the world to himself through the
death of Christ.* Paul here introduces his idea of the *new creation.* In
Christ, all has been made new. In this newness of life, the Christian has
acquired a new set of standards and values. He should no longer judge
people and events by old, conventional standards.

One of the key words in this passage is *reconciliation.* 'God, through
Christ, was reconciling the world to himself.' Notice the imperfect
tense. Can Paul intend by this to include all of Jesus' earthly activity in
the great act of reconciliation? Certainly in his lifetime, Jesus broke
down barriers, social, religious, political. And the climax of this work of
reconciliation was the Cross. To participate in this work of reconciliation is one of the most important tasks of the apostle.

FIRST READINGS, Year 2 (1 Kings)

Monday (1 Kings 17:1-6). *Drought for a wicked king.* The prophet
Elijah announces to King Ahab of Israel (874-853 BC) a long drought as
punishment for the worship of the Canaanite god Baal which Ahab,
urged on by his Tyrian Queen Jezebel, had allowed to take root in Israel.

Several of the narratives about Elijah (and Elisha) tell of unusual, even miraculous, happenings (here the ravens). The historical figure of the prophet tended to take on legendary proportions among the disciples of the prophets (see 1 Kings 20:55; 2 Kings 2:3) where these stories were transmitted.

Tuesday (17:7-16). *The miracle of the flour and the oil.* Elijah who so bitterly opposed the introduction of Canaanite cults into Israel is shown here as Yahweh's instrument for saving the life of a Sidonian (Canaanite) woman and her son during the long drought. The Lord's providence for his prophet reaches out to non-Israelites (see Lk 4:25-26). The edifying narrative insists on the fulfilment of Yahweh's word as uttered by the prophet—a constant theme in the Deuteronomic writings.

Wednesday (18:20-39). *Yahweh or Baal: which is God?* Elijah's opening words show what is at stake in this dramatic confrontation: Yahweh cannot be served alongside Baal; a choice must be made. The frantic clamour of the Baal-prophets meets with stony silence from their Baal, but Elijah's prayer is answered by an incontrovertible display of Yahweh's power. The wood, the holocaust, and the very water (an added obstacle) are all consumed by lightning. Confronted with different but no less insidious idols, Christians today must base their choice too between powerless pretenders and the living God.

Thursday (18:41-46). *Rain from Yahweh.* The rain-god Baal has been shown up as a powerless nullity (yesterday's reading). It is Yahweh who grants rain and all other blessings to Israel. King Ahab learns this lesson here from Elijah who announces the end of the fast called to prepare for sacrifice and to implore rain.

Friday (19:9, 11-16). *Elijah's experience of God.* Driven out of Israel by the threats of Queen Jezebel, Elijah travels south to Mount Horeb (called Sinai in other Old Testament traditions), and at this historic spot learns that henceforth Yahweh will reveal himself not in the spectacular phenomena of storm, earthquake, and fire (see Judg 5:4-5), but in the gentle sound of intelligible communication to his prophets. The commission given to Elijah at the end is an example. In fact it is his successor Elisha who will install Hazael and Jehu (2 Kings 8:7-13;9:1-10).

Saturday (19:19-21). *The call of Elisha.* Since the cloak symbolised the personality and status of the owner, Elijah's action means that Elisha is called to be his successor in the prophetic mission. Elisha's request to kiss his parents seems to be granted only grudgingly by Elijah, who perhaps expected a more immediate response on Elisha's part (see Lk 9:61-62). In any case, Elisha's slaughter of the oxen and burning of the plough mark his break with his old manner of life (compare Mk 1:16-20).

GOSPEL READINGS (Matthew)

INTRODUCTION TO THE GOSPEL ACCORDING TO MATTHEW

For full seventeen centuries in the history of the Church Matthew outweighed all other gospels in the readings for Sundays and holy-days. Among the Fathers it is the most quoted gospel from the second century on. Today there are few enough who might pick Matthew as their favourite gospel. Perhaps the reason is that so much attention has been given to the other three gospels that Matthew's popularity has waned. But over the past ten years or so a vast output of articles and books on Matthew have rediscovered him and encourage us to have a rethink and a new understanding of his gospel.

The Person of Christ. If we approach the readings from Matthew with an open and prepared mind we can discover special insights about the person of Christ and what it means to be a Christian which we do not find in other gospels. Each evangelist sets his sights on particular aspects of Jesus and his teaching. Matthew dwells on the *power* of Jesus. 'All power' has been given to him by the Father. Like Yahweh he is Lord of 'heaven and earth' (28:18). He is powerful in word and action. He is the teacher *par excellence* who comes to reveal God's will for humanity, especially in those long discourses which are a feature of this gospel. He has only to speak a word and men, women and children are healed, even at a distance. He manifests his power to forgive, to heal and overcome any distress or evil that crushes man (9:6; 10:1). In those stirring scenes on the Lake of Galilee (chs 8 & 14) he has power over nature; he is Lord of the wind and the waves. Here, too, he is Lord of his people, the Church, which is symbolised by the boat tossed about by the waves. This stress on the power of Jesus points for Matthew to the mystery of his person. It reflects the faith of the early community in their Lord. Jesus is the expected one of his people, the Messiah, Son of God. The constant references to the Old Testament point to him as the one who fulfils the high expectations of his people.

He is the one to whom God has given extraordinary authority, a Son of Man (Daniel 7:13f). Constantly throughout the gospel he is addressed as 'Lord'; people 'worship' him. This shows him to be a divine Son. Matthew projects the power and majesty of the risen Lord back into his earthly ministry. That is why, as contrasted with Mark, he will often tone down the limitations and human reactions of the earthly Jesus. Jesus is the teacher with authority and the commanding Lord. Yet a person of power without compassion, the man who shows power without sharing it or placing it at the service of those in need would be an awesome and uninspiring figure. For Matthew Jesus is the compassionate Servant of God who is touched by distress and takes it away by his healing power (8:17; 9:36). He shares his teaching and healing power with those who continue his mission (10:1; 28:20). All power and compassion come together in him.

Lord of his people. Jesus cannot be separated from his people. The whole gospel is summarised in the concluding three verses (28:18-20): Jesus is the Messiah and King to whom the Old Testament looked forward; he has all power in the Kingdom; he forms a new community. This community consists of 'disciples' from all nations. This universal gathering is the Church. Those who are baptised so that they now belong to the Father, Son and Spirit and who live the teaching of Jesus ('all that I commanded you') are disciples. The gospel has often been called 'ecclesial' because it describes more than any other gospel what the Christian community, the Church is. It is a new 'people' which has grown out of an old Israel and 'produces the fruit' of the Kingdom (21: 43). Jesus is Lord of this new people. He who was rejected by his own has, through his death and resurrection, become the 'corner-stone' of the new building, the new temple which is the Church. He gives stability to and binds together his people (21:42). Life in this community is constituted by personal relationships. The Christian is a disciple who does the will of the Father; he has a close, personal relationship with Jesus who manifests this will. He is baptised into the name of the Father, Son and Spirit, that is, into a relationship by which he belongs to them. Christian community is a life of brotherhood which is expressed in mutual service and support, personal care and forgiveness 'from the heart' (12:46-50; 28:19; ch. 18).

This new people is very much in continuation with the old people, the Israel of the past. And yet it is born out of Jesus' rejection. As Matthew was writing for Jewish-Christians, his view was influenced by the contemporary situation. Many gentiles were entering the Church whereas official Judaism was opposed to the new community. He writes to convince Christian Jews and Pharisee-led Jews that the Christian community alone represents the true Israel of God. Jesus' rejection is a shadow which appears throughout the gospel. The atmosphere of conflict and rejection is more striking in this gospel than in any other. Yet Matthew does not dwell on the rejection of Jesus as a meaningless tragedy. It is foretold in Scripture and therefore it belongs to God's plan not only for Jesus but also for his people. He who was rejected becomes the centre and Lord of a worldwide community. The Christian, too, is invited to share in that rejection which leads to resurrection.

While rejected by the religious leaders of his time, the life and work of Jesus are rooted in the history and culture of his people. At times readers will find the gospel difficult because its language and atmosphere reflect Old Testament Judaism much more pronouncedly than any other gospel. Matthew is writing for Jewish-Christians in their terms and categories. He quotes the Old Testament so frequently because he wants to show that the life, teaching and destiny of Jesus are somehow foreshadowed in Scripture. It is also his way of saying: all that happened to Jesus, particularly his death and resurrection, are part of God's plan for him from the beginning. The language is very Jewish, for example, expressions such as 'Kingdom of heaven' (the Jewish frequently substituted other names for God), the constant references to Jewish customs and law, a preference for certain numbers (three and seven). Jesus is a Jewish rabbi who gathers disciples and instructs them. His mission is to his own people of Israel. During his lifetime they have a prior claim. It is his Father's plan that the Kingdom be opened to the whole world. Jesus is a man of his own people and yet a Messiah for the whole world who forms a new brotherhood which embraces all peoples.

The power of his word. Jesus is inseparable not only from his own people but also from his message. He has come to accomplish his Father's will (26:42). A disciple is one who understands and 'does the will of my Father' (12:50). The main reason why Matthew's gospel prevailed in the liturgical readings for a long period of history was that it contains so much teaching of Jesus. Matthew structures his gospel by alternating narrative with discourses. There are five major discourses (chs 5–7; 10; 13; 17:22–18:35; chs 24–25) preceded and followed by narrative sections which are connected with them. Between the introduction to the gospel (chs 1–2: the infancy account) and the concluding section about the passion and resurrection (chs 26–28) there is the central part consisting of *five* sections (chs 3–7; 8–10; 11:1–13:52; 13:53–18:35; chs 19–25) all of which contain a narrative account (chs 3–4; 8–9; 11–12; 13:53–17:21; chs 19–23) leading into a long discourse. This is the basic plan of the whole gospel. The weekday readings are taken from the central part of the gospel (chs 3–25), beginning with the Sermon on the Mount.

In order to profit from those readings which deal with the sayings and discourses of Jesus it is helpful to keep in mind some of the key points of Jesus' teaching:

(a) His teaching continues and develops that of the Old Testament. Jesus views the Old Testament ('the law and the prophets') not as a book or code of laws. As a whole it expresses God's will for man in its essential intention. He brings to a more complete expression God's will or 'law'. Christian life consists in living out this new law or teaching of Jesus. It is a life of 'righteousness'.

(b) This life of 'righteousness' is explained as doing the Father's will (clarified by Jesus), having right relationships with God and our fellow-men or actively loving God and our neighbour. To be 'perfect' is to be obedient to this will of the Father, to lead a God-centred life, to imitate his perfect love which is all-embracing and does not discriminate against any class or race, not even against the sinner or the unjust. This active love finds its expression above all in mercy and forgiveness because the Father himself is merciful and forgiving.

(c) Christian living is shown in action not just in expressions of our faith. This action must be accompanied by a process of interiorisation. The important thing is not so much what a person does but rather what he is. Sin and holiness are rooted in the heart, deep within ourselves. The Christian is called to a life of wholeness. He integrates attitude with external action.

Conclusion. There is a striking unity about the whole gospel. The same ideas and expressions recur. These sometimes indicate that the gospel reflects a developed stage of the Jewish-Christian community for which it was written. The mission to the gentiles was well under way. The baptism of Christians included a profession of faith in a Trinity of persons (28:18-20). A commonly accepted view today is that the gospel in its present form was composed sometime in the 80's (AD) by a converted Jewish rabbi or at least a highly educated Jewish-Christian who had at his command a considerable knowledge of rabbinic learning and teaching skill. At the same time it contains traditions which are apostolic and which are associated with an apostle, Matthew.

Some years ago a friend gave me this rhyme:

> Matthew gives us five discourses,
> In threes and sevens he likes his sources,
> He writes to show what the Old Testament meant
> With an ecclesiastical (i.e. ecclesial) bent!

This may not appeal to our poetic sense. But it does summarise much
of the truth about Matthew. It makes a lot of sense provided we remember that the focus of the gospel is the person, work and teaching of
Jesus, the Lord of his new people, the Church.

Further Reading: P. F. Ellis, *Matthew, his Mind and his Message,*
Collegeville, Minnesota, 1974. H. Wansbrough, 'St Matthew' (commentary on the gospel), *New Catholic Commentary on Holy Scripture,*
Nelson, London, 1969. A. M. Hunter, *Design for Life* (An Exposition
of the Sermon on the Mount), London: SCM, 1969.

* * *

The readings over the following three weeks are taken from the Sermon
on the Mount (Mt 5–7). Here Jesus gives a sketch of the Christian life
and its new demands. The Sermon is a 'design for life' (A. M. Hunter), a
magnetic force which has drawn politicians, writers, radicals and
reformers of many cultures, for instance, Tolstoy and Gandi. Its key
feature is the stress on inwardness. Undoubtedly, Christianity is a
matter of action, not just religious verbiage. But as regards this lived
faith in action, the emphasis is on our attitudes, on how we stand
before God, on our heart and inner wholeness. For Jesus the good and
the evil life flow outwards from within ourselves. Even the best
behaviour is worthless when it is not an expression of our inner selves.
Christian life is like fruit on a tree. It you want good fruit, first make
sure that the tree itself is sound. What matters is what a person really is,
not so much what he does.

Monday (Mt 5:1-12). *In search of happiness.* Jesus speaks to that deepest longing in each man's heart—his search for happiness. To be 'blessed'
or happy is to experience God's special love and favour. On the face of
it, it might appear as if the beatitudes look for happiness all in the
wrong places—in the struggle for peace, in rejection, in doing what is
right, in 'mourning'. But this Christian happiness is no pie in the sky. It
is something within ourselves, something for which and towards which
each person keeps working. It comes with the conviction that God's
kingdom, his saving life and love, is present to us and will finally en-
compass us if we respond to the word and example of his Son. Jesus
lived and taught what it means to trust the Father (poor in spirit), to
lead a God-controlled life (meek), to have a single-mindedness and
sincerity in the service of God (pure in heart), to make and preserve
peace among men and to have that outgoing kindness of the heart of

God (mercy). Hope and God's strength are held out to sad and suffering disciples.

Tuesday (Mt 5:13-16). *The mission of the Christian.* No man can be a disciple of Jesus unless he is a source of strength and light to his fellow-man. Read any of those countless cookery books available today and you will notice how often salt is recommended! It gives flavour and 'punch'. It can become tasteless, too, from the damp. The world with its needs looks forward to being strengthened by the example and concern of those who claim they have experienced Jesus and his message in a real way. The genuine disciple will not pass unnoticed. His inner experience and convictions spontaneously express themselves in lived faith and active concern for the world about him. He does not want to be listless or bury himself in isolation and introspection. He tries to share his strength and his talents with others. How can *I* bring light and strength to another human being today?

Wednesday (5:17-19). *The mission of Jesus.* Jesus' background, upbringing and life were deeply rooted in his own people. He does not knock down all those religious traditions which were the heritage of his own culture and race, specially beloved by his Father. As a man born and reared in Judaism, the most treasured part of his heritage was the Old Testament, 'the law and the prophets'. He speaks about the Old Testament as a whole, as governing man's activity and not as a book of codified laws. For him it expresses God's saving love or will in its essential intention. The mission Jesus has received from his Father is to bring to a more complete expression God's will for man. In Gethsemane he shows that his own life was dominated by a desire to do his Father's will: thy will be done (26:42). Jesus' words on the Mount clarify what the Father wills for and from his own brothers, Christian disciples.

Thursday (5:20-26). *An affair of the heart.* Christian living is 'righteousness'—a matter of having right relationships with God and our fellow-men. It is a life pleasing to God, lived according to Jesus' radical view of God's will for man. It goes beyond Christian words and actions. It comes from the heart, from deep within ourselves. It calls for attitudes and a morality in the blood and bone. A purely legalistic religion attacks the problem of right and wrong from the outside and proceeds to lay down rules. Jesus tracks sin to its lair within the heart of man. The law, he says, condemns murder. I condemn deep-seated hate, that is, in the mind, will and emotions combined. Our worship is valueless if not sustained by a Christian spirit of reconciliation. Before entering

into God's presence let us be right with our neighbour. We are invited
not to leave quarrels unrepaired.

Friday (5:27-32). *Wholeness and inwardness.* The examples given by
Jesus illustrate that Christian discipleship surpasses the religious laws of
his own culture and affects the depths of man's being. It is a life of
wholeness and inwardness. If affects the whole person, our attitudes,
our living and thinking. A fleeting external gesture, such as a look, may
reveal a deep-seated selfishness and evil gnawing at us inside. The figurative sayings about the offending eye and hand teach that, since man's
heart is the source of good and evil, an inward self-discipline is necessary
for our life with God. Jesus' words affect not only man's inner self in a
radical way; but also the most intimate of his human relationships, his
married life. Here Jesus goes far beyond the thinking of his own day.

Saturday (5:33-37). *The Lord of all my life.* Jesus criticises certain
practices of his day which encouraged insincerity and dishonesty. People
were in the habit of excluding the divine name from oaths and sub-
stituting other words so as to evade the truth. The disciple is to speak
truthfully and live honestly because he is dealing with God in all areas
of his life. He is the Lord of all his life; he is 'acquainted with all my
ways' (Ps 139). We do not welcome him just into certain areas of our
life and keep him out of others. Because he is everywhere, all through
life and every activity, we want to bring him into every transaction.
Christian integrity means to stand by our words and actions in his
presence and to offer him an invitation to everything in our life. All
doors are opened to him.

ELEVENTH WEEK OF THE YEAR

FIRST READINGS, Year 1 (2 Corinthians)

Monday (2 Cor 6:1-10). *Paul reminds the Corinthians of the trials and
humiliations which the apostles have to suffer.* See further, Friday of
Tenth Week, p. 125 above.

Tuesday & Wednesday (2 Cor 8:1-9; 9:6-11). *An exhortation to contri-
bute generously to a Church collection.* Christ became poor to make us

rich; those with some wealth should help their less fortunate brethren. Very often in missionary work today, financial support comes from the 'sending church'. In Paul's situation, the reverse was the case. Corinth was a far more wealthy place than Palestine and Paul is here requesting financial assitance for Jerusalem from the people he had evangelised in Corinth. It has been suggested that the collection was intended for the contemplative wing of the Church, the ideal community which is described early in Acts as having all things in common and being 'of one heart and soul'. Whatever its purpose, the suggestion of this collection reveals a practical side of Paul's character and a very genuine concern for those in need.

Thursday (11:1-11). *Paul preached the gospel free of charge.* Paul reminds the Corinthians of their dignity as Christians. Their believing community is the bride of Christ and it was Paul himself who arranged the marriage ceremony in Corinth. He is now afraid that his enemies in Corinth will alienate them from himself and from Christ.

Friday (11:18, 21-30). *Paul speaks of his anxieties for the churches he has founded.* In their attempts to discredit Paul, his enemies at Corinth boast of their own qualifications and achievements. Paul now counters these attacks. On the purely human side he has better testimonials than any of his adversaries. He goes on to tell the Corinthians how much he has suffered for the sake of the gospel.

Saturday (12:1-10). *God's grace works best through human weakness.* Fr Lyonnet called this passage 'the fundamental law of the apostolate'. Paul is aware of his spiritual gifts, but to bring him down to earth, he suffered this 'thorn in the flesh'. The 'thorn in the flesh' has been variously interpreted as blindness, or some other physical defect, sexual temptation and so on. Fr Lyonnet interprets the phrase in its context. For him, the thorn in the flesh is the frustration experienced by Paul in his apostolic ministry: his failure on several occasions to win people over to Christ, the difficulties in the churches he founded, desertion by some of his fellow apostles. Paul beseeches God to take away this 'thorn' from him. But the answer comes as unmistakable as it is mysterious: 'My grace is enough for you; my power is at its best in weakness.' The apostle is now reassured. He can even rejoice now in his frustrations, in his own very weakness, because it is right there that the power of God becomes incarnate.

Paul is here very much in line with at least one current of Old Testament spirituality: it is that which was summed up by Libermann in his

death-bed aphorism: 'God is all, man is nothing'. It is particularly prominent in Isaiah, where the power of God is often contrasted with the
frailty, helplessness and transitoriness of man (see the very beautiful
lines in Is 26:16-19). It is, however, important to remember that there
are other kinds of spirituality in the Old Testament, where man's
dignity and responsibility are stressed, as for example, in the Wisdom
Books, some of the Psalms, parts of Kings.

FIRST READINGS, Year 2 (1 & 2 Kings)

Monday (1 Kings 21:1-16). *Naboth's vineyard.* The attachment of a
free Israelite land-owner to his ancestral property comes into conflict
with King Ahab's wishes. The king though much chagrined appears to
accept Naboth's refusal, but his foreign wife Jezebel is decidedly less
scrupulous. Not for the last time in Biblical history a false accusation
makes possible a legal condemnation of an innocent man. Since the
property of an executed criminal reverted to the crown, Jezebel is able
to present Ahab with the coveted vineyard. Might seems to be right.

Tuesday (21:17-29). *God's sentence on Ahab and his house.* The
powerful ones of the earth are not exempt from God's judgement. The
judicial murder of Naboth and the seizing of his property draw an immediate response from the Lord through Elijah. The terrible sentence
is delayed in part because of Ahab's repentance; it is in the time of his
son Jehoram that Ahab's entire family will be wiped out (2 Kings
9—10), but Jezebel will die as the Lord's word foretold (2 Kings 9:30-
37) and the dogs did lick Ahab's blood (1 Kings 22:38).

Wednesday (2 Kings 2:1, 6-14). *The assumption of Elijah and succession of Elisha.* After the parting of the waters of the Jordan (compare
Ex 14—15 and Josh 3—4), Elisha asks for a double share (the eldest
son's portion) of Elijah's spirit. His cry 'Chariot of Israel and its
chargers', as he sees Elijah being taken up amid the fire and wind
typical of divine interventions, means that the prophet is a better
defence for Israel than are military forces (see also 2 Kings 13:14).
    Later Judaism expected Elijah's return to usher in the Final Age of
God's rule: see Mal 3:23-24 (RSV 4:5-6) and Mk 9:11-13 (with parallels).

Thursday (Sir 48:1-14). *Praise of Elijah and Elisha.* This eulogy comes
from the second century B.C. Elijah's eschatological role is noted (vv.
10-11). The statement that Elisha's body prophesied in death refers to

the raising of a dead man to life by contact with Elisha's bones (2 Kings 13:20-21).

Friday (2 Kings 11:1-4, 9-18, 20). *The end of a wicked queen.* Queen Athaliah of Judah, a daughter of Ahab king of Israel (and therefore not of David's line), violently usurped the throne of Judah on the death of her son King Ahaziah, and introduced the cult of Baal. The account of her overthrow and execution seven years later notes the part played by Jehoida the priest and the professional soldiers and by the free citizens of Judah in the coup. The temple of Baal was destroyed, and the new king Jehoash of legitimate Davidic stock was installed with a solemn covenant renewal ceremony.

Saturday (2 Chron 24:17-25). *You have deserted Yahweh, now he deserts you.* Towards the end of the reign of Joash (or, Jehoash) the kingdom of Judah was invaded by the Aramaeans. The post-exilic author of Chronicles offers a religious explanation for this disaster. The king who had begun as a pious ruler and a friend of the priesthood later tolerated the wicked ways of the apostate Judeans and even murdered a prophet in the temple (see Mt 23:35; Lk 11:51). The Aramaean invasion and Joash's violent death followed as Yahweh's punishment. One can contrast the more laconic account in 2 Kings 12:18-22.

GOSPEL READINGS (Matthew)

Monday (Mt 5:38-42). *Resentment and retaliation.* Jesus outlaws 'tit-for-tat', measure for measure which appears in the Old Testament, Greek and Roman law. He criticises the spirit of vindictiveness in cases of personal wrong. He drives this home with four images which are not to be applied literally. They are an appeal for a spirit of forgiveness, of non-resentment, of non-retaliation and of generous giving. The Christian is not denied his human rights, the right to protect himself against violence and injustice. But he is not an avenger, a man of heartless attitudes who always insists on his own rights. We do not forfeit our rights; neither do we think of our right to do as we like but always our duty to help.

Tuesday (5:43-48). *The perfect lover.* In Jesus' time loving the neighbour belonged to the essence of Jewish religion. But the neighbour was limited to those of one's country or religious community. Jesus' doctrine of the extra goes far beyond that. The 'enemy' is now a neighbour. The

Christian is a man for all others, for those of other nations, creeds, even for those who are fair or unfair, kind or difficult because God's care embraces all humanity whether they are loving or unloving. The call to be perfect is not an invitation to strive with fanatical will power after some abstract ideal. It is to look at God, to see how perfectly he loves and then to try to imitate in our own human way the expansiveness of his love, his unconquerable good will. 'The man who cares most for men is the most perfect man' (Barclay).

Wednesday (6:1-6, 16-18). *The sincere lover.* Right attitudes and sincerity before God give meaning to our Christian practices. Charitable donations, attendance at prayer meetings and fasts which are influenced by the desire to be noticed and approved of are empty. They should be free from preoccupation with oneself as *the* great benefactor of society or with one's public. 'The difference between do-gooders and people who love is the difference between a life which is an on-stage performance and a life which is an act of love' (J. Powell: *Fully Human, Fully Alive).* In prayer, too, Jesus recommends forgetfulness of self and of admirers. He does not mean that one's room is necessarily the best setting for our prayer but rather that we do not make a theatre out of our prayer. We do not pray to the gallery. A Christian is not an actor, a 'hypocrite'. What counts is our sincerity before God.

Thursday (6:7-15). *The prayer of forgiveness.* God is not forced effectively by long prayers. It is easy to confuse a sincere prayer with verbosity. The Lord's prayer contains six petitions which bring the whole of life into the presence of the Father. The first three have to do with God and his glory; then come requests for our human needs: provision, pardon and protection. The petition for forgiveness is further developed to bring home to us that God's mercy and our own mercy towards one another are interlinked and interdependent.

Friday (6:19-23). *The God-controlled life.* Christian living is the God-controlled life. Once a man looks for self-sufficiency in his own gifts or in preoccupations that exclude God, then he ceases to realise his utter dependence on him. The human heart longs for a focus, a centre of life. This centre has to be a personal relationship in which he can rest secure. This relationship, man's most treasured possession, is with God. It is the giving of the heart to him in right living and good works. When our vision of life is distorted by overconcentration on our possessions we find ourselves walking away from God into the darkness.

Saturday (6:24-34). *Do not be anxious.* The person who places all his trust in himself, in the works and wealth of his own making has ceased to recognise that God is in control of his life. Our lack of trust begins when we look for security in our own efforts. Jesus criticises feverish effort, anxious haste and worry in which God has no part. In fact, we are anxious people. But we sometimes increase anxiety by overanxiety. There is one main care and all else is subject to it: to recognise God's care and concern, his presence which delivers us from anguish. In the light of his love and support we can see our anxieties in their proper perspective. Here and now he is with us and we try to live in his protecting presence just for that here and now.

TWELFTH WEEK OF THE YEAR

FIRST READINGS, Year 1 (Genesis 12—18)

Monday (Gen 12:1-9). *The Call of Abraham.* With the call of Abraham the history of sin gives way to the story of salvation. Called from a world of sin and idolatry (cf. Joshua 24:2) sometime around 1850 B.C., Abraham received the divine promise of land and posterity. Abraham's response to the divine call was prompt and unconditional. The phrase 'Abraham went, as the Lord had told him' (v. 4) expresses an attitude of faith and trust that makes of the ancient patriarch a model for all believers.

Tuesday (13:2, 5-18). *The Generosity of Abraham.* This story is a true reflection of nomadic life. For the nomads often disputed among themselves about grazing rights in the unoccupied hill country. When Lot disputed with his uncle Abraham, the old patriarch acted magnanimously and gave the younger man whatever grazing land he chose to take. But if Lot gained possession of the best land for the time being Abraham received a new promise that all the land of Canaan would one day belong to his numerous descendants (vv. 14-17; compare 12:7).

Wednesday (15:1-12, 17-18). *A Covenant with Abraham.* When Abraham wondered if God was ever to fulfil his promise to give him a family of his own (v. 2) the Lord reassured him that his descendants would indeed be numerous (v. 5). He even confirmed the promise by a solemn covenant. The strange rite of cutting the animals in two (vv. 9-10) was a well-known form of ratifying covenants in the ancient middle east. The flaming torch passing between the divided carcasses (v. 17) symbolised God's confirmation of the covenant and his commitment to his promise.

Thursday (16:1-12, 15-16). *The birth of Ishmael.* When Sarah bore no children she followed the custom of the time and provided her husband with a concubine who would bear him a child. But when the concubine did conceive Sarah became jealous, and, contrary to accepted custom, she drove her from Ahraham's household. But the Lord came to the rescue of the offended girl, told her to return to her mistress Sarah, and assured her that her child would become a courageous and independent leader of a nomadic tribe (v. 12).

Friday (17:1, 9-10, 15-22). *A Covenant with Abraham.* This is the P version of the covenant recorded in Gen 15 (see reading for Wednesday). Verses 6-8 (omitted in our reading) repeat the promise of children and of land. Circumcision was to be the sign of the covenant. It would be a sign of God's care of his covenant partner, and a sign of the circumcised man's acceptance of the divine plan.

During the time of the Babylonian exile (587-539 B.C.) circumcision was to become a mark that distinguished the Jews from their pagan neighbours.

Saturday (18:1-15). *Sarah will have a son.* Abraham's hospitality to his unknown guests is described with consumate art. One of the guests, who turns out to be Yahweh, assures Abraham that his barren wife will bear a son. Even if Sarah laughs at the idea, the Lord will be able to fulfil his promise.

FIRST READINGS, Year 2 (2 Kings)

Monday (2 Kings 17:5-8, 13-15, 18). *The end of the northern kingdom.* The constant plotting of the Kings of Israel against their Assyrian overlords brought the final disaster upon their kingdom and Samaria its capital (721 BC). The deportation of defeated populations was a common Assyrian practice.

The theological explanation of the Deuteronomic writers notes that the disaster was due to infidelity to Yahweh's covenant. The Lord had often warned the people through his prophets but they refused to listen. From now on the Lord's saving plans will be operative only in Davidic Judah.

Tuesday (19:9-11, 14-21, 31-36). *Yahweh saves Jerusalem.* Some decades after the fall of Samaria King Hezekiah of Judah rebelled against the Assyrian overlord. A powerful enemy force under King Sennacherib moved against Jerusalem. In this desperate situation Hezekiah prays to Yahweh and consults the prophet Isaiah who transmits to the king an oracle of hope. Human might is of no avail against Yahweh's will to save Jerusalem; the Assyrians suffer heavy losses in their camp (possibly as a result of a plague) and are obliged to retire.

Wednesday (22:8-13; 23:1-3). *Covenant renewal under Josiah.* King Josiah of Judah (640-609) took advantage of Assyrian weakness to remove Assyrian cults from Jerusalem. His subsequent general religious reform (of great importance in Biblical history) received its initial impetus from the finding in the Jerusalem temple of the Book of the Law (622 BC); this may have been an early edition of Deut 5–28, abandoned and forgotten during the reign of Josiah's irreligious predecessor Manasseh. Shaken by his new insights into the Lord's will as revealed in the book, Josiah orders the people to assemble for a solemn renewal of the covenant with Yahweh.

Thursday (24:8-17). *The first deportation from Jerusalem.* The young king of Judah, Jehoiachin, paid the price of his father's rebellion against the Babylonians who were by now the dominant power in the near east; Jerusalem surrendered to the Babylonians on 16 March 597. The king and many of his more influential subjects were deported to Babylon, and a puppet king was set up in Jerusalem.

The Deuteronomic writer notes that these calamities were due to the sins of the Judean kings especially Masasseh (24:3-4, 9). Isaiah's prophetic words to King Hezekiah (20:17) about the plundering of the temple have now been fulfilled.

Friday (25:1-12). *The end of the southern kingdom.* The puppet king Zedekiah foolishly rebelled against the Babylonians. A second siege of Jerusalem followed and the city fell in the summer of 586 BC (or possibly 587). Zedekiah suffered the cruel fate of a rebel vassal; the Babylonians sacked and burned the temple (and much of the city with it); more Judeans were deported to Babylon.

Monarchy in the land of Israel had come to an end, and the period of Exile began (587/6-538 BC). But when all seemed lost from a human point of view, the Lord did not abandon his people. His word, proclaimed to the exiles by Ezekiel and the prophet known as Deutero-Isaiah (Is 40–55), would bring a message of purification, hope, and new life.

Saturday (Lam 2:2, 10-14, 18-19). *Lament over fallen Jerusalem.* This deeply moving poem from the exilic period describes the wretched state of ruined Jerusalem punished by its outraged Lord. An accusing finger is pointed at those prophets whose false optimism had blinded the city to its sins and impending doom (for Jeremiah's encounter with one such prophet see Jer 28). However tears of grief and repentance may yet win the Lord's mercy.

GOSPEL READINGS (Matthew)

Monday (Mt 7:1-5). *The splinter and the plank.* Mercy is an inward quality. Jesus not only speaks of forgiveness that comes 'from the heart' (18:35), but also of mercy that has its roots in the mind. We feel happy in the presence of a counsellor and friend who is non-judgmental. The parable of the splinter and the plank tells us to be merciful in our judgments if we want to experience God's mercy. The over-critical eye detects the tiniest flaws outside itself. It is not a question of closing our eyes to others' failings but rather of pardoning them. The concern to criticise and reform others is often marred by an uncritical moral complacency as to our own lives. A look in the mirror, a glance at our own meanness, our own 'plank' dwarfs our brother's faults and helps us to become more accepting.

Tuesday (7:6, 12-14). *The golden rule.* The word of God is precious and not to be wasted. It is for those who are ready for and worthy of it. Living and communicating his word to others will bring rejection and failure. But this should not be provoked by tactlessness. Jesus' message about treating others as we would wish to be treated has been called the 'golden rule' of Christian living. 'So act as to treat humanity,' says the philosopher Kant, 'whether in your own person or that of another, in every case as an end, not as a means only.' The disciple does not just avoid doing things against others; he will always look for things to do for them. The way of lived faith and active concern for others is no easy road.

Wednesday (7:15-20). *Testing the message.* The inwardness of Christian living is once more underlined by Jesus. He warns against those who can mislead us under a pretence of good. The test of a man's message is the fruit of his own living. His inner wholeness appears in manifestly sincere attitudes. Christianity flows from within outwards. Man is in his works. We are what we do, not what we pretend to be. 'It is not good works which made a good man,' says Martin Luther, 'but a good man who does good works.'

Thursday (7:21-29). *Living the word.* A disciple's sincerity is proved not by fine words but by living the word of Jesus. The image of the wise builder describes doers of the word. They stand firm. Obedience to Jesus is the only sure foundation of their life. The Sermon on the Mount ends with this insistence on listening and doing. The Christian is for Matthew one who does the Father's will as manifested in Jesus. This Christian man of action is not just an extrovert. His activity springs from the inward hearing and self-appropriation of Jesus' word.

Friday (8:1-4). *The healing Lord.* So far the readings from Matthew have been taken from the teaching of Jesus. Throughout the gospel he is the expected one, the Messiah of his people to whom 'all power in heaven and on earth has been given' (28:18). He is 'Lord', powerful not only in word but also in deed. The two chapters following his message on the Mount show him as the Messiah and Lord of his people who manifests and shares his power in the many ways he heals and delivers from distress and fear. He is the Lord who saves, provided people trust in his power. He appears as the compassionate Servant of God who experiences and responds to the distresses of humanity.

First of all, Jesus heals ('cleanses') a leper. Jesus is the powerful, healing 'Lord' whom society's outcast approaches with a certain hope and trust in his power. Jesus speaks a commanding and healing word: 'Be healed...Go'. He is the commanding Lord who orders him to follow the law of his country. He must be certified as cured. Matthew contemplates Jesus as the Servant of God, gifted with power which he uses, not just for himself in order to manifest his might but in order to open up a new life to society's outcast. He shows that power is not for self but for service.

Saturday (8:5-17). *The compassionate healer.* Jesus is Lord, God's Servant who brings help and healing to 'all who were sick' (v. 16). His healing power is for all, especially for the ordinary and neglected people of his country—here for a mother-in-law and a foreigner. He is a Lord for the centurion who himself has power and authority. He can get certain things done merely with a word of command. If this is the case with him how much more can Jesus command and effect wonders by his word. He heals from a distance; he casts out evil spirits with a mere word. But his healing activity is conditioned by trust in his power. All who trust will experience the power of the compassionate Lord.

THIRTEENTH WEEK OF THE YEAR

FIRST READINGS, Year 1 (Genesis 18—27)

Monday (Gen 18:16-33). *A persevering prayer.* Abraham's urgent prayer on behalf of the wicked Sodom teaches that the God of Israel tempers justice with mercy. It also reminds the man of faith that he should never fail to pray for sinners.

Our's is a God who hears prayers (cf. Ps 65:2) and he does not reject those who turn to him with confidence.

Tuesday (19:15-29). *The destruction of Sodom and Gomorrah.* Having described Lot's hospitality to the visiting angels (19:1-3) and the wickedness of the men of Sodom (vv. 4-14) the author goes on in today's reading to describe the destruction of Sodom and Gomorrah.

Divine justice demanded that the wicked cities be punished. Only Lot and his family escaped the holocaust. The story of Lot's wife becoming a pillar of salt (v. 26) may reflect a folkloristic tale that explained the origin in the Dead Sea area of rocks that resembled a human figure. But in the present context it represents punishment for disobedience to the divine command not to look back at the city (cf. v. 17).

Wednesday (21:5, 8-20). *Isaac and Ishmael.* This story is very similar to that recorded in Gen 16:1-14 (see Thursday, Week 12). Here the accent is on the faith of Abraham who accepted God's promise that he would take care of Hagar's child and bless him. But it was through Isaac, the younger of Abraham's two sons, that the divine blessing was to be transmitted.

Thursday (22:1-9). *The sacrifice of Isaac.* Abraham had put all his hopes in Isaac, the child for whom he had so long waited. What a shock it was for him then to hear the command to slay the child (v. 2). Nevertheless, in a spirit of unshakable faith the old man prepared to obey the mysterious command. But seeing his trusting obedience the Lord revoked his command, spared the child, and rewarded Abraham's obedience by renewing the promises and blessings he had already given (cf. Gen 12:7; 15:18). The lesson is that the Lord calls for unquestioning faith, and that obedience to God's commands never goes unrewarded.

Friday (23:1-4, 19; 24:1-8, 62-67). *A wife for Isaac.* Following the death of Sarah Abraham sent one of his trusted servants to find a wife for his son Isaac in Mesopotamia. The lectionary only gives us snippets of this story which is one of the most beautiful and most artistically constructed in the Bible. The religious message of the story is that it was God who guided the quest from beginning to end (cf. v. 7).

Saturday (27:1-5, 15-29). *Jacob the Deceiver.* Jacob, egged on by his mother, deceived his aged father into giving him a blessing that belonged by right to his old brother Esau. The blessing (vv. 27-29) ensures Jacob that his descendants will enjoy the possession of fertile lands, and that they will have dominion over other nations. Another version of this deception story is given in 25:29-34.

FIRST READINGS, Year 2 (Amos)

INTRODUCTION TO THE PROPHETS

This week we begin a series of eight weeks' readings from the prophetical books, and this immediately after two long sets of readings from the historical books. This amount of Old Testament readings may well over-tax the endurance of the average churchgoer. The idea behind the plan of the lectionary, however, is praiseworthy. The Church wants us to hear the voice of prophecy resound against its original historical background. For this reason the lectionary first gives us the history of Israel from the time of the prophet Samuel and the beginnings of the Hebrew monarchy (eleventh century BC) right down to the fall of the monarchy with the destruction of Jerusalem by the Babylonia armies in 587 BC. Against this background we have the present readings from the prophets, given in chronological order: first the four brave men from the eighth century, Amos, Hosea, Isaiah and Micah. Next come readings from the prophets of the late seventh century and from the early period of the exile in Babylon: Jeremiah, Nahum, Habakkuk and Ezekiel.

Who were the prophets? For a long time a prophet was regarded as one who foretold future events—a foreteller. In more recent times emphasis was placed on the prophets as 'the men who spoke out', spokesmen for God on such matters as social justice, false religion, etc.—the prophets were forthtellers. The basic idea of the Greek word from which our term prophet is derived is indeed that of spokesman. In the biblical tradition, however, both are essential elements of prophecy. The prophets were spokesmen for God and foretold future events. When we speak of 'prophet', we generally mean such persons as Isaiah, Jeremiah, etc., those who would more precisely be designated 'classical prophets'. In the biblical tradition the term prophet is much broader than ours and could be used to designate others than these 'classical' prophets. The Hebrew notion of prophecy is linked with the more general desire of man to have contact with the divine through special persons and rites. Outside of Israel in the ancient near east kings and their diviners, augurs and seers who were believed to have special gifts for determining what the divine will was. Ordinary people, too, went to consult these privileged persons. The same was true in Israel and all or most of such persons could be classed as prophets. There were associations of prophets (called 'sons of the prophets' in the Bible), court prophets who were expected to reveal or divine God's will for the king, cult prophets in sanctuaries. Among these Hebrew prophets some were genuine, others false—oftentimes probably unconsciously so. This same term 'prophet' was then used to designate such men as Amos, Jeremiah etc., i.e. the prophets *par excellence* for us. What distinguished these latter from the others was their divine vocation which brought them into a very special relationship with God and made them aware of this relationship. God revealed his will and his plan for Israel and humanity to them. They 'stood in the council of the Lord' as some of themselves put it. They were filled with divine power and were given the strength to proclaim his word fearlessly. This special relationship with God called for sanctity on their part. They had to 'feel' their divine message as well as preach it.

The prophets were very much men of their own day, and the burden of their message depended on the circumstances of their time. When God's people were bent on rejecting the Lord or ignoring the demands of his law, the prophetic message was one of divine chastisement. This, in the main, was the case with the pre-exilic prophets. But the prophets' message was not merely one of doom. God's plans for his people were plans of welfare and hope. And when Israel was punished for her sins

by the exile, the prophetic voice brought consolation and encouragement and prepared God's people for the blessed age that was to come
and would be theirs if they were ready to accept God's ways with faith
and humility.

While the prophets were men of their own day, by virtue of the
word of God which they delivered to Israel they are men for all times.
This word is living and active and was intended to resound within God's
people long after the persons who first preached it had passed from the
scene. God has spoken at various times in the past and in various different ways through the prophets (Heb 1:1). Their voices still address us
today, and call for response, as we read their words or listen to them
being read in liturgical celebrations.

Monday (Amos 2:6-10, 13-16). *Divine election makes demands.* All this
week we have readings from the prophet Amos, who preached about
760 BC. In Amos' day the division of God's people (which began about
922) into the northern kingdom of Israel and the southern kingdom of
Judah was very much a reality. Amos was born in Tekoa of Judah, but
was sent by God to preach in Israel. The northern kingdom was then
flourishing materially. It was otherwise from the religious standpoint.
True, the liturgy and ritual of the central sanctuary at Bethel (where
Yahweh, God of Israel was venerated under the image of a young bull)
were impressive. The nation's prosperity was seen as a sign of Yahweh's
pleasure. His favours, it was believed, could be bought by sacrifice and
ritual, somewhat in the manner of that of Baal, the god of Canaan, and
irrespective of moral behaviour. All looked quiet in the northorn horizon. Then comes Amos, the prophet, as a disturber of the peace. And
he came right into the royal sanctuary of Bethel. In a telling passage we
have a series of his oracles against foreign nations, the enemies of Israel
(Am 1:2—2:5). This would have pleased his audience no end. It was
what they wanted to hear. But then Amos turned on themselves. God
will punish them as much as any other nation. They looked on themselves as God's chosen people. But this election, Amos reminds them, is
meaningless without a life in keeping with the moral law. Their immoral
lives, with their injustice, oppression of the poor, etc., make a mockery
of their profession of faith. The God who chose them will punish them.

Tuesday (3:1-8; 4:11-12). *'Prepare to meet your God'.* Amos the
prophet thunders on. He can do no other because of the divine power
that has taken hold of him as prophet. Israel shall indeed meet her God,
but God as he really is—the God of justice and truth—not the God they

believe him to be, i.e. the God who must shower material benefits on his people. Destruction is certain to come on the northern kingdom. Despite Amos' strong language, it seems that he also believed this disaster could be averted by repentance.

Wednesday (5:14-15, 21-24). *Liturgical celebrations without good works are an abomination to God.* This is one of the well-known prophetic condemnations of the cult (see also Am 4:4-5; Is 1:11-17; Mic 6:6-8; Jer 7:21-22). In Amos' day and in later pre-exilic times it was believed that lavish sacrifices in themselves could win divine favour—as if the God of Israel needed sacrifices like the gods of Canaan and other countries. The sacrifice pleasing to God is a true religious life, shown in respect for the rights of others. The responsorial psalm develops the point.

Thursday (7:10-17). *The prophetic voice will not be silenced.* Language as outspoken as that of Amos—and this in the very sanctuary of the king—was hitherto unheard of. It proved too much, or too dangerous, for Amaziah, the official priestly custodian of the shrine. In order to save the prophet, or more likely his own skin, from the king's anger, he tells Amos to return to his native Judah. But Amos is conscious of being a prophet in a manner different from the others who then bore that name. He is God's envoy; he has a divine message to deliver and this he will do, come what may.

Friday (8:4-6, 9-12). *The prophet once again condemns social injustice.* Punishment for their sins, Amos tells his audience, is sure to come. Through his prophet, God's word is addressing itself to them; this word they now reject. A day will come when divine guidance will be sought, but only too late. It will not be found. It is a very serious thing to reject divine guidance and divine grace.

Saturday (9:11-15). *Promise of a new age.* The book of Amos, almost totally devoted to threats and predictions of disaster, closes in a note of hope. God will usher in a new age for his people. The house of David will again be renewed. The passage looks like the words of a prophet after Amos' day, although it may conceivably come from Amos after his return to Judah from Israel. When the teaching of the prophets was being edited and put together in the books we now know, oracles of doom are very often rounded off by prophecies of welfare. God is always a God of hope.

GOSPEL READINGS (Matthew)

Monday (Mt 8:18-22). *The cost of discipleship.* The second group of miracles (8:18–9:17) are more than descriptions of Jesus' power as Lord of his people. They are also a call to follow him. Our attention is drawn to his word and action. His word makes radical demands on his followers (18-22), it calms the storm (23-27), it frees those possessed (28-34), it forgives sin and restores people to health (9:1-8). It summons a tax-gatherer away from his office (9:9). The two examples in this reading illustrate what discipleship means. It is to have faith and to follow wherever and whenever Jesus calls us. It is an invitation to share in his way of life, in his values and to face realistically the costs of our discipleship.

Tuesday (8:23-27). *Lord of our fears.* Jesus shows that he is Lord (v. 25). He is Lord of the wind and the waves. He is a saving Lord for disciples who cry out: Save, Lord, we are perishing. By a mere word he calms threatening forces. He is Lord of the Christian community, the Church, symbolised by the boat. He is Lord of our fears; he asks disciples why should they be afraid when he is present. The are 'men of little faith'—a frequent phrase in the gospel for those who lack trust in the Lord. When they experience his power they finally come to trust in him. The scene is a reminder for Christians to trust in his power, for he is actively present in the Church.

Wednesday (8:28-34). *The deliverer from evil.* This somewhat crude and puzzling story, which has most probably been influenced by popular story-telling, fixes our attention on one point: the power of Jesus over the force of evil. 'Have you come to torment us before the time?' It is true that a time will come at the end when there will be a complete conquest of evil and sin. But already in Jesus there is a power at work over sin. He communicates his power to us and dispels evil from the heart of man. The fear and negative reactions of people in the face of Jesus' power and compassion are a reminder of the rejection of Jesus, a theme which recurs throughout the gospel.

Thursday (9:1-8). *Healing forgiveness.* Jesus is not merely Lord over nature, evil and sickness. He now exercises and speaks about his power to forgive. His healing words and actions restore a man physically; more important, they affect him on the deepest level of his existence. Physical healing is a sign that he has divine power to communicate God's pardon to men. This is a story about God's forgiveness and man's trust. Without the faith and trust of his friends this man would never have been brought into the healing presence of Jesus. A man is saved by the faith of his friends.

Friday (9:9-13). *The call to discipleship.* Jesus is the Lord who calls disciples, in this case Matthew, to 'follow me'. Following Jesus is a committed attachment to his person, a life of listening and service. Matthew appears among those sinners and tax-collectors who share a meal with Jesus. In Jewish life sharing a meal was an expression of intimate communion and fellowship. He is also one of those 'sick' or sinful people whom Jesus came to call. The call to discipleship is a special experience of Jesus' mercy. It is an invitation to a life of communion with Jesus, to fellowship expressed in listening and serving. Jesus is a messenger of the Father's mercy. He does not bring rituals that create barriers between men. He does not come to call those who are self-satisfied and convinced of their own goodness. He invites those who are conscious of their sin and deeply aware of their need of a saviour. It is only those who know how much they need him who can accept this invitation.

Saturday (9:14-17). *Radically new.* Jesus explains the mystery of his person his suffering destiny and the meaning of his mission. He is a 'bridegroom'; in him God expresses his care for his people. His presence is a cause of joy and celebration. But disciples will feel his absence when he is violently taken away from them. The images of the patch and wine-skins illustrate how Jesus in word and action contributes something radically new to the meaning of human life, something utterly different from what went before him. The Christian disciple will ask himself: am I ready to accept the moments of Christ's joy-filled presence and the painful moments of his seeming absence? Do I allow Christ to change me radically, to renew me?

FOURTEENTH WEEK OF THE YEAR

FIRST READINGS, Year 1 (Genesis 28–50)

Monday (Gen 28:10-22). *Jacob's ladder.* Esau, understandably, hated his deceiving brother, and decided to kill him (cf. 27:41). In order to avoid Esau's anger, and in order to procure a wife from among his own kinsfolk, Jacob set out for Mesopotamia (28:1-5). Today's reading tells how the Lord appeared to him on the way, promised to be with him on his journey, and to bring him back safely to his homeland. God extended his favour to this schemer who was to become the father of the Israelites. Jacob was struck with awe in the presence of his God and consecrated the place to him.

Tuesday (32:23-33). *No longer Jacob, but Israel.* Gen 29:31 tells how the Lord favoured Jacob in Mesopotamia, so that he could, as today's reading says, return to Canaan with two wives, a large retinue, and many possessions. The puzzling story of Jacob's wrestling with a stranger who turned out to be God may be based on a legend about a noctural demon. But in the present narrative it is a reminder that we must all struggle with God in persevering prayer. The change in Jacob's name (v. 28) suggests that he owed his position as father of the Israelites to God alone.

Wednesday (41:55-57; 42:5-7, 17-24). *Joseph in Egypt.* The lectionary tells us nothing about Joseph's youth, about his being sold to traders, about his being taken to Egypt, or about his rise to power there (37:1–41:45). Today we read how his brothers came to Egypt for provisions and encountered Joseph without recognising him. When Joseph, who did recognise his brothers, ordered one of the family to be kept in prison until the youngest brother should be brought to Egypt the other brothers saw this as a punishment for their former treatment of Joseph.

Thursday (44:18-21, 23-29; 45:1-5). *God sent me before you to preserve your lives.* The story of Joseph's emotional encounter with Benjamin (43:11-34) is omitted in the lectionary. So also is the story of Joseph's ruse of placing his royal cup in the sack of Benjamin (44:1-17). Today's reading describes Judah's urgent plea for Benjamin who faced imprisonment because the royal cup had been found in his sack. Judah's love for his youngest brother and his pity for his father touched Joseph, who then dramatically revealed his identity. Joseph's declaration that all the events that had overtaken him were part of God's plan to save the family of Jacob (45:5) gives a religious meaning to the whole Joseph saga.

Friday (46:1-7, 28-30). *Jacob and Joseph meet.* When the brothers returned to Canaan and told Jacob that Joseph was still alive (45:26), the old man resolved to go and see him (v. 28). Today's reading tells how Jacob, encouraged by a divine vision, set off for Egypt with his family and possessions. There in an emotional scene he received a royal welcome from Joseph. The long Joseph saga had a happy ending.

Saturday (49:29-33; 50:15-25). *The death of Jacob and Joseph's magnanimity.* When Jacob died his sons feared that Joseph might seek revenge for their former cruelty to him. But Joseph reassured them, and explained that even their malice fitted into God's plan. As we complete our readings from Genesis, then, we admire the generosity of Joseph, and we wonder at the wisdom of God who guides all things according to his own purposes (compare Rom 8:28).

FIRST READINGS, Year 2 (Hosea, Isaiah)

Monday (Hos 2:16-18, 21-22). *God's love for Israel, his spouse.* The prophet Hosea was a younger contemporary of Amos, and like him preached in the northern kingdom of Israel. Like Amos, his message was one of condemnation. The whole tenor of his teaching, however, differed from that of Amos. Hosea regarded sin above all else as a rejection of divine love. The better to bring this message of divine love to God's unfaithful people, Hosea took the bold step of presenting Yahweh as the husband of Israel. He may have adopted this approach in order to counter the religion of Baal, the fertility god of Canaan, who was regarded as wedded to the land, and to whom Israel was paying homage. From Yahweh, the true God, says Hosea, and not from Baal, come welfare and fertility. In one branch of prophetic teaching the exodus from Egypt and the desert wanderings that followed came to be regarded as the ideal of time of friendship between Israel and her God. It was the period of her youth when her love for God was ardent, the time before she had corrupted herself with the religion of Canaan. In today's reading God says that he will once more win back his unfaithful people's affection.

Tuesday (8:4-7, 11-13). *As a man sows, so shall he reap.* The oracle was delivered by Hosea after part of the northern kingdom had been destroyed by the Assyrians in 732. It contains a condemnation of the worship of Yahweh under the form of a young calf or bull, as practised in the sanctuary of Bethel. While this worship was not in itself idolatry, in the climate of the time and area it led to it and left the door wide open to a wrong understanding of the God of Israel and the demands made by belief in him.

Wednesday (10:1-3, 7-8, 12). *Sow integrity; seek the Lord.* The Assyrian armies destroyed part of the northern kingdom in 732. Ten years later what remained was to fall to these same forces. This final disaster was imminent as Hosea spoke the words read today. The destruction came because of the people's sins. They are now called on to repent, to purify their hearts, to seek the Lord.

Thursday (11:1, 3-4, 8-9). *God's tender love for his people.* The emphasis is on God's love for his people in the days of its infancy, when he led them out of Egypt. Now that the nation is about to be destroyed, God says he almost finds it impossible to permit the disaster. But the destruction is for his people's good. The nation must now fall; new life can follow.

Friday (14:2-10). *An invitation to repent.* Over and over again the prophets had warned Israel that her sins would finally spell her downfall. And yet in this destruction lay salvation, but only if the nation would admit the iniquity of its ways, if only it would turn in repentance to the Lord their God, the one sure hope of salvation. God has revealed himself to man to bring him life, divine life that requires death to self.

Saturday (Isaiah 6:1-8). *Isaiah is called to be a prophet.* Today we begin a series of seven readings from the prophet Isaiah, a very limited number indeed in view of the size and importance of the book. The reason is that most of the readings for the Advent liturgy are from Isaiah, particularly from the second part of the work (Is 40—55). Isaiah is the greatest and deservedly the best known of the prophets. He came from the upper strata of Jerusalem society and was a highly cultured person. His prophetic ministry was carried out in Jerusalem intermittently over some four decades, from the time of his call in the year of the death of King Uzziah of Judah, about 742 BC to 700 or so. Before the commencement of Assyria's conquering push westwards, Judah, like Israel, enjoyed peace and prosperity. The penetrating glance of the prophet saw another picture: a religion at variance with Israel's beliefs, reliance on external religious rites; the perversion of justice; the oppression of the poor; worse still, hearts closed to God's word and divine grace. In his own life-time, Isaiah was a singular failure. His teaching was rejected. But he was a man of great faith, with an unshaken confidence that God would bring his own divine plan of salvation to completion when and how he saw fit. The book that bears Isaiah's name (with sixty-six chapters) is a combination of the prophet's own teaching and of generations of his disciples who shared his vision. The prophet's own oracles were put together in blocks, the oldest collection being possibly chapters 6–9 which begins with an account of his vocation. This we read today. The divine attribute which most struck Isaiah was God's holiness, stirring the prophet to a sense of his own sin and of that of the people. Isaiah is symbolically purified and sent as a messenger of the thrice holy God.

GOSPEL READINGS (Matthew)

Monday (Mt 9:18-26). *The healing touch.* A dead child comes to life when Jesus comes and takes her by the hand. A woman trusts in his healing touch. She believes that a single touch of his clothes will heal her. He, too, is touched by her faith and trust. He speaks to the paralysed man: take courage, have confidence. She experiences the power of his healing word. Jesus touched men, women and children and they were healed. He allowed himself to be touched by life when he saw their distress and had compassion. He was touched and broken on the cross. But by his wounds we are healed.

Tuesday (9:32-38). *Compassion and rejection.* The healing activity of Jesus provokes two opposite reactions. The crowds are overcome by his power. The religious leaders are threatened and accuse him of being in league with the powers of evil. We get a summary view of his ministry: he is a teacher, a healer and bearer of good news in word and work. He is a wounded healer because he is distressed to see the people without religious leaders to guide, comfort and strengthen them. He sees the crying need for people who not only listen to the good news but who are willing to share it with others. Jesus, the man of compassion is wounded by the distress of humanity. Even the man of compassion experiences rejection because he is a threat to those who lack compassion.

Wednesday (10:1-7). *Sharing power.* In the previous chapters Jesus has manifested his power to teach and to heal. Now he chooses men to whom he communicates this power. But they are called to share not only in his power but also in his own experiences of rejection. Jesus has compassion on his people who were lost and bewildered, 'like sheep without a shepherd' (9:36). He looks for men who will be devoted to the pastoral care of his people. Their mission is directed for the moment to his own people. Ultimately the gospel will through them come to all peoples. Those whom Jesus chooses for the task of manifesting the kingdom, God's life and love, are ordinary people. He always chooses such people not just for what they are but also for what they can become through the gift of his word and power.

Thursday (10:7-15). *Guidelines for mission.* The one sent by Jesus shares in his power; he continues Jesus' healing mission. The instructions about what the apostle should or should not take with him are not so much concerned with ascetical poverty as with disponibility necessary for effectively proclaiming the kingdom. He leaves aside anything that encumbers him in his mission. His gift to the people is the good news of God's life and love in Jesus, the kingdom, and all that this implies. This gift has been given to him freely; he should pass it on without seeking a reward. But those prepared to accept the teaching of disciples are asked to undertake the responsibility of helping to make their mission possible materially. The one sent is to be discerning in the way he exercises his mission. He remains to consolidate the word where he finds acceptance. (To shake the dust off one's feet means total rupture of communion and fellowship with another.) There is no point in continuing an obviously ineffective apostolate.

Friday (10:16-23). *Like doves and serpents.* The instructions of Jesus are influenced by the Church situation at the time of the author. Disciples who live and proclaim his message also share in the destiny of the man Jesus, in opposition and rejection. Discipleship and the apostolic life are an adventurous following that leads to life. Jesus offers his own hardship, 'blood, sweat and tears', even death. Disciples will sometimes find themselves among strangers, unaccepted, 'sheep among wolves'. They will be alone, unprotected as they are opposed even by those who are close to them. Yet they are to be 'wise' and 'simple': the Christian does not rashly make a martyr of himself. The life of every Christian witness is precious and he need not provoke people deliberately into action against him. He is prepared to stand by his faith in Jesus when the occasion demands, at whatever cost to himself. He knows that the time of trial is also a time of strength in the Spirit. This will be the Christian experience till the end of time. The man with a message from God is 'simple', sincere and right in his intention. He focuses on the good he has to accomplish in his mission, never on the evil he could do, even to those who reject him.

Saturday (10:24-33). *Faith casts out fear.* Repeatedly the disciple is told to have courage and not to fear or flinch before the costs of discipleship. He shares in the destiny of his Lord. When he lives and communicates the word which he has received, sometimes it will be unwelcome and rebound on him. But his faith in Jesus and the Father drives out fear. He lives and speaks with courage because he knows that whatever happens he cannot drift beyond the love and care of God. Even his experience of rejection falls within the Father's loving plan for him somehow. He declares solidarity with Jesus in word and action because he knows that the judgments of eternity will correct the judgments of those who reject him.

FIFTEENTH WEEK OF THE YEAR

FIRST READINGS, Year 1 (Exodus)

The *Book of Exodus* expands the basic tenet of Israel's faith: 'Yahweh brought us out of Egypt'. It describes the events which form the foundations upon which Israel's religious and social life rests. It tells of Moses who gave the Israelites a national identity, and who communicated the law and the covenant to his people. Old Testament prophets, preachers and writers continually refer to the Exodus themes as to the basis of all their teaching.

Monday (Ex 1:8-14, 22). *Reduced to slavery.* Exodus 1:1-7 forms a transition from Genesis to Exodus and tells of the extraordinary multiplication of the descendants of Jacob in Egypt. Today's reading takes up the story with a description of Pharaoh's efforts to curb the increase of the Hebrew population. It is probable that the Pharaoh who forced the Hebrews to labour on building sites was Rameses II (1290-1224 BC), a Pharaoh who was noted for building projects such as those mentioned in Ex 1:11.

Tuesday (2:1-15). *Moses saved from the Nile.* This well-known story which is very similar to the legend of Sargon of Accad (c. 2300 BC) must be regarded as legendary in character. It is meant to illustrate God's provident care of his chosen one, and it explains how a Hebrew child happened to receive an Egyptian upbringing (cf. Acts 7:22).

Wednesday (3:1-6, 9-12). *The Burning Bush.* Yahweh, who identified himself with the God of the patriarchs, gave Moses the task of leading the Hebrews into freedom, and assured him that he would always be with him to assist him in his task. Since, in the Old Testament, fire frequently signifies the presence of God (cf. 13:21; 19:16 etc.) the burning bush story must be regarded as a poetic statement of the fact that the Lord appeared to Moses and spoke personally to him.

Thursday (3:13-20). *Revelation of the Divine Name.* This passage links the name 'Yahweh' with the verb 'to be', and explains it as 'I am who I am'. This is a popular rather than a scientific explanation. The exact meaning of 'Yahweh' is unknown. But it seems to convey the idea that the God of Israel is always present among his people, always at hand to guide and assist them. Our present text (E) and Ex 6:2-3 (P) claim that the name Yahweh was first revealed to Moses, while J gives us to understand that God was worshipped under that name since the earliest days of humanity (cf. Gen 4:3).

Friday (11:10—12:14). *The Feast of Passover.* The lectionary omits the accounts of Moses' return to Egypt, of his encounter with Pharaoh and of the plagues (Ex 4:18—11:9). Today's reading tells of the origin and meaning of the feast of Passover. This feast was to become an annual memorial celebration of Israel's deliverance from Egypt. But it was more than a simple recalling of what happened in Egypt. It proclaimed that the saving power of the God who led the Israelites out of bondage was available to all generations of Israelites. It also raised hopes for the future since it looked forward to the final liberation of Israel in the messianic age.

At the Last Supper, which took place in a Passover context (cf. Mt 26:17-19; Mk 14:12-16), Jesus gave a new meaning to the Passover rite when he identified the bread and wine that were blessed with his own Body and Blood (cf. Mt 26:26-28).

Saturday (12:37-42). *A mixed multitude leave Egypt.* All authors agree that the statement that 600,000 men (and therefore about three million people in all) left Egypt is a gross exaggeration. It is more likely that about 5,000 people in all escaped from slavery. The annual Passover night was to become a 'night of watching' (v. 42) for the Israelites, a night on which they would recall and re-enact the saving events of their ancestors' deliverance from Egypt.

FIRST READINGS, Year 2 (Isaiah, Micah)

Monday (Is 1:11-17). *A prophetic call to Jerusalem.* Because of its iniquity, the 'Holy City' of Jerusalem is addressed as Sodom. Despite the gravity of their sins, the inhabitants offer lavish sacrifices in the temple, apparently without any qualms of conscience. In no uncertain terms the Lord rejects their sacrifices and prayers and calls for a change of life; see also Amos 5:14-15, 21-24—Wednesday, Week 13.

Tuesday (7:1-9). *Have faith; trust in the Lord.* The setting of this passage is the so-called Syro-Ephraimite war (734 BC) when the kingdoms of Damascus (Syria) and Israel (Ephraim) tried to force Judah to enter into their anti-Assyrian alliance. Isaiah called on Ahaz, king of Judah, to have faith in the Lord. The military and political crisis in question was but a passing one. Without faith in the true master of history, however, neither king nor people could remain faithful to the covenant with God. I need hardly recall that this passage is the setting for the Immanuel prophecy, omitted at this point in the lectionary because read on the Fourth Sunday of Advent.

Wednesday (10:5-7, 13-16). *The Lord will break the might of proud Assyria.* In Isaiah's day the Assyrian empire was conquering all before it. Its power could not be checked. These victories the Assyrians attributed to their own power and the might of their national god Ashur; see Is 37. But Isaiah knew that Assyria was but an instrument in the hand of God to punish sinful Judah. God would, in time, bumble Assyria as he had humbled Judah. Yahweh was the Lord of history, bringing down the mighty from their seats.

Thursday (26:7-9, 12, 16-19). *A persevering wait for salvation.* This passage was composed some centuries after Isaiah's day; the salvation of which he and other prophets spoke had not yet come. In the first section of the pericope, Israel speaks of her long, patient, wait amid trials for the coming, the birth, of the messianic age. She was like a woman pregnant with messianic salvation for the world. But this salvation, for so long awaited and often believed to be imminent, did not come. In the concluding section God bids Israel to have confidence. Salvation will surely come.

Friday (28:1-6, 21-22, 7-8). *Hezekiah, king of Judah, prays and is healed.* This passage also occurs in 2 Kings 20:12-17 and in modern versions of Isaiah the verses are rearranged in accord with this. It contains an example of the power of prayer. The miracle was worked on the ten steps of a sundial or a staircase built by Ahaz, Hezekiah's father and predecessor.

Saturday (Micah 2:1-5). *True religion implies social justice.* Today we begin a series of readings from the prophet Micah, Isaiah's contemporary who preached principally in Jerusalem. The first three chapters of this book contain Micah's preaching. Some, if not the greater part, of the remaining chapters are from later inspired writers, not from Micah himself. Today's reading contains a theme familiar to us from the early prophets. It is a condemnation of social injustice, greed and exploitation. The Lord is proclaimed as the punisher of these sins.

GOSPEL READINGS (Matthew)

Monday (Mt 10:35–11:1). *A gospel without compromise.* Dedication to any cause does not put up with half-measures. There is no middle of the road or half-way following of Jesus; his gospel calls us to take definite stands. A constant paradox in the life of the disciple is that he is a messenger of God's peace who causes division. Because of Christ man is divided and in conflict with himself; men are divided among themselves because of the values he proclaims without compromise. The decisions of a Christian may sometimes alienate him from those who are closest to him. Christian living is not safety first. It demands the removal of all obstacles that prevent one from making the right choices. Jesus promises peace and security to those who accept the price of discipleship. Finally, as the disciple shares in the work and destiny of his Lord, to welcome and accept him is to open oneself to Christ. A man's messenger is like the man himself. Anyone, no matter how insignificant, who shares the love and the word of Jesus, is his messenger.

Tuesday (11:20-24). *The tragedy of unbelief.* Characteristically, narrative parts and long discourse alternate. Jesus' 'apostolic discourse' is followed by another narraive (chs 11–12) which prepares for a discourse in parables (ch. 13). We have come now to a turning-point. The shadows begin to fall. The main theme of these two chapters has to do with the rejection of Jesus. They evolve in such a manner that the intensity of opposition against him mounts steadily, even though Jesus has come to his people with a ministry of healing and teaching (4:17, 23; 9:35; 11:1). He has empowered disciples to undertake an identical mission. But now the false Israel of the Pharisees rejects Jesus the Messiah, forcing him to turn to the gentiles. The movement in the readings from this section oscillates between belief and unbelief. Those who reject Jesus, the false Israel, are contrasted with the true disciples of Christ. They constitute the true Israel, the Church. All these passages invite us to reflect on the meaning and consequences of our discipleship.

Jesus expresses sorrowful pity and indignation that comes 'not from outraged pride but from a broken heart' (Barclay) that those who had been offered so many opportunities did not respond in faith. The cities where Jesus had worked, even Capharnaum, 'his own city' where he lived (4:13; 9:2) did not repent in response to his extraordinary work. Their experience of him should have helped them turn towards God. The special, even prolonged moments of God's presence among his people can become either occasions of deep conversion for those who are alert and open or simply missed opportunites for others who do not listen.

Wednesday (11:25-27). *The thanksgiving of Jesus.* Out of the experience of his mission Jesus prays in thanksgiving to his Father as the almighty creator and Lord of the universe. It was to the 'simple', the poor in spirit, people who were open because they realised their dependence on God, that God manifested himself in the person and words of Jesus. They are the ordinary people; they responded more than their religious leaders, the wise and understanding. These were ready to trust their own ability to understand God's will and ways. They go away empty-handed because they close their mind and heart to God's action and word in his unique revealer. They were unready to hear and learn anything new. The man with a mission not only sees acceptance and rejection as part of the Father's plan. He will also praise and thank him for those people whom the Father has touched through him. In addition, he experiences that the heart, not the head, is the home of the gospel.

Thursday (11:28-30). *A light load.* Jesus offers hope and courage to those ordinary people who are open to his message. Their religious leaders had made religion an intolerable burden by their legalistic and joyless attitude. It had degenerated into a load of countless regulations. They spoke of the 'yoke' of the law. Jesus tells the people to come to him because his yoke fits well. His following does make radical demands. But he does not crush his followers. He himself obeys his Father out of love and makes possible through his word and example a life of fidelity towards God. The disciple of Jesus is recognisable when his lived faith does not appear to oppress himself or others as a joyless imposition.

Friday (12:1-8). *Lord of the sabbath.* In this chapter opposition to Jesus is gathering momentum. He is pitted against the leaders of official

Judaism in situations of conflict. He has spoken about 'my yoke', his law or the way of Christian life as expounded particularly in the Sermon on the Mount. He now shows that his interpretation of God's law or will for man is sharply contrasted with that of the Pharisees. Their hostile reactions vary from suspicion, deep distrust, bitter prejudice to an evil determination to do away with him (v. 14).

First of all, Jesus is suspect as a teacher. He allows his followers disregard the host of tyrannical regulations about the observance of the sabbath. His reply shows the spirit of his teaching and the mystery of his person. He picks examples from his own tradition to show that the claims of human need and human hunger take precedence over any ritual custom or practice. He recommends the practice of mercy in contrast to that proud and hard-hearted inclination of the religious leaders to condemn those who do not submit to their regulations. Jesus is greater than the temple, the most sacred place in all the world. He is the place of God's presence. He is the centre of a true worship which is incompatible with a legality and narrow-mindedness that overshadows the living service of the heart and turns Christian life into the service of ritual rather than the service of human needs.

Saturday (12:14-21). *The compassionate servant.* Jesus seemed to have dominated all the difficult situations of his ministry. But now he follows an obscure path where he seems to have succumbed to opposition. He withdraws. Is this a sign of failure? Has he given up before the relentless power of the rejection he faces? Rather it all points to him as a true Servant of God who has the Spirit and brings God's saving love and life to men in his own unique way. There is a certain quiet unostentatiousness about his work. He does not enter into endless debate or loud contestation. There is a deep inwardness about his activity. His mission is to raise up what is cast down, to heal, encourage, not to treat the weak with contempt but with understanding and to bring hope beyond all barriers of language and culture which divide men from one another.

SIXTEENTH WEEK OF THE YEAR

FIRST READINGS, Year 1 (Exodus)

Monday (Ex 14:5-18). *Pharaoh pursues the Israelites.* Pharaoh regretted his decision to grant freedom to his Hebrew slaves. When he pursued them to bring them back the Hebrews fell into a panic and complained against Moses. But Moses reassured them that God would not abandon them. God himself then assured Moses that he would 'get glory over Pharaoh and all his host' (v. 18), that is, that he would manifest his power by destroying Pharaoh and his army.

Tuesday (14:21–15:1). *The miracle at the sea.* The story of the crossing of the Red Sea makes it clear that Israel's liberation was entirely God's doing. Israel owed her existence to God who brought her into being. This is the message of today's reading which was meant to arouse faith in Israel's Redeemer rather than give a factual account of an actual event. The deliverance from Egypt was to become the model of later saving acts of Yahweh (cf. Is 40:3-4; 43:17-19 etc; 1 Cor 10:1-5).

Wednesday (16:1-15). *Manna and quails.* The provision of manna and quails for the complaining Israelites was a sign of God's continual care for his people. Even if we take the manna to be a sweet substance found on the tamarisk shrub in the desert, and even if we accept that quails are migratory birds that can easily be caught in the Sinai Peninsula in autumn, we must admit that the biblical author regarded the manna and quails as a miraculous sign of God's provident care for Israel. Christ saw in the manna a foreshadowing of the Eucharist (cf. Jn 6: 31-33, 49-51).

Thursday (19:1-2, 9-11, 16-20). *The Covenant.* The recently liberated slaves encountered their God at Sinai. There, in a dense cloud, amid thunder and lightning, in fire and smoke (vv. 9, 16-19) God spoke to them and gave them a new destiny and a new understanding. The extraordinary natural phenomena, and the ritual purification which the people had to undergo (vv. 10-11), convey the idea of God's holiness and man's need for reverence in his presence.

Friday (20:1-17). *The Decalogue.* The privilege of being God's chosen people and a holy nation (cf. 19:5-6) involved precise obligations. These are clearly summarised in the Decalogue. It is generally agreed today that the Ten Commandments, apart from minor additions, can be reasonably attributed to Moses.

Saturday (24:3-8). *The Covenant is ratified.* When the people agreed to regulate their lives according to God's will (v. 3) Moses sealed the covenant by sprinkling the blood of sacrificed animals (v. 5) on the altar—which represented God—and on the people (vv. 6, 8). The Lord and his people were thus symbolically united. The bond of unity was further symbolised by the eating of a meal (v. 11) at which God was regarded as an unseen guest. When Jesus inaugurated a new covenant he sealed it in his own blood with words that clearly refer to the Sinai ritual (campare Mt 26:28 and Ex 24:8).

FIRST READINGS, Year 2 (Micah, Jeremiah)

Monday (Mic 6:1-4, 6-8). *This is what the Lord requires: to act justly, to love him tenderly and to walk humbly before him.* Following what is known as a law suit pattern, Yahweh calls on Israel to make answer for her sins: the mountains and hills will be the witnesses (cf. Is 1:2; Ps 48[49], etc.). On his part, God has shown Israel nothing but kindness, especially on her exodus from Egypt, the great event of her history. Israel then asks what offering would be a pleasing response to God. The prophetic reply, in the best prophetic and priestly tradition (Is 1:11-17; Jer 7:22; Hos 6:6; Ps 49[50]:7-15,etc.),indicates in what true worship consists. We have an anticipation of Jesus' words (Jn 4:24).

Tuesday (7:14-15, 18-20). *A humble prayer for pardon.* A magnificent prayer for pardon. Bashan and Gilead, to the east of the Sea of Galilee, were former Israelite possessions. They were conquered by the Assyrians in 732 BC.

Wednesday (Jer 1:1, 4-10). *Jeremiah is called by God to be a prophet.* Today we begin a series of fifteen readings from the book of Jeremiah. Jeremiah, who was from Anatoth a few miles north of Jerusalem, was called to prophesy in 626 BC during the reign of the pious king Josiah. Babylon and Media were then in the process of destroying the Assyrian empire, a task completed in 605 when Nebuchadnezzar came to the throne of Babylon. Jeremiah's early preaching occurred during the reign of Josiah. In 622 this king introduced a religious reform. The prophet's real activity, however, began with the death of Josiah in 609, when Jehoiakim, Josiah's son, came to the throne and the reform programme was abandoned. From then until the fall of Jerusalem to the Babylonians in 587 Jeremiah preached repentance, but with very little apparent success and with much suffering. He had a sensitive nature and disliked his prophetic calling which obliged him to preach divine punishment on his own people. By nature, he was a warm character. He also had a message of hope for Israel. After her purification she would enjoy a glorious and happy future. The purified people would be restored to new life. He wrote the first edition of his book in 609 BC (Jer 36). This was destroyed. The present book of Jeremiah had a complicated history of composition. It contains genuine oracles of the prophet and much information concerning him, but has also material from a later date.

The account of the prophet's vocation, read today, contains the essential themes of the book. Jeremiah was set aside in the divine mind for his work before his birth. He was to preach God's word concerning Israel and the pagan nations (in which sense he is 'a prophet to the nations'), prophecies which God would bring to pass. He was thus set over these nations to pull down and build up.

Thursday (2:1-3, 7-8, 12-13). *By sinning we forsake God, the source of living water.* This is an example of Jeremiah's early preaching, influenced by Hosea (cf. e.g. Hos 11). Israel is regarded as Yahweh's bride; the days of her youth were those of the exodus and desert wanderings. The riches of the promised land, which the Lord gave her, served only to alienate her from him.

Friday (3:14-17). *The restoration of Israel foretold.* This passaage is most probably an inspired post-exilic prose text, not from Jeremiah himself. The ark of the covenant (containing the two tables of the law), above which the Lord was regarded as enthroned, was destroyed together with the temple in 587 BC. There was no ark in the second temple completed in 515 BC and its absence was keenly felt. The message of the present text is that there will be no need of ark. Jerusalem in its entirety will be God's throne and the centre of worship for pagan nations. This note of universalism characterises exilic and early post-exilic prophecy.

Saturday (7:1-11). *Jeremiah condemns superstitious belief in the temple.* This episode is recounted again in ch. 26 (cf. Saturday, Week 17). The year in question was 609 BC, the year of Josiah's death, of the deposition of his successor Jehoahaz by Pharaoh Neco and the beginning of Jehoiakim's reign as king of Judah. While the inner court of the temple served for worship, the outer court was a place of concourse. There various groups would meet and prophets would address them, etc. The people believed that the temple itself, with the ark and the divine presence, was a guarantee of their safety, irrespective of their moral conduct. Jeremiah disabuses them. Jerusalem and its temple are no more immune from destruction than was Shiloh, the earlier sanctuary of the ark in the time of Samuel (cf. 1 Sam 1–4). The actual destruction of Shiloh is not recounted in the Bible and scholars are not certain with regard to the event referred to by Jeremiah.

GOSPEL READINGS (Matthew)

Monday (Mt 12:38-42). *The sign of contradiction.* Jesus confronts those who reject him. They lack faith because they are looking for a special sign, unconvinced that he is the sign of God's presence among them. The only sign he offers is their own very rejection of him, the greatest teacher and prophet of their nation. He will find greater faith outside the land. Sometimes we seek sensational signs and revelations or we want religion to be always exciting; we can miss the more obvious places of God's presence and the more routine invitations to love.

Tuesday (12:46-50). *The identity of the disciple.* Jesus points to his companions and explains who and what is a disciple. He is the one who has a personal relationship with Jesus; he is adopted into his family and is at home with him. If Jesus is his brother, then like Jesus himself, he does the will of the Father. This will is expressed in the person and teaching of his Son. Discipleship, then, is a personal, active relationship with the Father and Son.

Wednesday (13:1-9). *Listening to the word.* This parable discourse (13:1-52) is a turning point in Jesus' ministry. He has been rejected by the religious leaders of the land. Earlier in the gospel we saw him teaching in the synagogues. Now, banished from the official 'church' of his day, he delivers his message in the open by the seashore. He speaks in parables. These reveal truth to those who are open to it; they conceal it from those who do not want to face it. Matthew has Jesus outside the house (13:1) speaking to those who do not understand, who neither know nor do the Father's will (vv. 1-35). Then, inside the house he speaks to disciples who represent the Christian community, the Church (vv. 36-52). He instructs them about what God's will implies. All the parables are about the Kingdom. The Kingdom is the 'area' or the presence of God's saving life and love. It is God's saving intervention through Jesus in the lives of men, which is conditioned by their response.

By knowing and doing God's will as manifested in Jesus, man truly belongs to the Kingdom. Therefore, the unifying theme of the parables is knowing and doing God's will.

This parable focuses on Jesus and also on his word. It is a story of growth and contrast. Some seeds perish, others produce fruit. Jesus liberally communicated the word of his Father and his message lives on. But while some stifle its growth in their hearts, the true disciple is a real hearer—he listens, understands and obeys.

Thursday (13:10-17). *The gift of hearing.* Disciples are privileged because they have received the word of Jesus. This word tells about the mysteries of God and his will for humanity. It is pure gift. Yet Jesus promises that more, full happiness itself, will be given to those who are receptive. Those who refuse to listen remain outsiders. For them Jesus' message is a riddle. But the person who is willing to follow him in faith can share even in the mysteries of God.

Friday (13:18-23). *Hearing and understanding.* God's saving love and life, his Kingdom, comes to us through the word of Jesus. There are various reactions in us to his word. The faithful disciple is the one who 'hears the word and understands it'. True understanding takes place when what is grasped by the mind affects our whole, inward self. It effects a spiritual renewal which translates hearing into action. Obstacles to this renewal through the word are disobedience to the Father's will communicated to us in Jesus, external pressures and an over-involvement in other affairs which crowds out the more important things.

Saturday (13:24-30). *Reserving judgment.* The man of fidelity receives the word and it bears fruit in good works, particularly in works of love on behalf of others. There are those who are not faithful. Ultimately, God will separate the faithful from those who are unfaithful. The parable is a reminder that in the end there is the judgment of God. He reserves judgment to himself. Those who recognise the sovereign will of God and acknowledge that only he knows what is in the heart of each man will not take rash measures against their brother.

SEVENTEENTH WEEK OF THE YEAR

FIRST READINGS, Year 1 (Exodus, Leviticus)

Monday (Ex 32:15-24, 30-34). *Rebellion and pardon.* The newly-formed people of God soon forgot their allegiance to Yahweh and fell into idolatry. Seeing that the people had broken the covenant, Moses smashed the tables of the Law which no longer had any significance. Yet he felt compelled to pray for his rebellious people. Indeed, like the suffering Servant (cf. Is 52:13—53:12), and like Jesus, the righteous one who died for the unrighteous (cf. 1 Peter 3:18), the innocent Moses was willing to offer his life for his people.

Tuesday (33:7-11; 34:5-9, 28). *The Tent of Meeting and new Tables of the Law.* Today's reading is a combination of three passages that are in no way inter-connected. The first passage (33:7-11) tells how in the Tent of Meeting Moses used the receive divine oracles which he communicated to the people. The pillar of cloud symbolised Yahweh's presence to Moses. The second passage (34:5-9) contains a declaration of God's mercy and justice, and it records Moses' prayer to the Lord to accompany the stubborn Israelites in their wanderings. The final verse (v. 28) tells that the Tables of the Law which Moses had broken (cf. Ex 32:19—see Monday's reading) were replaced.

Wednesday (34:29-35). *Moses' shining face.* This curious story conveys the idea that after his forty-day stay in the presence of God (cf. 33:28) Moses' face reflected the glory of Yahweh whom he had been privileged to see. St Paul refers to this episode in a passage in which he wishes to show that the covenant inaugurated by Christ is superior to that instituted on Sinai (cf. 2 Cor 3:4-13).

Thursday (40:16-21, 34-38). *The Tabernacle.* The Tabernacle was the place of God's invisible presence among his people. It was also known as the Tent of Meeting (cf. e.g. 40:12, 22), that is, the tent where Yahweh met his people. The *ark* was a small portable box which contained the *'Testimony'*, that is the two tables on which the law was written (cf. 31:18).

Friday (Lev 23:1, 4-11, 15-16, 27, 34-37). *Feasts of Israel.* Today and tomorrow we read the only two passages from *Leviticus* that are included in the yearly weekday cycle. These passages deal with Israel's principal feasts.

The feast of *Passover* (23:5) and *Unleavened Bread* (vv. 6-11) were originally two feasts. But since they both occured in the spring they were combined into one feast at an early stage of Israel's history. (For *Passover*, see above—Friday, Week 15.) The feast of *Unleavened Bread* (vv. 6-11) originally celebrated the beginning of the barley harvest. The first bread of the new crop was eaten unleavened, that is without the addition of a piece of dough from an earlier baking in which the yeast had developed. The Israelites celebrated the feast as a commemoration of the Exodus (cf. Ex 12:17). The feast of *Weeks* (vv. 15-16) celebrated the harvesting of the wheat, the latest crop to ripen. The *Day of Atonement* (v. 27) was a day of fasting. This was the only day in the year when the High Priest entered the Holy of Holies. The ritual for the day is described in Lev 16. The feast of *Tabernacles* (vv. 34-36) or the feast of Ingathering (Ex 23:16) celebrated the completion of the harvest.

Saturday (25:1, 8-17). *The Jubilee Year.* This was a year of liberation which was celebrated every fifty years. During that year the land was left fallow (vv. 11-12), land that had been sold was restored to its original owner (vv. 13-17), and Israelite slaves were set free (vv. 39-41). The reason for these observances was that the land and people of Israel belonged to God alone (vv. 23, 41). He alone had the right of absolute ownership.

FIRST READINGS, Year 2 (Jeremiah)

Monday (Jer 13:1-11). *A symbolic action indicating the corruption and ultimate fate of Judah and Jerusalem.* The symbolic action made clear to Jeremiah (and possibly also to his listeners) the nature of Israel's sin. Israel, the Lord's pride and glory, had become corrupt and useless. If by the Euphrates the Mesopotamian river is meant, the action must have taken place in prophetic vision, not in reality. The name 'Euphrates' here, however, may be merely a variant of Parah or Perath (cf. Josh 18: 23), the present-day wadi Perat about six miles north of Jerusalem.

Tuesday (14:17-22). *Jeremiah asks God to spare his people.* As prophet, Jeremiah interceded for his people. Here we hear him pray during some unspecified and unidentifiable occasion of drought and war.

Wednesday (15:10, 16-21). *Jeremiah laments his plight as God's prophet.* This is one of the passages known as 'The Confessions of Jeremiah'.

(The others are 11:18—12:6; 17:14-18; 18:18-23; 20:7-18). In these 'Confessions' Jeremiah reveals his innermost communions with God. In the present text he complains of the trials which his prophetic vocation has brought on him. They had practically led him to abandon his prophetic mission. God's answer is in stern language: Jeremiah's thoughts are base ones and unworthy of the noble prophetic calling. God's spokesmen must think noble thoughts. So, Jeremiah must repent and return to the Lord if he is to continue to act as God's mouthpiece. Only through union with God can he have the purity of intention and the strength required for his task.

Thursday (18:1-6). *God moulds human history as a potter moulds his clay.*

Friday (26:1-9). *Jeremiah preaches against false trust in the temple.* The same episode as in chapter 7—see above, Saturday, Week 16. The repitition is an indication of the nature of the present book of Jeremiah, made up from different collections of the prophet's oracles and discourses and from narratives concerning him.

Saturday (26:11-16, 24). *Jeremiah's life is spared.* His attack on the temple brought Jeremiah into conflict with the priests and false prophets, custodians of the popular myth. It is the princes, the civil rulers, who see him freed. These cite as precedent (vv. 18-19) the case of the prophet Micah (Mic 3:12) a century earlier. Ahikam, earlier a minister of king Josiah (2 Kings 23:30), whom Jeremiah admired, was friendly towards the prophet; see also Jer 36. We should note the dignity and modesty of Jeremiah's reply to his accusers. It was prudent, humble and firm (St Jerome); the prophet was conscious that he spoke not in his own name but in the name of God who had sent him.

GOSPEL READINGS (Matthew)

Monday (Mt 13:31-35). *Growth in the Kingdom.* The Kingdom, that is the presence of God's love and life in and among us, starts from apparently insignificant beginnings with one man, Jesus and his small group of companions. The growth of this small group around Jesus into a vast world-wide community is like the living seed that becomes a tree or like the effects of a fistful of yeast that helps to make enough bread to feed about a hundred. The work of God through his Son begins modestly. The disciple knows that tiny beginnings and minor signs of his own growth are a promise and a hope of a final transformation.

Tuesday (13:36-43). *Sons of the Kingdom.* Jesus explains and develops the parable of the weeds in the wheat. It is a call to be 'sons of the Kingdom', to do the will of God. Such people are called 'righteous' (a favourite expression in this gospel). To be righteous is to be obedient to the word of God as interpreted by Jesus, particularly through works of love on behalf of a brother (25:35); it is to lead a life of inwardness which is expressed in Christian action (5:20), to have one's relationships right with God and with our fellowman. It leads to a life of sharing in God's own glory and happiness.

Wednesday (13:44-46). *A full investment.* A poor labourer finds a priceless treasure in a field; he gives away everything to buy that field. Pearls of the finest quality from the Indian Ocean fisheries were bought by rich businessmen. A financier invests all he has to acquire a special pearl. These images illustrate that the Christian has discovered the find of a lifetime in the Kingdom, in Jesus who manifests the life and love of God. He invests all of himself in it; he makes it the centre of his life. His total investment consists in his response of doing God's will as revealed in Jesus. Christian living means a total investment of oneself.

Thursday (13:47-53). *The righteous and instructed disciple.* In its mission the Church gathers together people of all kinds, people who respond in varying degrees to the Father's will. As the Kingdom has a present and a future, there is a time for gathering and a time for sorting out. God is the ultimate judge of the heart of man. The hope of happiness in God's presence encourages the disciple to lead a life of righteousness here and now. The final image describes the true disciple: he is one who really understands. He has accepted the word of the Kingdom. As the host brings out of his stores all kinds of everything for his guests, so also the disciple who has listened to and obeyed the Father's will in Jesus draws from his heart and manifests the riches of God which have been imparted to him through Jesus.

Friday (13:54-58). *Rejected at home.* After the parable discourse, there follows another major section of the gospel, consisting as usual of narrative (13:53–17:21) leading up to a discourse (17:22–18:35–this deals with the community aspect of Christian life). In all this section Jesus directs his attention more to disciples. He instructs them about himself and what it means to follow him. He is the Messiah who suffers and who invites disciples to share his suffering and glory (ch. 16). He describes the community spirit of disciples (ch. 18). For Matthew disciples represent Christians of all time.

The suffering in store for Jesus looms on the horizon. Already Jesus has been rejected by the religious leaders of the land. Now his own townspeople 'take offense at Him'. Their questioning registers their lack of faith and trust. While they are deeply impressed by his teaching and the reports of his miracles, they cannot accept that he could be at one and the same time one of themselves and one fully authorised by God, the hoped-for prophet and liberator of his people. Their unbelief, not his own inability, make it impossible for Jesus to work miracles there. These are conditioned somehow by man's openness and trust. Lack of trust and confidence creates barriers which restrict God's action in our lives.

Saturday (14:1-12). *The way of the prophet.* Jesus' rejection is connected with the fate of John the Baptist. Not only the religious leaders and his own townspeople reject the prophet. The official secular authorities of the country in the person of Herod show complete lack of understanding for the prophet, who went before Jesus and whose work and destiny are closely linked with Jesus. John follows the same path and meets the same fate—the death of a prophet. John, like Jesus, delivers his message with courage. There is no disguising it. He did not compromise (11:7). He protested against injustice and corruption. He was God's messenger who followed the dangerous occupation of telling the truth and of exposing corruption when he thought it was right to do so. Like Jesus he speaks out the truth and suffers for it. The voice of the prophet who prepares the way for Jesus and who follows a similar path is silenced by those who do not like to hear the truth.

EIGHTEENTH WEEK OF THE YEAR

FIRST READINGS, Year 1 (Numbers, Deuteronomy)

The four readings from *Numbers* (Monday–Thursday) that occur in the weekday lectionary all describe situations in which the Israelites complained against Moses.

Monday (Num 11:4-15). *I am not able to carry this nation.* When the

Israelites murmured about the tastelessness of the manna Moses,turned
to God in despair. How could he continue to lead such a stubborn
people? The lectionary passage does not go on to tell Yahweh's response to Moses' appeal. In fact, God transferred some of Moses' responsibility to seventy elders who he endowed with the Holy Spirit (vv. 16-
17, 25).

Tuesday (12:1-13). *Miriam's leprosy.* When Miriam and Aaron disputed
Moses' position of authority the Lord proclaimed that Moses was the
greatest of all prophets. Others might see God in visions and dreams,
but Moses alone saw him face to face (cf. Ex 33:20). When Miriam's
rebellion was punished with leprosy Moses was generous enough to
intercede with God on her behalf.

Wednesday (13:1-2, 25–14:1, 26-29, 34-35). *We are not able to go up
against this people.* When the Israelites who had been sent out to spy
the land of Canaan reported that the inhabitants of that country were
men of mighty stature who were firmly established in strong cities the
people refused to attempt to take the land. For this failure to trust in
Yahweh they were condemned to wander for forty years in the wilderness, so that those who left Egypt never entered the Promised Land.

Thursday (20:1-13). *Water from the rock.* As in Ex 17:1-7 this miracle
is said to have taken place at Meribah, a place-name which means 'Contention', and which suggests Israel's contention or complaining against
God. The present narrative adds a puzzling explanation of the fact that
Moses and Aaron were not allowed to enter the Promised Land. The
text says that the two leaders did not believe in Yahweh (v. 12). Some
commentators explain this by saying that Moses showed a lack of faith
when he struck the rock twice. But this is not a very satisfactory
explanation, and we must admit that the reason for the exclusion of
Moses and Aaron from Canaan remains obscure.

Deuteronomy: the Book of Covenant Religion. The Book of Deuteronomy contains a legal core (chs 12–26) within a framework of homiletic narration and exhortation (chs 1–11 and 29–34). The legal part of
the book is substantially the 'law book' that was found in the temple in
621 BC (cf. 2 Kings 22:8-10). At about the same time the homiletic
sections were added to this legal book by the so-called Deuteronomic
(D) writers. The selection of readings from Deuteronomy are, as one
might expect, taken from the homiletic section of the book. They insist
on God's choice of Israel and on Israel's duty to respond in loving
obedience to so gracious a God.

Friday (Deut 4:32-40). *God's love for Israel.* God's personal revelation to Israel, the miracles that accompanied the Exodus, and the settlement of the people in Canaan, are proofs of God's love for his people, of his power, and of his goodness. Israel's response to such a God should be one of obedience and love.

Saturday (6:4-13). *A statement of faith.* Verses 4—9 of this passage form part of the *Shema*, a prayer or profession of faith which every devout Israelite recited daily. They proclaim that Israel must offer exclusive worship to Yahweh. Each Israelite must instruct his children in the law, and he himself must be continually mindful of the commandments of God.

FIRST READINGS, Year 2 (Jeremiah, Nahum, Habakkuk)

Monday (Jer 28:1-17). *True prophet and false prophet confront each other.* In 597 king Jehoiakim died and was succeeded by his son Jehoiachin. That same year Nebuchadnezzar, king of Babylon, laid siege to Jerusalem which had rebelled some years earlier. Jehoiachin surrendered and was exiled to Babylon together with princes, craftsmen and others besides (cf. 2 Kings 24:8-17). Zedekiah, Jehoiachin's uncle, was placed on the throne of Judah by Nebuchadnezzar. The populace, however, pitted their hopes on Jehoiachin's return from exile through a miraculous divine intervention. This vain hope found a spokesman in the false prophet Hananiah, who, like Jeremiah, used prophetic symbols to convey his message. Although Hananiah's message ran counter to Jeremiah's, the latter could only hope Hananiah was right. It is what he himself would wish. The Lord proves the Jeremiah, not Hananiah, was the true prophet.

Tuesday (Jer 30:1-2, 12-15, 18-22). *A prophecy of better days to come.* This passage comes from a collection of oracles known as 'The Book of Consolation' (Jer 30—31). Despite the inevitable punishment which their sins would bring on them, God's people had a future. God's plans for Israel were plans of welfare, not destruction, to give them a future and a hope (Jer 29:11). Their fortunes would be restored and they would have native not foreign (Babylonian) governors. They would again be God's covenanted people. ('You shall be my people and I will be your God' is the covenant formula.)

Wednesday (Jer 31:1-7). *Israel will find favour with God in the wilderness.* The desert wanderings, after the exodus, were regarded as a time of special intimacy between God and Israel (see Jer 2:1-3—Thursday, Week 18). This initimacy would be renewed in the exile and Israel would return joyfully to her homeland.

Thursday (Jer 31:31-34). *The prophecy of the new covenant.* The readings from Jeremiah appropriately end with this high-point in Old Testament revelation. Authors, however, are divided on whether this prophecy is actually from Jeremiah himself or comes from some later exilic or post-exilic inspired writer. It is similar to Ez 36:24-28 (read Thursday, Week 20). In any event it is one of the most important texts of the book, and indeed of the entire Old Testament. Jeremiah saw the end of the old order in the destruction of Jerusalem in 587. The failure of the Sinai covenant is here attributed to its external nature and to man's innate weakness. The new covenant, here prophesied, would be a power within man. This prophecy was fulfilled in Christ's death and resurrection and in the gift of the Holy Spirit (cf. Mt 26:28; 2 Cor 3:6; Heb 8: 6-13).

Friday (Nahum 2:1, 3; 3:1-3, 6-7). *A prophecy on the destruction of Nineveh, for long the oppressor of Judah.* Nineveh, the capital city of Assyria, was destroyed by the combined forces of Babylon and Media in 612 BC. The book of Nahum, written shortly before the destruction of the city, is entirely devoted to a description of the event. In today's reading we sense the jubilation of the people of Judah on the downfall of the detested city which had ruled their country as overlord since king Ahaz had become Assyria's vassal in 734. Nineveh itself had become a symbol of oppression and godlessness, as Babylon and Rome would at a later date.

Saturday (Habakkuk 1:12—2:4). *It is hard to understand why God permits injustice. Salvation lies in faith.* The prophet Habakkuk was a contemporary of Jeremiah. He probably preached during the reign of king Jehoiakim (609-597 BC) when Judah was oppressed by this unjust king and by the Chaldaean (i.e. Babylonian) armies. The oppression of the just by the ungodly and of sinners by greater sinners posed a problem for Habakkuk. How could the just God of Israel permit this? The book opens (1:2—2:4) with a dialogue between the prophet and God on the subject; a curse on the oppressor by the prophet follows (2:5-20). The work closes with a psalm (ch. 3) on the final triumph of God.

In today's reading the prophet first seeks an explanation of divine providence. He apparently looks on the Chaldaean armies ('this people') as God's instrument to punish Judah. Yet, the Chaldaeans themselves are arrogant and murderous, and sacrifice to their own gods and power. Habakkuk seeks a divine answer, figuratively ascending his prophetic watchtower to receive it. The content of this reply is not altogether clear but the substance of it is that God's word and promise will be fulfilled in God's own good time. Lack of faith spells personal disaster; faithfulness to God and faith in the living and true God will bring life, in the full, open-ended meaning of this term. The New Testament will spell out what this life consists in and the prophet's words on faith will become a key text for St Paul; cf. Rom 1:17; Gal 3:11; see also Heb 10:38.

GOSPEL READINGS (Matthew)

Monday (Mt 14:13-21). *Power and compassion.* Despite his rejection and the news of John's violent end, crowds gather around Jesus, the man of compassion. He who commands has also compassion; he gives thanks to God for the food he provides. The miracle-accounts in this chapter strengthen our faith in the power of Jesus. Through various undertones we are reminded that Jesus is the leader of his people, the expected one who provides special nourishment from God, who prepares a feast and gathers his people together. 'He looked up to heaven... and blessed and broke and gave the loaves to the disciples': Jesus' compassion in feeding the hungry crowd foreshadows the constant giving of himself in the Eucharist.

Alternative Reading *(This gospel may be read when the above gospel is read on the Sunday in Cycle A).* (14:22-36). *Walking on the waters.* Jesus not only provides for those who are hungry. He also cares for and delivers his companions from distress. He is the Lord who saves by his power. He also gives disciples a share in this power when he invites Peter to walk with him on the waters. Disciples are afraid. Peter does not trust in the power of his Lord and goes under. He is the man 'of little faith'. Jesus is the Lord who takes away our fears: It is I; fear not. He reaches out a hand to show disciples that they can trust in him as the Lord of his Church, symbolised by the boat. The poet Francis Thompson expressed his faith in the presence of Jesus' power in our lives when he wrote: 'And, lo, Christ walking on the waters, not of Gennesareth but of Thames'.

Tuesday (14:22-36: cf. above).

Alternative Reading *(This gospel may be read when the above gospel, i.e. 14:22-36 is read on the previous day in Year A of the Sunday cycle.)* **(15:1-2, 10-14).** *The state of man's heart.* Jesus along with disciples, for whom he is responsible as their teacher, is accused of laxity with regard to some external practices, which were a matter of life and death for the religious authorities of his day. He defends the people against a false understanding of religion. What matters, he says, is not the state of a man's practices but the state of a man's heart. Christian life must pierce the skin as far as the core of his being and change him inside. Jesus dismisses religious authority when it does not faithfully represent God's plan for his people. Those who show by their attitudes and actions that they themselves do not know the way to God cannot show the way to others.

Wednesday (15:21-28). *Persistent faith.* The story is a reminder that Jesus' healing power is for all. It is also an instruction on faith and trust in his power. For this woman Jesus is 'Lord', one from whom she hopes for 'mercy'. She wins it through her persistence. Jesus did not refuse faith wherever he found it. The disciples tried to get rid of her. Jesus says that the first priority in his mission are the needs of his own people. Like the centurion this woman has 'great' faith; it occasions a response from Jesus which exceeds all expectations. The healing word of Jesus cures her daughter from a distance. Faith here is the persistent trust in the Lord's compassion and healing power.

Thursday (16:13-23). *The way of suffering.* Peter, in the name of the disciples, confesses faith in Jesus. But Jesus shocks their faith in him by revealing his tragic destiny. Peter is congratulated for his faith in Jesus and rebuked for his lack of it. He is congratulated because he has responded to that faith inspired in him by the Father. He is to be the foundation or source of cohesion for the community of disciples, the Church. His authority involves some power as regards membership of the community and teaching. On the other hand, Peter does not understand the mystery of the cross. He pits his own will against the Father's will for Jesus and tries to deflect Jesus from the way of God. Peter, who is given special responsibility in a community of believers experiences himself the darkness of faith.

Friday (16:24-28). *Discovering life.* Jesus tells disciples what his way of the cross means for them: they deny themselves, take up their cross and follow him. Self-denial and suffering are not an end in themselves. The Christian finds in Jesus a new centre of his life. He follows the wishes and destiny of another. He accepts the most radical insecurity, even death itself in order to give testimony in his life to Jesus. The man who risks for Christ finds himself and finds the true and lasting life. The only possibility of finding this lies in the following of Jesus.

Saturday (17:14-20). *Doing the impossible.* This healing is a lesson to the disciples about the need of faith and trust in the power of Jesus. Jesus is Lord and healer from whom this man expects healing mercy for one of his family. Disciples who lack trust cannot heal. Jesus trusts in his Father and speaks the healing word. Even if disciples have a minimum of faith, God will make possible for them what is humanly impossible. A little faith and trust go a long way. Through his faith and trust the disciple comes to share in the power of Jesus himself.

NINETEENTH WEEK OF THE YEAR

FIRST READINGS, Year 1 (Deuteronomy, Joshua)

Monday (Deut 10:12-22). *Love the Lord and keep his laws.* Christ's words 'If you love me you will keep my commandments' (Jn 14:15) might be regarded as a summary of this passage.

Tuesday (31:1-8). *The Lord will conquer.* The ageing Moses assures his followers that the Lord will give them possession of the Promised Land. He will eliminate the inhabitants of that land who might resist Israel's settlement as he had destroyed Sihon and Og who had resisted Moses' passage to Canaan (cf. Num 21:21-26, 33-35). Having given this promise Moses installed Joshua as leader of Israel. As a *Responsorial Psalm* to this reading we have part of the *Song of Moses* (Deut 32), a canticle which proclaims the great things that Yahweh had done for his people.

Wednesday (34:1-12). *The death of Moses.* Our final reading from Deuteronomy portrays the tragic scene of Moses surveying the land of Israel which he was not destined to enter. The great leader who had brought the people out of slavery was denied the joy of seeing them settled in the land that had been the goal of all his journeyings. But then, the role of the servant of God is not to enjoy rewards but to fulfil his mission faithfully.

Readings from the books of Joshua, Judges and Ruth. Joshua and Judges form part of the Deuteronomic history. An introduction to this has been given above under Week 1, Year 2, pp. 74-75.

Thursday (Josh 3:7-11, 13-17). *Entry into the Promised Land.* After the long years of desert wandering the Israelites, under Joshua's leadership now, are at last within sight of the land promised by Yahweh. The solemnity of the moment is marked by the liturgical atmosphere of the narration and by the similarity between the drying-up of the Sea of Reeds during the Exodus and of the Jordan now. The Ark of the Covenant, carried by the priests at the head of the procession, is the symbol of God's helping presence with his people and of their commitment to him.

Friday (24:1-13). *God's benefits proclaimed to the community.* The group of Israelites led by Joshua have secured a foothold in the land, and here they meet in cultic assembly at Shechem in the centre of the land with other related groups who had not experienced the events of the Exodus and Sinai. Joshua proclaims Yahweh's saving deeds on behalf of the people: he called them out from a pagan existence across the Euphrates and then brought them out from Egypt the land of slavery to the Promised Land. The recalling of God's benefits, then and now, is the prelude to a choice set before the beneficiaries.

Saturday (24:14-29). *We choose Yahweh!* After the recital of Yahweh's saving deeds the hearers must decide whether they will join Joshua and his immediate followers in whole-hearted service of the Lord or continue serving alien gods. The choice is a serious one: Yahweh is a holy God, inaccessible to human manipulation; he is a jealous God, brooking no compromises in his call for exclusive service. The New Testament will throw further light on the mystery of God's forgiveness, but God remains the Holy One: '. . . hallowed be thy name'.

FIRST READINGS, Year 2 (Ezekiel)

Monday (Ezek 1:2-5, 24-28). *The prophet Ezekiel has a vision of the divine glory.* The prophet Ezekiel was a younger contemporary of Jeremiah. As it now stands, the book that bears his name has an orderly arrangement: an introduction on the prophet's call (chs 1–3); reproaches and threats against his people, mainly before the fall of Jerusalem in 587 BC (chs 4–24); oracles against foreign nations (chs 25-32); oracles of consolation and welfare for Israel, mainly after the fall of Jerusalem (chs 33–39); a detailed description of the new restored Jerusalem and Judah (chs 40–48). In the framework of the present work the whole ministry of the prophet is set among the exiles in Babylon between 593 and 571 (the first and last dated oracles of his). The book received its present arrangement, however, after Ezekiel's day and some of its contents come from his disciples. The actual history behind the composition of the book is a very complicated one and some scholars believe that part, if not all, of Ezekiel's ministry was in Palestine. It appears more likely, however, that Ezekiel's ministry was entirely among the exiles in Babylon, first among those exiled in 597 and later among those exiled after the destruction of Jerusalem in 587. Ezekiel himself was probably exiled to Babylon with the first group. He had a very important role to play in preparing his people for the future that awaited them if they would only turn to God in their time of trial. Before the final destruction of Jerusalem his main preoccupation was to convince both the exiles and those still in Palestine that the catastrophe was inevitable. He also had the task of preparing them spiritually for the disaster. After Jerusalem fell he had to show them that this was not the end. God would restore them to new life.

The vision mentioned in today's reading is dated 593-592 BC, the fifth year of King Jehoiachin's exile. The reigning monarch Zedekiah did not count; Jehoiachin was still regarded as true king of Judah, even if in exile. The river Chebar, where the exiles were, was a navigable canal, south-east of Babylon and connected to the Euphrates river. In his vision of the Lord in glory, Ezekiel saw God seated as king in a mobile throne. This vision of God's glory he had in a pagan land. This is significant. God's glory was transcendent; it was not limited to Jerusalem or the temple. It could equally well be with the exiles in Babylon. This was highly important teaching for a people whose faith was unduly centred on the temple in Jerusalem; see Jer 7 and 26.

Tuesday (2:8–3:4). *The prophet Ezekiel is sent by God to preach to Israel.* The burden of Ezekiel's preaching will be 'lamentations, wailings, moanings', written on the scroll which in vision he was given to eat. The task seemed pleasant to him, but he is forewarned that the people will reject his message. However, the very fact that he has forewarned them will prepare them for conversion when the catastrophe comes.

Wednesday (9:1-7; 10:18-22). *A vision of the sins of Jerusalem and of the destruction of the city.* Here we have two visions which are to be dated some time before the city's destruction or possibly immediately following on it. The destruction is attributed to the appalling sins of the people. The lives of those who are dismayed at the people's guilt will be spared. The destruction of the temple, however, will not be the end for Israel. The glory of the Lord which dwelt in the temple is seen preparing to leave its seat in Jerusalem. It will move eastwards to be with the exiles in Babylon in order to prepare the creation of a new nation.

Thursday (12:1-12). *By a symbolic action Ezekiel mimes the imminent exile.* The wall Ezekiel pierced through was probably made of sun-dried clay bricks. Exiles would be able to take with them only the bare necessities of life. The 'ruler' mentioned at the end of the passage is king Zedekiah, who escaped through the wall as the city was being captured by the Babylonian army; cf. 2 Kings 25:5-7.

Friday (16:1-15, 60, 63). *Jerusalem, the Lord's unfaithful wife.* This allegorical history of Jerusalem (which stands also for Israel) tells of the Lord's loving care for her. Ezekiel reminds the people of their mixed origins. The Amorites and Hittites are in the Bible regarded as the pre-Israelite inhabitants of Canaan. From these, and not from Yahweh's word, Israel drew her inspiration. Her true origins as God's people lay in the desert after the exodus from Egypt. There the Lord found her helpless and reared her tenderly to womanhood. But she responded to his love by prostituting herself to her pagan neighbours. Her loving divine husband is, however, ready to pardon her.

In case this reading should prove too much for particular congregations, an **Alternative Reading (16:59-63)** is provided. It speaks of God's readiness to renew his covenant with faithless Israel. Jerusalem's elder and younger sister are, respectively, Samaria and Sodom (16:46-47).

Saturday (18:1-10, 13, 30-32). *Each person will be punished by God for his own sins, not for the sins of his forebears.* Jerusalem and Judah and God's people may have inherited the sinful ways of their fathers and of their Amorite and Hittite predecessors. These, however, were only an environmental influence; each individual remained personally responsible for his own sins. At the time of Jeremiah and Ezekiel the question of personal responsability was coming to the fore and both answer it in similar fashion. The popular proverb cited by Ezekiel is also found in Jeremiah (31:29). The earlier emphasis in Israel was on collective responsibility. Even after Ezekiel and Jeremiah this principle retains a certain validity. One generation does effect the next, but despite this each individual remains personally responsible for his actions.

GOSPEL READINGS (Matthew)

Monday (Mt 17:22-27). *The new community.* The fourth long discourse of the gospel (17:22-18:35) is about life in community, about those qualities which mark the personal relationships of the disciple. It is influenced by the concrete situation within the Jewish-Christian community for which the gospel was written. However, it speaks to us about attitudes and values which Christians of all time seek to realise in the Christian community and also in their relationship with the world community of man.

The announcement of Jesus' death and resurrection in connection with the temple tax shows that the temple has ceased to be the centre of community. Through his death and resurrection the temple is replaced by the new community with Jesus as its Lord. The temple tax once symbolised allegiance to the religious centre and cult of Jerusalem. Disciples are now 'sons' of the Father; they are 'free'. Their worship is no longer limited to one place. What unites us as Christians is that Jesus is our brother and his Father is our Father.

Tuesday (18:1-5, 10, 12-14). *Like Jesus and the Father.* To be like a child has nothing to do with naivete or self-effacement. It means not 'acting great' towards others or lording it over them. It is to be like Christ himself, to be open and generous in our service of one another. It is to be like the Father by welcoming or receiving others and showing personal care, like him, towards those who are in need of our support and understanding.

Wednesday (18:15-20). *A life of brotherhood.* The main point of this difficult reading is that one should try everything in one's power to bring about reconciliation between people whenever there are breaches of relationships within the community. The first step in 'winning back' a brother is to make a personal approach to him. The power to 'bind and loose' refers to the power within the community to effect reconciliation not only between a brother and the community but also him and the Father. Faith in Jesus and our coming together to express this faith binds us into a community of brotherhood. The Father listens to those who come together out of faith in his Son in order to express their needs to him.

Thursday (18:21—19:1). *From the heart.* The Christian is inspired not only by the Father's personal care for each member. It seeks to put into practice the words of the Our Father: forgive us as we forgive others. We say this prayer repeatedly and we want it to be a prayer that comes from the heart. Living the spirit of our Father means offering forgiveness, like him, not just once but repeatedly and from the heart—from sincere dispositions of love and mercy.

Friday (19:3-12). *Marriage and celibacy.* In another narrative section (chs 19—23) which leads up to a discourse (chs 24—25) Jesus is on his last journey from Galilee to Jerusalem, the place of his death. In more controversies and discussions with the religious leaders he continues to stress the difference between true and false discipleship.

In this confrontation he speaks about the new order of things for marriage, the restoration of God's original purpose for it and celibacy. The following of Christ finds expression in a man's fidelity to his wife. God's intention concerning their personal union is realised through a life-long self-giving in love and forgiveness. There are also people who 'make themselves' unmarriageable 'for the sake of the Kingdom', that is, because they have experienced the Kingdom, the power of God's love in Jesus. Celibacy is not just a matter of giving up something. The celibate has discovered someone, God's love in Jesus to such a degree that marriage is no longer possible. The experience which leads to and which helps him to live out a decision not to marry is as intimate and incommunicable as another's decision to prefer his wife over all others.

Saturday (19:13-15). *A blessing for children.* After his strong words about the Father's will concerning the relationship between husband and wife, and in particular, about the dignity of woman within this relationship, Jesus now shows in action and attitude his own concern and that of his Father about another area of family life. The doctors of the law held that religion was chiefly a man's business. Women and children were a negligeable quantity in social life; their role was to listen and to learn. In blessing the children Jesus teaches that it is not so in the life of Kingdom. On his way to death he has time for all those who approach him, those who are sick, the insignificant people of society. He wishes to show that the life of the Kingdom, God's love and care is for all without exception.

TWENTIETH WEEK OF THE YEAR

FIRST READINGS, Year 1 (Judges, Ruth)

Monday (Judg 2:11-19). *The sour fruits of infidelity.* The Deuteronomic editors give a schematic theological interpretation of the period of the Judges (12th-11th century BC). The people's first fervour (see Josh 24) has become a dim memory. Time and again they relapse into worship of pagan fertility gods, but the only fruit they gain is enemy oppression. Yahweh raised up charismatic military leaders (the 'Judges'); the people listened to these during their life-time but afterwards relapsed. The pattern of apostasy, oppression, rescue, and relapse repeated itself, but this dismal tale of infidelity may yet stimulate the people to turn whole-heartedly to their only Saviour.

Tuesday (6:11-24). *Called to rescue Israel.* The incursions of nomadic Midianite hordes have reduced Israel to dire straights. Yahweh seems to have abandoned his people to this oppression because of their sins of idolatry. But he who saved them from Egyptian oppression long ago is ready to repeat his saving deeds. The call comes to an insignificant farmer's son (compare 1 Cor 1:26-31). Yahweh's envoy (=angel) bears patiently with Gideon's cautious reactions and brings him gradually to recognise the tremendous fact of a personal vocation from God.

Wednesday (9:6-15). *A fable against a self-made king.* Abimelech son of Jerubbaal (identified with Gideon) persuaded the leading men of Shechem to murder his seventy brothers and proclaim him king, a title which Gideon had refused (Judg 8:23). Jotham, the youngest son of Jerubbaal, who also escaped from the massacre, expresses in the present fable a judgement on Abimelech's kingship.

The olive, the fig, and the vine—all valuable to men—refused the kingship as a useless thing; only the worthless thorn-bush can be found willing to accept the role of king. The final words (v. 15) foreshadow the war between Abimelech and his former supporters of Shechem (9: 22-27). God's saving purposes are not served by blood-stained usurpers.

Thursday (11:29-39). *The tragedy of a victor's vow.* Jephthah, chosen by Yahweh to rescue the Israelites of Transjordan from the attacks of the Ammonites, makes a desperate vow before the decisive battle, and the reading tells of the tragic outcome. Human sacrifice, well-known

among neighbouring peoples (see 2 Kings 3:27), was condemned by the
Law (Lev 18:21; Deut 12:31; and compare Gen 22). The present text
makes no explicit judgement on Jephthah's extraordinary action. His
misguided zeal inspires horror, but there is also something admirable in
the way Jephthah and his daughter submit to God's will as they understand it.

Friday (Ruth 1:1, 3-8, 14-16, 22). *A foreigner chooses to live among
Yahweh's people.* The book of Ruth (see p. 75 above) does not seem
to share the attitude of Deut 23:3-6 where Moabites are excluded from
the assembly of Yahweh. Ruth is a young Moabitess who chooses to
leave her own land across the Jordan and accompany her aged mother-
in-law Naomi back to Israel, to Bethlehem. This generous self-forgetful-
ness will be rewarded by Yahweh who will make of Ruth an ancestress
of David and of the Son of David (see Mt 1:5).

Saturday (2:1-3, 8-11; 4:13-17). *Ruth, ancestress of David.* Ruth's
future is prepared in what seems an ordinary, even coincidental, way,
but the Lord's providence is at work. She finds security in her exile
through marriage to Naomi's kinsman, Boaz; their child, Obed, is
reckoned as continuing the line of Naomi's husband. And future horizons, which far transcend the simple setting of rural Bethelehem,
emerge in the closing note about Obed's grandson, David. The Lord's
plans move ahead in the quiet of everyday events.

FIRST READINGS, Year 2 (Ezekiel)

Monday (Ezek 24:15-24). *Ezekiel becomes a sign for Israel. The death
of his beloved wife foreshadows the destruction of the temple.* The destruction will be so disastrous that the inhabitants will have no time for
mourning.

Tuesday (28:1-10). *The proud ruler of Tyre will be humiliated.* The
city of Tyre (on an island off present-day Lebanon) was in antiquity
renowned for its trade. Situated on its island a half mile off the coast, it
considered itself impregnable. Daniel (more properly written Danel; see
also Ezek 14:12-23) was a legendary figure of Phoenician legend and is
now known from the Ugaritic texts (14th century BC), found at a site
north of Lebanon. The capital sin of the ruler of Tyre in Ezekiel's eyes
was pride, which had him regard himself as a god. It was the sin of
Eden, and, in fact, the continuation of this passage (28:12-19) should be
compared with Gen 3.

Wednesday (34:1-11). *The God of Israel is to become a true shepherd to his people.* This prophecy, which is to be dated after the fall of Jerusalem, is one of hope and consolation. Israel's shepherds (her kings and princes) had played her false and had been the cause of her exile. Yahweh himself would now become her shepherd and tend to her needs as these had failed to do. This is the first of Ezekiel's major prophecies of the restoration of Israel. Jesus will later declare himself to be the Good Shepherd (Jn 10:11-18).

Thursday (36:23-28). *The new Israel is to be given a new heart and a new spirit.* This beautiful passage is Ezekiel's counterpart of the prophecy of the new covenant of the book of Jeremiah (Jer 31:31-34 — Thursday, Week 18). God's people are to be taken home from exile; their sins are to be forgiven and they are to be endowed with a new internal principle of spiritual life: a new heart and a new spirit. That a new covenant is intended, even if not explicitly mentioned, is clear from the covenant formula: 'You shall be my people and I will be your God' (cf. Jer 31:33). All the elements of this new covenant are gifts of God, to be accepted through the obedience of faith.

Friday (37:1-14). *In exile Israel looked as a dead nation. The spirit of God will bring them back to new life.* This magnificent vision of the dry bones speaks of the resurrection of Israel as a nation after the exile. Jesus will later proclaim himself to be the resurrection and the life (Jn 11:25-26).

Saturday (43:1-7). *The glory of the Lord returns to the new temple in Jerusalem.* Ezekiel 33—39 contain prophecies on the restoration of Israel from exile; chapters 40—48 are devoted to a detailed description of the newly constituted Israel, especially to the new temple. The glory of the Lord, sign of God's presence with his people, had abandoned the temple at the destruction of the city to go eastwards and be with the exiles in Babylon (see Monday & Wednesday, Week 19). Ezekiel now sees this same glory of the Lord return to the new temple in Jerusalem. The work of restoration, of the assembling of God's scattered children, was completed—at least in vision. In reality this came through the death and resurrection of Jesus and through the gift of the Holy Spirit. And this left the man-made temple of Jerusalem without further purpose. The risen Christ was the new temple, accessible to all through faith. And at the death of Jesus the veil of the temple, indicating the presence of the divine glory, was rent. The divine presence was henceforth elsewhere, in fact everywhere to those who believe.

GOSPEL READINGS (Matthew)

Monday (Mt 19:16-22). *Freedom for God.* Christians are called to be 'perfect'. This means following Jesus and realising through his word and example the invitation to make our lives God-centred, to learn where the real treasure is. To be perfect, to follow Jesus is the free act of a man who places his entire existence at the disposition of his Saviour, Jesus. He tells the young man that so long as his possessions create a self-sufficiency which divides his heart and prevents him from being God-centred he does not possess that freedom and openness which the Christian life demands.

Tuesday (19:23-30). *The need of God's riches.* The following of Jesus is a radical way of life. It is directly opposed to that self-sufficiency and sense of power which human avarice, selfishness and over-preoccupation with riches can create. When a man feels that his needs are satisfied by his many possessions he can easily think that he does not need God. The invitation to follow Jesus is a call to believe more and more in the greater riches of God and in his generosity which always surpasses that of man. God's standards do not regard what a man possesses but what he is and what he becomes through his experience of complete dependence of God.

Wednesday (20:1-16). *A grace, not a reward.* Rewards in the Kingdom will not be in proportion to earthly status. The key figure in the parable is the householder (one of Matthew's favourite images for God). We are invited to reflect on the greatness and universality of God's love and compassion, the gratuitousness of his gifts. The point is: God's gifts come from his goodness. We cannot earn them. 'What God gives is not pay but a gift; not a reward but a grace' (Barclay). The call to share in his friendship, whenever it comes, is his free gift. We cannot quarrel with his right to be generous towards whomsoever he pleases. The householder's kindness and generosity show up the selfishness and lack of generosity of those who complain about the mercies which others have received.

Thursday (22:1-14). *Call and response.* The call to follow Jesus is an invitation of grace. It is not based on prerogatives of race or class. His Church is an open door. Those called in from the highways and byways have no claim on the king. But following Jesus is more than a matter of enjoying a grace. A grace is also a responsibility. The wear and tear of Christian living means persevering in our response to the concrete demands of the gospel. We are invited not only to come to Christ but also to allow ourselves to be constantly changed by him.

Friday (22:34-40). *The whole truth.* The sum and substance of Christian living is active love of God and of our fellowman. Concern for humanity is 'like' the commandment to love God, that is, of the same quality. There is really only one commandment; there is no love of God without love of neighbour. The meaning of this love is explained by the whole gospel account of Jesus' person, work and teaching.

Saturday (23:1-12). *True and false religion.* At first sight, this chapter is the most frightening chapter of the whole New Testament. Jesus appears so unsparing and forcible in the extreme. Yet he is here taking a stand on behalf of his people against attitudes and a type of religious leadership which makes religion an intolerable burden and encourages hypocrisy. Jesus as prophet speaks strong words of warning. Religion, he says, is not a load of obligations and prohibitions; it is not a means of drawing respect or attention to oneself. In the Christian community there is no place for authoritarianism because it is a life of brotherhood.

TWENTY-FIRST WEEK OF THE YEAR

FIRST READINGS, Year 1 (1 Thessalonians)

INTRODUCTION TO THE LETTERS TO THE THESSALONIANS

The two letters to the Thessalonians which date from about 50 AD, twenty years after the death of Jesus, are the earliest of the New Testament books. These letters must be read with imagination like listening to one side of a telephone conversation. They are not careful theological treatises composed in the calm of a study but are written with typical Pauline urgency to a young church in need of guidance and a deeper understanding of the Christian message. These letters are a very interesting example of the interest and care with which Paul instructed one of his early communities.

Paul was led by the Spirit to Europe somewhat against his inclinations (Acts 16:7ff) and Thessalonica, the Roman capital and chief seaport of Macedonia, was his second foundation after his 'departure' from

Philippi. Paul had spent at least three Sabbaths there (Phil 4:16) and worked there to support his mission (1 Thes 2:9). These two letters are written in Corinth after another hurried departure from Thessalonica and brief stays in Beroea and Athens. Timothy had just arrived back to Paul (1 Thes 3:1, 6; Acts 18:5). He had been sent from Athens to strengthen the Thessalonians in their afflictions and to report the situation to Paul.

The first letter gives us an invaluable summary of Paul's teaching to a mainly gentile audience (1 Thes 1:9-10) and its problems were mainly dealing with the second coming of Christ and the end of the age (i.e. eschatology). Other problems were persecution (1 Thes 1:6, 22), Paul the dictator and charlatan (2:6, 7, 11), immorality (4:3-8), division in the church (4:9; 5:13), authority (5:12-14).

Second Thessalonians, written shortly after First Thessalonians, gives a further explanation of the manner of the coming of Christ and attempts to correct the idleness of many of the Thessalonians and their reliance on a false letter from Paul (2 Thes 2:2).

Further Reading: New Testament Reading Guide, No. 6. W. Barclay, *The Daily Study Bible.*

Monday (1 Thes 1:2-5, 8-10). *Thanksgiving and encouragement.* Paul the good psychologist begins on a positive note of thanksgiving and encouragement for the suffering Thessalonians even as he prepares the ground for his subsequent corrections. God loves them. Their response is described in the famous triad (1 Cor 13:13) which describes the Christian life: a faith which shows itself in action, a love in work, a hope in endurance. They have that joy which comes from the Holy Spirit. Paul recalls them delicately to their already famous conversation *from idolatry to the service* of a *living* God. A Christian is one who is waiting for the coming of the risen Jesus who *delivers* him from the coming judgement.

Tuesday (2:1-8). *The Ideal Pastor.* Paul gives a beautiful picture of how to preach the gospel, his tender affection for his *brothers* and his self-lessness. He sought no glory from men but only to please God. He drew courage *from God* to preach good news in the face of great opposition.

Wednesday (2:9-13). *The word of God not of men.* Paul gives a brief apologia of his irreproachable character probably in answer to some insinuations that he was like many of the wandering charlatans that we read about in the literature of the times. By trade a tent-maker (Acts 18:3) he insisted on preaching the gospel at his own expense (Acts 20:

34; 1 Cor 9:18) and *hard work*. Like a father to his children, he *encouraged* and *pleaded* for a life worthy of God who calls to glory. He *thanks* God that they recognised God's word.

Thursday (3:7-13). *A plea for growth in love.* It is touching to read of Paul receiving comfort from a young church to face his own distress and trials. Timothy had brought good news but there were shortcomings. Paul begins his correction with *thanks*, joy, a desire to meet face to face and a prayer which goes to the essentials and asks the Lord for an increase in love. He concludes with recalling the coming of Jesus which would of course mean judgement on the kind of lives which they were living.

Friday (4:1-8). *What God wants is holiness.* Paul recalls them to the teaching which they had received. Holiness or being like God consists in what pleased God not what is customary, popular or what can be determined rationally or scientifically. Like the modern world, the Hellenistic world was much more tolerant in sexual conduct than Paul or the biblical tradition. A Christian should remember the coming judgement, God's call, the gift of the Holy Spirit which he has received.

Saturday (4:9-12). *Love, work, good example.* Evidently some Christians through false zeal were disturbing others and becoming spongers on their love. Paul often insists on the good example by which Christians would command the respect of outsiders—love, minding one's own business, doing one's work.

FIRST READINGS, Year 2 (2 Thessalonians, 1 Corinthians)

INTRODUCTION TO FIRST CORINTHIANS

This letter was written probably in the early part of 54 AD. It was written to a Christian community whom Paul himself had founded, but among whom others like Apollos and maybe even Peter also worked. Living as they did in a very wealthy and, we are led to believe, immoral city, the Christians in Corinth were bound to find the ideals put before them by Paul somewhat exacting.

What we find in this first letter is a series of practical answers to the problems which presented themselves to the Apostle: strife and division in the Corinthian church (1:4-9), public litigation among the members (6:1-8), questions about sexual morality and marriage (5:1-5; 6:12-20; 7:1-40), the eating of food that has been sacrificed to idols, questioning of Paul's own claim to the apostleship (4:3, 15; 9:1ff.). This by no means suggests that the first letter to the Corinthians is lacking in depth of thought or spiritual insight. The opening chapter is one of the finest passages ever written on the meaning of the cross; Paul's understanding of the Eucharist, of the Mystical Body of Christ and of the Resurrection; his beautiful lyric on the greatest of the Christian charisms—love— all these save the first letter to the Corinthians for falling into the dreadful category of a catechism of questions and answers.

Monday (2 Thes 1:1-5, 11-12). *Thanksgiving and praise.* We easily pass over such beautiful words as Paul's greeting of grace (God's favour and generous gift of a new covenant in Christ) and peace its result (forgiveness, reconciliation with God and one's fellow man and fullness of life). Then Paul begins as his custom was on a positive note of thanksgiving and encouragement—a model for us to follow in our letter writing. A beautiful prayer combines God's grace and power with man's desires, his human efforts at prayers and his suffering for the kingdom.

Tuesday (2:1-3, 14-17). *Stand firm, keep the traditions.* The obsession and hysteria about the coming of Christ had not subsided despite Paul's first letter. The coming is not yet says Paul. He therefore urges them to stand firm, to keep the traditions and instructions which he has already given them and not let themselves be deceived by any contrary prophecy, or rumor or even a letter purporting to come from Paul himself. Paul prays that they may be given enouragement and strength in every good deed and word.

Wednesday (3:6-10, 16-18). *Discipline the idlers.* Some had given up work and were disregarding Paul's own example and teaching—'busybodies instead of busy'. Paul's advice is blunt. 'No loaf for the loafer.' Religious enthusiasm is no excuse for neglecting one's earthly duties or disturbing others. But Paul warns them not to treat such a member as an enemy but to correct him like a brother (3:15). As forgeries were circulating in his name. Paul puts the final greeting clearly in his own handwriting.

Thursday (1 Cor 1:1-9). *Paul chosen by God himself.* The very first reading shows Paul's concern about his own status vis-a-vis the Corinthian church. He was well aware that he had not been one of the Twelve. He was, in fact, a johnny-come-lately on the apostolic scene. His vocation, in fact, is none the less real for that. It depended not on a choice made or approval given by men: it came directly from God himself. This is a very important point for Paul. It is the only authenticity he can claim for his message. The Twelve might point to their investment with authority by Jesus and to the acceptance of this fact by all of Jesus' followers; Paul could point only to what happened invisibly between him and his God. This was no public guarantee. That is why it is of paramount importance to Paul to win the faith of his hearers not only in what he preaches but in himself.

Friday (1:17-25). *The folly of the cross is the wisdom of God.* The second reading from this letter launches us right into the heart of Paul's doctrine of the cross. When one comes to talk of the cross, the Apostle reminds us, all philosophical systems are both useless and helpless. There really is no way of explaining the crucifixion. To the Jews it is a scandal because for them, the very idea of a crucified Messiah was a blasphemy. The cross for them was a punishment, a divine judgement on the man Jesus whom they saw not only as a figure who had met with human failure but as a perverter of the people. The contrast between his claim and his shameful death *had* to be interpreted now by every faithful Jew as the judgement of God. To the Greeks, and by Greeks are here meant 'gnostics', those who believed that by sheer speculation, they could attain divine wisdom, the cross is obviously folly. It is a reversal of all human specualtion because the cross (like the incarnation in John's gospel) means not that man has reasoned his way up to God but that God has reached down to man in his frailty. The cross is therefore the crystallisation of the freedom of God to move beyond the categories in which man had hitherto known him. There can be only one response to it, and that is faith, trust, wonder.

Saturday (1:26-31). *Worldly standards are overthrown.* From the paradox of God's action in the cross, Paul moves to the illustration of this paradox in the make-up of the church (1:26-31). There were slaves in the Corinthian church, and even though there were also wealthy people, Paul can still remind the Corinthian Christians that when they took on Christianity, not many of them were wise, not many influential, not many of noble family. Again, the conventions of the world are overthrown.

GOSPEL READINGS (Matthew)

Monday (Mt 23:13-22). *Worship in truth.* Intransigence, legalism and various forms of religious fanaticism create barriers and mislead those who are searching for God. A religion which is marked by hair-splitting, casuistry and insincerity is not genuine worship. God seeks a response from man's heart in truthfulness and sincerity.

Tuesday (23:23-26). *A sense of proportion.* Obsession with the minutiae of our religion is futile if it makes us neglect the more important matters. It is possible to observe all the outward actions of religion and yet to be completely unchristian in the things that matter—in doing what is right, kindness to those in need of help, integrity in our dealings with one another. The example of straining wine on the lookout for a small insect is the picture of someone who has lost his sense of proportion. Besides, religion is not a mask or a Sunday suit. It engages the whole person who responds to God and men from the heart, from deep within himself.

Wednesday (23:27-32). *To smile and be a villain.* For Matthew hypocrisy is the fundamental sin. It is an attitude which is opposed to doing God's will. It is a denial and contradiction of true love. The word 'hypocrite' means an 'actor'. There is a conflict between inside and outside. Hypocrisy is a loveless interior attitude beneath the disguise of pleasing appearances. It is to preach without practising, to smile and be a villain. We can preach without remorse against others for doing what we do ourselves. We can judge the sins of past history without thinking that history some day will judge us. Those who put the Son of God to death condemn those who maltreated prophets.

Thursday (24:42-51). *Waiting and watching.* The next three readings which belong to the last great discourse of the gospel (chs 24—25) are parables advising Christians to use well the time intervening before the final coming of Christ.

First of all, the Christian life is a constant preparation for the full manifestation of Jesus. The disciple can never lull himself into a sense of security. When his vision excludes his eternal destiny, his life becomes laden with unhappiness and grief. He begins to run away from himself. Jesus pronounces a blessing on the Christian who waits and watches. It is a watching of eager expectation for the fullness of life which results from a life of faithfulness to God and man. No life happens without waiting. We wait for life to reveal its meaning and we know that one day light will dawn without fail.

Friday (25:1-13). *On being ready.* Already in the Sermon on the Mount Jesus has contrasted the 'foolish' with the 'wise'. The Christian who lives the word is like a 'wise' builder whose house is on a solid foundation. The 'wise' bridesmaids are those who have lived the word; they are the true servants of God, friends of Christ who have the resources with which to meet the Lord when he comes. The resources of the Christian are a life of faith translated inot action. Jesus comes to patient and prepared hearts. His coming does not happen according to our schedule.

Saturday (25:14-30). *The faithful servant.* The parable describes what it means to be a 'good and faithful servant'. Christian discipleship is more than professing faith. Lived faith is an active response to Christ and our fellowman according to the measure of the grace and gifts we have received. It is a creative life, filled with unending possibilities for further growth and service. God does not demand from us graces and gifts he does not intend for us. Yet the faithful servant does not lean back and rest on his oars or shut his mind to new and challenging possibilities. He builds his hopes on who he is, on what he has been given and on what he can become. When he has no more to give he passes into the Kingdom of someone who will be as faithful with him as he was with others.

TWENTY-SECOND WEEK OF THE YEAR

FIRST READINGS, Year 1 (1 Thessalonians, Colossians)

INTRODUCTION TO THE LETTER TO THE COLOSSIANS

On Wednesday of this week we begin the reading of the letter to the Colossians. The letter was written by Saint Paul to a Christian community in the Lycus Valley within modern Turkey. A Jewish colony existed there whose way of life, as we gather from the ideas attacked in this letter, resembled closely the people of the Dead Sea Scrolls. Thus, we find Paul stressing the primacy of Jesus over the angels. The Essene emphasis on angelology is well known. Similarly any insistence on dietary laws, a sacred calendar, indeed any formal observances (especially circumcision cf. 2:11-13), is condemned in this letter. We might read 2:16-23, not included in the daily readings, to see the kind of regulations which Paul opposes, because they do not conquer the weakness of the flesh.

Christ is the head of the body. We are saved through our belief in him, and through any external laws. Indeed, as in the Prologue of Saint John, we are told that all things were created through him. The forces for estrangement in the world are conquered by the blood of his cross so that now everything becomes reconciled to the Father. We are called upon to join in that re-creative activity through a share in the sufferings of Christ. We are enabled to do so because we possess his risen life, and become peace-makers. Easter living and worldly living are set out in sharp contrast. A decision for either begins in the home.

We might note at the end that the practice of reading the Pauline letters within different churches is recommended: the beginning of the *Corpus Paulinum.*

Monday (1 Thes 4:13-18). *We shall stay with the Lord for ever.* A new problem had arisen—the fate of those who had died before the Parousia. They will rise *first* says Paul, using the traditional imagery of trumpet, cloud, meeting the Lord in the air—between earth and sky, etc. His basic comforting teaching is that all will stay with the Lord forever.

Tuesday (5:1-6, 9-11). *Preparation for the Second Coming.* The date of the Parousia (Daniel 2:21; Acts 1:7) cannot be calculated although a recent book *The Late Great Planet Earth* proclaiming that the time has come as we approach the year 2,000 has sold more than 8 million copies. Paul uses the same simile as Jesus 'like a thief in the night' (Mt 24:43-44; Lk 12:39-40). The emphasis in Paul is on the surprise and suddenness element—inescapable like the labour pains of a pregnant woman. But a Christian belongs to the day and lives in constant anticipation of it by a sober and watchful life (1 Peter 1:13; Mk 13:32ff). Therefore he will not be taken by surprise because he knows that God is on his side.

Wednesday (Col 1:1-8). *Thankfulness to God for the faith, hope and charity of the Colossians.* The apostle thanks the Father for the gift of the Good News which he has bestowed on the Colossians. Already their belief in Jesus Christ has shown itself in their total giving to one another, caused by their hope in heavenly fulfilment. The Gospel of our forgiveness through Jesus Christ continues to spread, and was in fact taught to them by Epaphras, one of Paul's collaborators, who reports to him on their progress.

Thursday (1:9-14). *Paul prays for the continuing fruitfulness of the Colossians.* He asks the Father that this community may be open to his saving will, understand what is the best thing for them to do, and then carry it out in every way. Thus, they grow up in their knowledge of God. Their activity will show forth God's life in them because he continually strengthens them. They are to thank him for liberating them from the darkness of the unredeemed into the light of those redeemed from sinfulness, through the work of his beloved Son.

Friday (1:15-20). *A hymn which describes the creating and reconciling work of Jesus.* Jesus Christ shows us perfectly in external form the invisible God. All things were make through him, and this includes the angels. He precedes them in time and dignity. In fact, everything depends on him. He is head of the Church (which Paul now clearly calls his body) both in authority and as principle of life. God fills the world with his saving presence through him, and the same world is reconciled to the Father through his peace-making. This activity reaches its final stage in his death through crucifixion.

Saturday (1:21-23). *Paul contrasts the former and present state of the Colossians.* In the past, this people were outside the saving way of God because of their sinfulness both in thought and in deed (cf. also 1 Cor 6:9-11). The Father has now brought them back to himself, the source of their being, through the death of Christ become human as they are human. No angel could save them, only he who could suffer and die like themselves, and for their sakes. He encourages them to persevere in their faith, and not to drift away from the promise of their eternal reward. Paul is the servant of this Gospel to the peoples (cf. Acts 26:16-19).

FIRST READINGS, Year 2 (1 Corinthians)

Monday (1 Cor 2:1-5). *Paul preached Christ, and Christ crucified.* The practical implications of salvation through the cross for Paul's teaching are set forth in 2:1-5. If human philosophy is unable to explain the paradox of the cross, then to use philosophical arguments and rhetorical devices is to no avail. If God chose to reveal his power in weakness, then the weakness of the preacher, where oratory and argumentation are concerned, must be yet another 'incarnation' of the power of God's Spirit. It is on the power of the Spirit, ultimately, not on the strength of logic and rhetoric, that faith must be based. Paradoxically, the preaching of the feeble and senseless message of the crucified Christ proves to have a power and a wisdom no human eloquence possesses, because it is the power and wisdom of God himself.

Tuesday (2:10-16). *Only through the enlightenment of the Holy Spirit can we understand Christianity.* In this passage the reason is given why someone can see God's hand at work in such mysterious things as the crucifixion. The Christian sees with the vision of the Spirit, not with merely human eyes. He can therefore see more and at greater depth than any philosophy has dreamed of. Nor is he to fear contradiction from the man of pure reason. The latter is on a different wave-length: he has no right to question what comes from stations and from media to which he has never tuned in. It is not that the 'spiritual' man is infallible (cf. 14:29); what Paul is saying here he also says in 4:3ff: human condemnation and human acquittal are nothing to him; his only judge is the Lord.

Wednesday (3:1-9). *The progess of the Church comes from God alone.* Paul now turns on his audience. From their conduct, their wrangling, jealousies, rivalries, he concludes that they are not spiritual men. As Christians they are very immature. And so he scolds them: how can he speak spiritual truths to them if they are not of a mind to begin to understand them? In a situation where there were different 'gurus', Paul again comes back to the centrality of God. In the long run, it is God's work; Paul, Apollos and Cephas are merely his instruments. To create disunity by following one over against another is therefore not only unchristian; it is positively stupid. What suffers in the end from such rivalries is the community itself.

Thursday (3:18-23). *An exhortation to work for God alone.* Progress in the Christian life comes from God alone. Christ was made man to promote God's glory; Christians are servants of Christ for this same end. Christianity has no place for personality cults.

Friday (4:1-5). *The preacher of the Gospel must be a servant of Christ.* It is only fitting that Paul having disabused the Corinthians of their ideas about Church leaders should now go on to define the essential role of the minister of the Gospel (4:1-5). The preacher of the Gospel must be a servant of Christ, a steward (literally 'housekeeper'—think of the image of the Church as God's household in 1 Tim 3:15). That is, the preacher has no significance of his own; he points from himself to Christ. He is the person, in the original meaning of that word (the mask) through whom Christ speaks. Therefore, his primary duty is to *be faithful.* The preacher of the Gospel must be trustworthy, that is, he must be relied upon to deliver Christ's message, not his own. He must not exercise his own initiative merely, but what is perhaps more important, he must not act or speak on his own authority. Surely, a sometimes much needed reminder in our day too of the danger of authoritarianism which runs counter to the authentic power of Christ which was based on and marked by gentleness.

Saturday (4:6-15). *The apostles are weak instruments to reveal God's power.* The personal note is sounded even more loudly in 4:6-15. For all his insistence that he does not care how people judge him, Paul is here at pains to vindicate himself in the eyes of his critics in Corinth. He points out his own style of life, his role of a 'fool' in the divine drama, his poverty, his hard work, his gentlemanliness. Here again, we have Pauline paradox at its best: the apostles are poor men who make many rich, they are the scum of the earth, yet they lead it to salvation. There is a certain pathos in these lines of Paul. He so identified his message with himself that now, criticised as he seems to have been by certain members and maybe even groups within the church at Corinth, he views this criticism as an attack on the very message he preached, the core of which was Christ crucified.

GOSPEL READINGS (Luke)

INTRODUCTION TO THE GOSPEL ACCORDING TO LUKE

As the final part of the ferial Lectionary unfolds, the Gospel of St Luke is read semi-continuously. In order, then, to make the best pastoral use of this section of the Lectionary's presentation of the word of God, it is necessary to have a clear idea of the structure and theological interests of this gospel.

The Evangelist. Saint Luke's own character comes across quite clearly when we consider the nature and atmosphere of his work, allowing for the fact that in addition to the gospel he wrote the Acts of the Apostles. That he came from a background which was very different from the Judaism out of which primitive Christianity grew is clear enough; that his association with Saint Paul in the gentile mission left is mark upon him seems equally clear. Perhaps it is this combination of circumstances that makes his gospel more accessible to us in many respects by comparison with the others. One area of pauline influence might well be the vision he has of Christ as the 'reconciler' of God and men; in fact, there is a sense in which his gospel could be definied specifically as 'the gospel of reconciliation'.

At the start of his work, he tells us that he set out to write 'an ordered account', 'after carefully going over the whole story from the beginning' (1:3). What enabled him to introduce an element of order into the gospel story was his clear concept of *movement* and *direction.* The whole of his work is about movement: in the gospel it is the movement of Jesus from Galilee to Jerusalem where the paschal mystery is fulfilled; in the Acts of the Apostles, the scene shifts and the movement concerned is that of the Church, from Jerusalem through Judaea and Samaria to the ends of the earth.

Within this framework, he has set out to recount the words and deeds of the Saviour, for 'the Gospel of Luke could well be resumed in this one sentence: Jesus Christ is the Saviour of men' (Lagrange). However, Luke himself would have been careful to add 'of *all* men'; there is in his work a universalism, a vision of Good News destined for all men of all races and ages and conditions, no matter how poorly equipped to receive it from the human point of view. It is this universal appeal which has given form to the Lukan portrait of Christ; it is an engaging and attractive portrait, one that all of us can feel at home with. This is what earned Luke the title of 'Scribe of the gentleness of Christ' given to him by Dante.

In the same way a modern writer has said: 'The Jesus of Luke, one feels, might well have uttered the words written on the Statue of Liberty in New York harbour—"Give me your tired, your poor, your huddled masses yearning to breathe free. Send these, the homeless, tempest-tost to me"' (W. D. Davies).

But, as in everything else that Luke wrote, the gospel presents a diptych; there is parallelism at work all the time. Just as the whole of the gospel itself is paralleled to the Acts of the Apostles, the image of the gentle Christ within the gospel is paralleled with another portrait. It is a further image of one whose time is short, whose demands on his followers are total, whose work is urgent. We would ignore one of these sides of the diptych at the risk of falsifying Luke's overall picture. Both have to be taken together, because they are complementary one to the other. This explains why Luke's gospel is also the Gospel of Renunciation and Perseverance. What he offers us, in the long run, is a catechism of christian discipleship, with all of its consolations and privileges, but also with all of its dangers and temptations.

The Structure of the Gospel. When we look at the shape and structure of the gospel of Luke, we can gain some insight into the way the evangelist sees the message and mission of Christ. After the *Infancy Gospel* (chs 1–2) which features so largely in the Lectionary for Advent and Christmas, he tells us of the *Galilean Ministry* (chs 3–9) in a way which resembles the story as told by Matthew and Mark (and yet even here his own hand betrays itself in those passages which he has included and the others do not have). However, it is only when we come to the end of chapter 9 that Luke really lets himself go, and provides us with an insight that is not matched in any of the other gospels. The whole of the central section of his version of the gospel story (chs 9–19) is taken up with the story of Jesus' journey to Jerusalem; here, his idea of movement and direction comes into full play. The central section is therefore knowns as the *Travel Narrative,* and it leads us to the heart of Luke's theology, for it is precisely in this section that Luke has chosen to gather together all the material which he contributes to the gospel tradition. Most of the passages in this section have no parallel in the other gospels at all; parables, controversies, sayings, miracles tumble over one another in a magnificent panorama of the active Christ welcoming those who come to him, teaching those who stay with him, arguing with those who would betray the nature of true religion. The rest of the gospel, the *Jerusalem Ministry* (chs 19–21) and the *Passion Narrative* (chs 22–24) rejoins the common tradition, even though Luke continues to tell the story in his own way. By the end of the last chapter, he has reached the place where he set out to be at the start, Jerusalem, the Holy City, the place of destiny for Christ and the Church.

The Theology of Luke's Gospel. The most obvious characteristic of Luke's gospel is that it is *the gospel of the poor.* The outcast, the people who are looked down upon by others—Jesus, according to Luke, deliberately seeks out and comforts; hence, there is an interest in this gospel in the 'sinners'. Time and time again we find the Christ of Saint Luke seeking out and saving what was lost. The burden of his message is the forgiving love of God. This explains why the parable of the prodigal son (or 'prodigal father' as it might be more properly called) is a theological centre of the Gospel. The Samaritans, the widow of Naim, the lepers—all of them have a special place in the concern and affection of Luke's Christ. In this connection, it is especially noteworthy how Luke introduces us to a great number of feminine characters that we would otherwise not have known. Running through much of the gospel is the confrontation between the disciple of Christ and riches. Money is one of Luke's concerns, but perhaps not in the way that it has become a concern for so many of us. He does not resolve the problem of Christian poverty and the harsh realities of economic and business life, but he does raise the issues clearly.

Another of Luke's points of interest is the presence and activity of *the Holy Spirit.* Not only in the developing mission of the Church, but more especially in the ministry of Jesus himself, the Spirit is at work and the prophecy of Joel is being fulfilled. Coupled with this is his emphasis on *prayer:* its place in the life of Jesus himself is clearly pointed out to us; its corresponding place in the life of the disciple of Christ is likewise underlined. Convinced as he was that Christ had ushered in the messianic age, there is an element of *joy* running through the gospel of Luke in such a way that it becomes characteristic of all who encounter Christ.

Side by side with these themes, there are others that belong to the second part of his diptych. He insists on the fullness of *renunciation—* we are to carry our cross after Christ; but he goes a stage further, in that he says we are to carry our cross 'daily', and so his is the gospel of *perseverance.*

Running through everything, however, is a major idea—that of *reconciliation.* In Christ, God and man come together in such a way that we can perceive in God our loving Father. From the first encounters with people to the end of his earthly life (where he reconciles the repentant thief) Jesus comes across clearly as the One through whom men find their way back to their Father. And this goes for *everyone:* rich and poor, great and small, sinners and just, Jews and gentiles, men and women together.

The Gospel of Luke in the Ferial Lectionary. The period covered by the Gospel of Luke in the ferial Lectionary runs from Monday of Week 22 to Saturday of Week 34, i.e. the final thirteen weeks of the liturgical year.

From Monday 22 to Monday 26 inclusive, the Galilean Ministry is presented in considerable detail. From Tuesday 26 to Wednesday 33 inclusive, the Travel Narrative is presented in even greater detail. The sequence is completed by a selection of nine readings from the Jerusalem Ministry.

The presentation in this book is as follows: firstly, a summary delineates the situation of the readings for the entire week within the gospel as a whole; secondly, a list is given of Reading headings; thirdly, a theological and pastoral scenario draws out day-by-day implications.

Luke 4:16—6:5. Beginning with the 'programmatic episode' of the visit to Nazareth, where Jesus assumes the role of the Servant of the Lord, the ministry rapidly develops. At Capernaum, there are crowds and cures; the sick are healed and the demons are overcome. The mission of Jesus, however, is urgent, and he has to be on the move, preaching the Good News to all. At this point, he encounters Simon Peter who begins to recognise him; so much so, that he and the others who worked with him leave their previous way of life and become Jesus' disciples. After the call of Levi, Jesus is found with the sinners at table; to those who complain, he speaks of his coming as the messianic age, when people are expected to be joyful. This begins his controversies with the religious leaders.

Monday (4:16-30). *The Programme of Jesus' Ministry.*
Tuesday (4:31-37). *The Ministry gathers momentum.*
Wednesday (4:38-44). *The Gospel destined for everyone.*
Thursday (5:1-11). *The first disciples are called.*
Friday (5:33-39). *The beginning of controversy.*
Saturday (6:1-5). *Controversy gathers momentum.*

The theological riches of these passages are quite considerable. The programme which Jesus takes upon himself in the synagogue at Nazareth *(Monday)* is one of liberation. The 'freedom of the sons of God' is the gift of Christ; this is why the demons are so clear that Jesus has come to destroy them *(Tuesday)*. The short summary statements *(Wednesday)* enable us to identify Jesus for the first time: 'You are the Son of God', and this conviction is what drives Jesus forward to go to the other towns and villages. The miraculous draught of fish *(Thursday)* is only the prelude to something more important—the calling of the first disciples. Peter and James and John are destined to find that their lives will never be the same. It is typical of Luke's gospel that we should find Jesus at table with sinners and 'undesirables'; he defends himself, because his presence ushers in a new age when there will be mercy and forgiveness for all *(Friday)*. Obviously, such an attitude was bound to cause trouble; therefore, the controversy between Jesus and the religious leaders starts—he proclaims himself 'Lord of the Sabbath' and this again puts him in the position of defending his disciples and at the same time revealing the nature of true religion *(Saturday)*.

TWENTY-THIRD WEEK OF THE YEAR

FIRST READINGS, Year 1 (Colossians, 1 Timothy)

Monday (Col 1:24–2:3). *The sufferings of the apostle help the growth of the Church.* The difficulties endured by Paul help the Church to deepen and to grow. Christ has begun the redemptive process in time, but the kingdom (the rule of God) has still to come fully (cf. Phil 3:10). Paul has received from God the commission of preaching his plan of salvation to the gentiles. This has been fulfilled in Christ, who is their hope of glory. He has the words of eternal life which Paul teaches, often wearily, but always strengthened by him (cf. also 1 Cor 15:31, the 'daily death'). He struggles to maintain the truth in all the churches, even those he has never met. He wants to keep them together in love, and bring them to a full understanding of God's will.

Tuesday (2:6-15). *We have been saved from the effects of ours sins through the cross of Christ.* Paul encourages the Colossians to commit themselves totally to the Jesus in whom they believe. Their wisdom is Christ, and not any philosophy of this world. He represents the fulness of God, and gives us of this fulness. Our fulfilment will not be found in any other force. We are saved not through the small 'flesh-stripping' involved in circumcision, but rather through the complete 'flesh-giving' of Christ's death on the cross. Now we are united to the Risen Christ in baptism. All the debts owed by our sins have been wiped out through his triumphant death.

Wednesday (3:1-11). *The glory of our heavenly lives with Christ will be revealed when he comes again.* Our sights must be set on the heavenly, not the worldly, because we were baptised into our crucified Lord. We must kill all forms of self-centredness within us. We note especially covetousness, a worship of material things belonging to others, and which we want for ourselves. We reject the motto, 'Don't delay, grab today'. We must also control our speech, and as new creatures be open to every man for Christ is in us all.

Thursday (3:12-17). *The virtues of the Christian life give thanks to God.* We are set apart to serve God. All the attitudes here concern building up relationships; real mercy where there is suffering, a goodness that is kind about the feelings of others, a courageous stance without violence, a readiness to accept any situations whatever the provocation, a continuing forgiving, an absolute giving. The real tranquillity will be achieved. Peace: the fulness of God's promise (in its various aspects, spiritual, material, emotional, mental, physical) will be effected in others through us. All such living, in the power of Christ, says, 'Thanks be to God'. In this way the liturgical celebrations mentioned in verse 16 are brought into our daily lives.

Friday (1 Tim 1:1-2, 12-14, 15-17—*See pp. 118-119 for Introduction*). *Paul's apostolic credentials.* Paul uses the customary letter-opening formula of his day (X to Y, greetings!) but enriched with affectionate blessings, typical of early Christian writings: he wishes Timothy, his well-loved disciple, grace, mercy and peace. Both in the opening verse and in verses 12ff a primary concern is to establish Paul's credentials as an apostle of Christ by the direct will of God. If his letter is to strengthen Timothy's position as leader of the church at Ephesus, it must first be clear that Paul himself had been entrusted with apostolic mandate. Apart from actually affirming this mandate, Paul portrays himself as a living sign of the gospel message—namely, the forgiveness of sins. Hence his strong affirmation (v. 15) 'I am the foremost of sinners'; his forgivenss by Christ and subsequent zealous ministry were tangible evidence for the fundamental doctrine that 'Christ Jesus came into the world to save sinners'. The contrast between his former state (blaspheming, persecuting, etc.) and his present role in Christ's service is not substantially weakened by the mention of his previous 'ignorance' (v. 13); 'it only helps explain how this mercy was made possible—Paul ranges himself among those for whom Jesus prayed on Golgotha' (J. Jeremias). Profound awareness of mercy underlies all the spirit of pastoral responsibility which runs through this letter. As Aquinas noted, the apostle 'feels keenly in his own experience what he once was, under the law, and what he has become under the influence of grace'. A majestic thanksgiving-doxology (v. 17), which may have already existed in the early Christian liturgy, provides the perfect finale to this passage (notable is the emphasis on monotheism, and the rather metaphysical tone of the adjectives 'immortal', 'invisible').

Saturday (1:15-17). *Jesus Christ came into the world to save sinners.* Explained under yesterday's reading.

FIRST READINGS, Year 2 (1 Corinthians)

Monday (1 Cor 5:1-8). *The Christian community must purge itself of destructive elements.* In 5:1-8, Paul turns his attention to sexual morality. On this point, many of the Corinthians, influenced as they seem to have been by gnosticism, were libertines. A man was living with his father's wife (probably his step-mother, since Paul does not call the sin incest; the woman's husband was either dead or divorced, otherwise Paul would have spoken of adultery) and the Corinthians looked upon the situation with tolerance. They were, Paul rages, even arrogant about their liberal view of sexual morality. He therefore castigates (a) the man in question; (b) the Christians at Corinth for what he sees to be arrogance as well as immorality. Granted this justification of most commentators' defence of Paul's severity on this occasion, his words of condemnation nevertheless have a harsh ring. The fact is that Paul had a very narrow view of sexual morality, and the erection of this view into a norm for Christian hehaviour had, in my view, a stifling effect on the Church's understanding of sex down the centuries. Paul ends this passage by resorting to paschal imagery. The purpose of this is clear: the Christian sacrifice has been offered; Christians are participating in a feast which demands purity of character and conduct, therefore 'the leaven of malice and wickedness' must be (like the leaven used in the period before Passover) thrown out and replaced by unleavened loaves of sincerity and truth.

Tuesday (6:1-11). *Believers should solve their problems within the Christian community.* Paul now passes on to deal with yet another practical problem: public litigation among Christians. When this takes place, when disputes are not settled out of court, then, Paul claims, love has died, and Christians have ceased to be Christians.

Wednesday (7:25-31). *The values of Christian celibacy.* The reading from chapter seven is part of that section that deals with Christian perfection. Paul is here considering celibacy and marriage. He makes a case for both. He gives first of all *ascetical reasons for celibacy.* Then he proceeds to give an eschatological argument in its support. Celibacy in this world is a reminder of a world and life beyond where, to use Luke's phrases, 'they shall neither marry nor be married'. The latter argument is the more important in this entire passage. Life, Paul reminds us, must be seen in perspective, *sub specie aeternitatis.* Thus seen, it appears as something very brief indeed. It may well be, of course, that Paul expected the end of the world to be imminent. That may well explain his words: 'the time is short'. But even if this is no so, his argument still has force. The unfortunate thing is, of course, that the view expressed here by Paul can create a misunderstanding of the world, of time, of the present. If Paul is here addressing himself to one kind of dis-ease, namely living in exile *in* the present as if the present were the only moment of human time, we need to be aware of another kind of dis-ease, namely living in exile *from* the present 'as if the present were only a way-station on the road to the future, or were merely the repetition of life patterns established in the past' (Sam Keen, *To a Dancing God*).

Thursday (8:1-7, 11-13). *Rules on Christian freedom.* Yet another practical problem is dealt with in 8:1-7, 11-13, the problem of whether it is right for a Christian to eat meat that has been used in pagan sacrifice. Paul's solution of the problem is as practical as the problem itself. It is not wrong in itself, he teaches, for a Christian to eat such meat. Yet some people believe it is wrong. Therefore, lest such people be upset, it is better even for those who see no wrong in eating the meat to refrain from doing so! A practical solution, yes, but dangerous also. How often must more liberal and liberated members of a community have either to yield to the wishes of those of stricter views or have recourse to subterfuge to do what they know is for them is good and right? However, one cannot fault Paul's plea for consideration of the other person ('knowledge puffs up. but *love* builds up') which is, I think, the point he really underscores in this passage.

Friday (9:16-19, 22-27). *The dignity and demands of the apostolate.* Here Paul again talks about his call to the apostolate. This time he describes his apostolic calling as a destiny, a kind of pull which he could not resist. He is, as it were, enslaved by Fate, and he sees himself precisely as 'a slave to all men in order that I might win the more of them'. Here in this passage, we meet the well-known words of Paul: 'I have become all things to all men in order that at all events I might save some. . . to the Jews I became a Jew. . . to those who were outside the Law (i.e. of Moses) I became as if I were outside the Law, . . . to the weak I became weak.' Paul, as C. K. Barrett points out (*First Corinthians*, p. 214), can adopt his varying attitude—to the Jews as a Jew, to the gentiles as a gentile—because he recognises not a smaller but a greater debt to God than legalism implies. He is not related to God by legal observance, but by grace and faith, and in Christ, only; but precisely in this non-legal relationship, he is Christ's slave, who owes absolute obedience not to a code, but to Christ as a person, and to the absolute principle of universal love, which Christ both taught and exemplified. Paul now turns to the games, well-known in Corinth, for a metaphor for Christian living. Just as in the games, it is not enough to enter the arena, one must strive with all one's might towards victory, so too in Christian life, it is not enough to enter Christianity through baptism; one must try with all one's strength to keep on the right way. Paul's thought here comes very close to that of Matthew for whom 'fruits worthy of penance' are far more important than baptism or charismatic shouts of 'Lord, Lord'.

Saturday (10:14-22). *The Eucharist is the sign of the Church's unity.* Much of what follows in the remaining readings has to do with *unity.* 'The fact that there is only one loaf means that though there are many of us, we form a single body because we all have a share in this one loaf.' That is, as one loaf was broken and distributed, those who partake of the one loaf are in spite of their plurality, one body. This theme will be continued in next week's readings from the letter.

GOSPEL READINGS (Luke)

Luke 6:6-49. The whole of this week is taken up with Luke's 'Sermon on the Plain'. It has the same function as the Sermon on the Mount in Matthew's gospel—an original expression of the basic attitudes of Christian discipleship, a 'design for living'. It is typical of the gospel of Luke that it is prefaced by a night spent in prayer and the choice of the Twelve. The sermon itself is simple and at the same time profound; it ranges from the apparently outrageous sentiments of the beatitudes and the woes, which seem to turn human values upside down, to the demand that those who would follow Christ properly must take the word he speaks to heart and actually put it into practice. Here, we are to discover in a nutshell what it means to be a follower, to live the life of the kingdom of God. He gives us his gift of grace and then makes plain to us the way we should go.

Monday (6:6-11). *Controversy over healing.*
Tuesday (6:12-19). *Jesus prays and chooses his Twelve.*
Wednesday (6:20-26). *The Sermon on the Plain (1).*
Thursday (6:27-38). *The Sermon on the Plain (2).*
Friday (6:39-42). *The Sermon on the Plain (3).*
Saturday (6:43-49). *The Sermon on the Plain (4).*

Theologically, the Sermon on the Plain touches on many topics. The passages which introduce it are instructive: the healing of the man in the synagogue *(Monday)* again points us in the direction of a discovery of the nature of a true religion of the spirit. To make institutions more important than people is the ultimate betrayal of the will of God. The preparation of Jesus and his work is completed; his prayer is the prelude to another important stage in his life, and this we will note throughout the gospel *(Tuesday)*. The Twelve are named, and right away they are caught up in the hurly-burly of the public ministry; they are to share the life of Jesus to the full. When the Sermon on the Plain itself begins *(Wednesday)* the beatitudes spell out for us a series of seeming paradoxes which warn us that the following of Christ is not to be an easy effortless thing. What human nature takes as standard, Jesus rejects, and presents us with another set of values altogether. The great commandment of love is spelled out in such a way that all its scope and all its challenge emerges in a few short sentences *(Thursday)*. The important point for Luke is that all of this is merely the reflection of the mercy and love of God himself. The series of short parables with which the sermon ends are equally instructive: they lead us into the area of our relations with one another *(Friday)* and present us with two alternatives *(Saturday)*. Either we take Christ seriously and make his words the foundation of our lives, or we let all of it wash over us in such a way that our lives are not changed. The choice is 'make or break' for the whole of our spiritual relations with God.

TWENTY-FOURTH WEEK OF THE YEAR

FIRST READINGS, Year 1 (1 Timothy)

Monday (1 Tim 2:1-8). *The Christian community at prayer.* This chapter lays down instructions for good order within the liturgical assembly, and recalls the still earlier instructions given to the Corinthians for their prayer-meeting: 'all is to be done decently and in order; our God is not a God of confusion, but of peace' (1 Cor 14:40, 33). When compared with the rather free charismatic prayer-forms of the early Pauline communities, however, today's text marks a development towards more formal liturgical order. It designates the kinds of prayers that must be said (for all men, for kings and rulers, etc.), and the deportment to be observed by the believers during this prayer-meeting (hands upraised, no quarrelling; the women modestly adorned, etc.). One can detect here the end of the primitive epoch of 'enthusiasm', especially when chapters two and three are read together, and it is remembered that the care of the community is placed firmly in the hands of official ministers.

In commending such prayers by the assembly on behalf of all men, the author includes a profound reflection upon God's universal salvific will (vv. 3-6). Christians, willing what God wills, must desire that all men be saved and come to knowledge of the truth. The motive is reinforced with a reference to the one mediator, Christ Jesus 'who gave himself as a ransom for all' (v. 6—a phrase which evokes the Lord's own saying at Mk 10:45). Knowledge of God's truth is also linked with salvation in the concatenated text of Rom 10:13-15 (sending, preaching, hearing, believing, calling on the Lord's name) as well as in Col 1:7; 2:2, 7; Eph 1:9; 4:13 etc. Obviously what is meant is something more than speculative understanding, but an acknowledgment of truth that leads to conversion. He wills both Jew and gentile to attain this salvific knowledge (cf. Rom 3:29f); but Paul's specific role in this process is to be 'teacher of the gentiles in faith and truth'. Indeed, he characterises himself with a triple function: apostle, herald, teacher (v. 7; cf. 2 Tim 1:11), each denoting a distinct aspect of his ministry: the divine sending, the initial proclamation, and the subsequent detailed application of the message to particular communities and individuals.

Tuesday (3:1-13). *Personality outline for local church officials.* This section follows smoothly from the preceding; instructions on public worship lead on to the qualities required in the officials who must conduct it. It is significant that 'nowhere else in the New Testament do the church's office-bearers receive such detailed treatment as in the Pastorals' (J. N. D. Kelly). Yet, what our text describes are not the precise functions, but rather the personal qualities of these officials. While *episkope* (oversight, bishopric) is called a 'noble task', we can only infer something of what it involved from the kind of person thought fit to exercise it. He must be a steady family man, dignified and temperate, of good reputation, and not a recent convert. Clearly, he plays a twofold leadership role: first within the community itself, and then as its representative towards society at large. A somewhat similar personality outline is traced for deacons; again the emphasis is on dignity, moderation and reliability. In both cases mention is made of having their family in good order. The Pastoral author apparently considers the local Christian community as an extended household whose well-being requires wise and kindly discipline from a paterfamilias and his helpers.

Wednesday (3:14-16). *Christ, the heart of the Church.* Amid the many items of detailed paractical advice in the Pastorals, these verses glow with a particular brilliance, stating the profound nature of the community as 'household of God', 'church of the living God', founded on the mystery of the incarnate Christ, once lowly but now glorified. Though brief, this passage is 'the culminating doctrinal point of 1 Timothy, and the very key to the three Pastorals' (C. Spicq). A reference to Paul's delay introduces the passage, and provides a motive for reminding Timothy (and the other readers of the letter!) of the deepest realities of ecclesial life. The rhythmic scheme (3 sets of contrasting phrases, applied to Christ) in verse 16 is quite possibly a citation from a previous source—for example, from a hymn already in use at the liturgy. At any rate, its function at this point in the letter is to affirm the presence and power of the Lord, at the heart of the Church.

Thursday (4:12-16). *Duties of a pastor.* There is much useful material here on the authentic fulfilment of pastoral ministry. Paul exhorts Timothy—whom he as formally appointed to church leadership at Ephesus (taking 2 Tim 1:6 as a further specification of 1 Tim 4:14)—to earn the respect of the community by appropriate personal behaviour. It is not enough to proclaim the message to others, as his public role demands; he must also adhere faithfully to its spirit, in his own life, Both aspects coalesce in the phrase: 'Let nobody despise your youth' —Timothy would have been about thirty-five years old by then, if the letter comes from Paul; cf. Acts 16:1, referring to 49 AD. He must become a model for Christian imitation (cf. 2 Thes 3:9; Phil 3:17), in keeping with his public function: (liturgical) reading of the Scriptures, preaching the subsequent sermon, and giving catechetical instruction (probably outside of liturgy). Verses 15-16 continue this theme, linking Timothy's pastoral effectiveness with his personal fidelity as a Christian. Verse 14 adds his formal ordination as a particular motive for zealous ministry. Without detailing the various possible interpretations of this verse, we simply express our view: public installation to ministry came by a visible rite, whereby the elders (presbyters) imposed hands and prophetic words (of prayer) were spoken; Paul himself was the primary elder, in the ordination of Timothy (cf. 2 Tim 1:6); this rite either conferred or confirmed an effective ministerial charism, henceforth capable of constant exercise to the extent that it was not 'neglected' by the ordained minister.

Friday (6:2-12). *True and false riches.* In his deep concern for orthodoxy of belief, the Pastoral author allows himself some scathing attacks not only on the ideas, but on the character and motives of heretical teachers. They are 'swollen-headed', 'devoid of real knowledge' and estranged from the truth; indeed, their primary purpose is to make religion into a source of profit! This prompts him to an edifying reflection on true and false riches: religion really is a source of great profit, but only in a personal and spiritual sense, bringing inward contentment to the believer despite (or rather because of) the frugal simplicity of his lifestyle. The true 'man of God' pursues the authentic values of righteousness and eternal life, through the struggle of fidelity to his Christian (and ministerial) vocation.

Saturday (6:13-16). *This sacred trust.* Coming to the conclusion of this letter, Paul lays on Timothy a most solemn injunction to fulfil his ministry (that is the primary sense of 'keep the commandment', in context of all the preceding chapters). Apart from the actual verb used (*'paraggello*, a word of authoritative command as in 1:3), the importance of this trust is further underlined by the double formula 'in the presence of'. Reference to the 'good confession' of Christ before Pilate (cf. Jn 18:36f) offers an inspiring motive for courageous ministry; the motive of eschatological hope is added in the following verse (a similar use of *epiphaneia* for our Lord's second coming occurs in 2 Thes 2:8), and leads into an exultant doxology (vv. 15f) upon the omnipotence of God, and the majesty of his unfathomable being. Notice that while the doxology is a highly compressed reflection 'De Deo Uno', it is prefaced by the usual New Testament attribution of the title 'Kyrios' to Jesus. We are here quite close to the soteriological insight of Jn 1:18.

FIRST READINGS, Year 2 (1 Corinthians)

Monday, Tuesday, Wednesday (1 Cor 11:17-26, 33; 12:12-14, 27-31; 12:31–13:13). *Various aspects of the unity of the Church.* Disruption of this unity, splitting into factions, renders useless the very celebration of the Eucharist (11:17-26, 33) which, as a *mere* sacrament, with no reference to society and community, is in Paul's eyes, meaningless. 12:12-14, 27-31 comes back to the same theme; the Christian community is like a body, each member having its own part to play in making the body function as one loving whole. The community is made up of people with different gifts or charisms. Not everyone has the same gift. The one gift, the greatest of all, which is available to all, is *love* (12:31 – 13:13).

Thursday (15:1-11). *Christ has truly risen from the dead. Paul has seen the risen Saviour.* Paul introduces the resurrection of Christ here as a prelude to the teaching on the resurrection of Christians of which he is going to speak at some length.

Friday (15:12-20). *The resurrection of Christ is the basis and guarantee of the resurrection of Christians.* The Greek Corinthians found it difficult to believe in a resurrection of the body to new life. At Athens, Paul had been politely dismissed when he proclaimed the resurrection of Christ (Acts 17:31-32). Belief in both the resurrection of Christ and of his followers is central to Christian faith.

Saturday (15:35-37, 42-49). *Our risen bodies shall be like that of the risen Saviour.* If First Corinthians opened with a discourse on the cross, it ends with Paul's reflection on the meaning of the resurrection. 'If Christ has not been raised, then our preaching is useless and your believing is useless.' For Paul, as for John, the only guarantee of the rightness of one's faith is the person believed in. If that person is not living but dead, then indeed he cannot be the object of faith. The resurrection is not something which affected only Christ. Christ is really the *first-fruits* of resurrected mankind. What resurrection means for each Christian is the topic of the last reading from First Corinthians. Death means change. Resurrection means transformation. At the resurrection, Christians will exchange their natural bodies for spiritual bodies and become a race of heavenly men.

GOSPEL READINGS (Luke)

Luke 7:1–8:15. The direction of the Gospel to all men receives a tangible expression in the cure of the centurion's servant. This gentile manifests the faith and humility that Jesus seeks among his own people without finding it. The restoring of the widow of Naim's son to life is another manifestation of the great compassion of the Father revealed in his Son. Yet there are people who will not accept the love of God: the image of the children in the market-place sums up the problem of the hardness of the human heart. Jesus' attitude to the 'woman who was a

sinner' is in stark contrast to the way of thinking of those around him.
He detects the love that animates her action. The women who follow
Jesus are mentioned briefly, but they are an important part of Luke's
story—these are the people who will be at the foot of the cross. The
teaching in parables begins with the parable of the sower and its interpretation: a precious insight into the way Jesus sees his own mission
and its fruits.

Monday (7:1-10). *The Centurion's servant healed.*
Tuesday (7:11-17). *The widow of Naim.*
Wednesday (7:31-35). *Hardness of heart.*
Thursday (7:36-50). *The woman who loved much.*
Friday (8:1-3). *The woman who followed Jesus.*
Saturday (8:4-15). *The Parable of the Sower.*

When we consider the theology of these readings, then there are
several important points to be touched on.

The attitude of the centurion *(Monday)* is not recorded for its own
sake, but rather as an example for ourselves; Jesus is searching for faith
and for that openness that the centurion possessed. It is no wonder that
his words of humility have been immortalised in the liturgy itself,
because they are a model for all of us. The raising of the widow's son at
Naim *(Tuesday)* points to the great compassion of God, but it also
raises the question of recognition; there are those present who are able
to discern the real meaning of what they have witnessed—God has visited his people. Like so much of the miracle-tradition of the gospels,
therefore, this one is really a revelation of Jesus himself. The puzzlement expressed in the gospel over the harness of the human heart
(Wednesday) is something that brings us very close to the humanity of
the Son of God. There are those who will not accept God's way, no
matter what he does. They are anxious to have God in their own image
and likeness; they are anxious to have their own good recognised; they
are anxious to have others punished. For them mercy and forgiveness
and the closeness of God himself are unintelligible. The wonderful story
of the 'woman who was a sinner' is almost a paradigm of what Luke's
writing is all about. The difference in attitude between Jesus and his
host is too noticeable to pass without comment, the first loving and forgiving and the second hardened and judicial. Salvation comes to the
woman through her faith which she has had the courage to demonstrate
before the world. Thus we can see the reality of God's dealings with
humanity *(Thursday)*. The short passage which introduces the women

friends of Jesus *(Friday)* is instructive; they remained faithful to him in a way that was not matched by some others who might have been expected to stand by him. The parable of the sower is profound *(Saturday)*. It challenges us to rethink over and over again our own reactions to the word we have received.

TWENTY-FIFTH WEEK OF THE YEAR

FIRST READINGS, Year 1 (Ezra, Haggai, Zechariah)

For the next three weeks we have readings from the post-exilic period of Israel's history—in fact a happy blend of passage from the historical and prophetic books. (The pre-exilic history of Israel is given in the readings from Weeks 1-5 and 10-12 of Year 2; there are readings from the pre-exilic and early exilic prophets during Weeks 13-20 of Year 2. The readings from Deutero-Isaiah, i.e. Is 40—55, the major late exilic prophet occur during the Advent season.)

Monday (Ezra 1:1-6). *The temple is to be rebuilt and prophecy fulfilled.* Jerusalem and the temple were destroyed by the Babylonian armies and the real exile commenced in 587-86 BC. All now seemed lost; the covenant made with Moses and the promises to Abraham looked like things of the past. The prophet Jeremiah, however (Jer 25:11-12; 29:10), had reminded God's people that the supremacy of Babylon would last only seventy years (a round number). After this Israel would return to her homeland and to a glorious future. And in fact Bablyon was conquered by Cyrus king of Persia in 539. The following year Cyrus permitted—even exhorted—the exiles to return home and rebuild the temple. What seemed like a dream *(responsorial psalm)* had come to pass.

Tuesday (6:7-8, 12:14-20). *The new temple is completed and the passover celebrated.* The return in 538 BC was not as glorious as the prophets had predicted. The area occupied by the new Israel was no more than 25 miles by 20 or so, with a population of about 20,000. Too engrossed with affairs of ordinary living (Hag 1—2) and hampered by

Samaritan opposition the repatriated Jews had made little progress by 520. In that year the prophets Zechariah and Haggai spurred on the returned exiles and the building of the new temple was completed on 1 April, 515 BC. A new beginning was made and the passover solemnly celebrated. This 'second' temple stood for 585 years. It was remodelled by Herod the Great and destroyed by the Romans in 70 AD.

Wednesday (9:5-9). *Ezra makes confession of his people's sins.* Ezra actually lived much later than the rebuilding of the temple (probably around 398). In his day the problem confronting the religion of his people came from the pagan wives the returned exiles had married. It endangered the work of restoration begun with the rebuilding of the temple. Israel had been punished, indeed almost destroyed, for her sins in the past. This was in danger of occuring again. See further G. von Rad, *The Message of the Prophets* (Old Testament Theology, vol. II), London: SCM, 1968, pp. 247-257.

Thursday (Hag 1:1-8). *A prophetic exhortation to rebuild the temple.* Zerubbabel, grandson of the exiled king Jehoiachin (cf. 1 Chron 3:17; Mat 1:12) was civil administrator for the newly returned community. The religious administrator was Joshua the high priest. The date is August 520 BC. The glory of the Lord, sign of his presence in the temple of Solomon, would also reside in the new building.

Friday (Hag 1:15-2:9). *The messianic age is about to dawn.* This exhortation came two months after the preceding one—October 520, on the last day of the feast of Tabernacles. The building had only begun and it was obvious that the finished structure would fall far below the splendour of Solomon's building, destroyed sixty years previously. Some of those present would have seen this temple. In exile and later, Deutero-Isaiah and his disciples (Is 56:1-8; ch. 60) had prophesied concerning the new, glorious Jerusalem and Israel, and the advent of God's universal kingdom with Jerusalem as its centre. Present reality seemed to give the lie to this vision. Morale was at a low ebb. In today's reading the prophet Haggai tries to arouse the people's hope. The new temple would be glorious; the promises would be fulfilled. Haggai linked the advent of the messianic age with the completion of the temple. In actual fact, this was to come in the crucified and risen body of Christ, the true temple, and with the destruction of the material building then being erected. Not even Haggai could foresee the real manner of fulfilment.

Saturday (Zech 2:5-9, 14-15). *The Lord is the glory and protector of the new Jerusalem.* The edict of Cyrus permitted the rebuilding of the temple, not of the city's walls. A walled city would present a danger to Persian and Samaritan power and permission was granted to rebuild Jerusalem's walls only later with Nehemiah (ca. 445 BC). In today's reading the prophet Zechariah, Haggai's contemporary, tells Jerusalem that even the absence of walls has messianic significance: it symbolises divine protection and the extent of the new Israel.

FIRST READINGS, Year 2 (Proverbs, Ecclesiates)

INTRODUCTION TO THE BOOK OF PROVERBS

Proverbs is in the nature of an edited collection of lists of sayings which are easily recognisable as expressing thought and guidelines for everyday living. Their origin is ultimately the experience of man living in society. Every nation has its own maxims and wise sayings and Israel was certainly no exception to this rule. The Hebrews shared the common life experiences of the ancient Near East and it is not surprising that she shared and even borrowed the wisdom sayings of her neigbouring countries, notably Egypt and Mesopotamia. Israel's own tradition held Solomon as the archetype of the wise man. It is understandable therefore that a work like Proverbs should be attributed to him, even though the format of the present work very probably comes to us from the post-exilic era.

The period after the exile was a time when the Israelites, both in Palestine and Diaspora, became more aware of what they had in common with other nations. Created reality was thought about to a greater extent than heretofore. Where Israel had formerly dwelt on God's working in their history, she now concentrated to a greater degree on the goodness of God's creation and tried to detect the order and also the patterns which were apparently inherent in created beings, and especially in man's experience. Man's experience was seen as something good and useful. Therefore, the final editor of Proverbs brought together as he saw them the collected experiences of man and proposed them to the society of his day, adding his own specific contribution, especially in the first nine chapters of the book.

It is relatively easy to see the major divisions of Proverbs although the headings assigned to each section are of little value as regards the material covered. Nine sections are normally proposed when dividing the book:

I   Introduction: the value of Wisdom (1:1–9:18)
II First collection of proverbs attributed to Solomon (10:1–22:16)
III Sayings of the Wise (22:17–24:22)
IV Other sayings of the Wise (24:23-24)
V   Second collection attributed to Solomon (25:1–29:27)
VI The words of Agur (30:1-14)
VII Numerical proverbs (30:15-33)
VIII The words of Lemuel (31:1-9)
IX The ideal wife (31:10-31).

We will deal briefly with each section.

I. Introduction: The Value of Wisdom (1:1–9:18). The first seven
verses of chapter 1 which introduce the book are interesting because of
the terms used as synonyms for wisdom, words such as 'discipline',
'understanding', knowledge', 'sense', all showing that the concept of
wisdom defies exact definition.

Verse 8 opens the remainder of this section with the picture of a
father advising his son, or perhaps a teacher his pupil. The general
theme of these nine chapters is to urge man, especially the young to
value and try to attain wisdom. Specific to this section is what is called
the 'anthological style'. Briefly, the phrase means that the author describes wisdom on the same terms as the word of God, the spirit of God
and the activity of God are described in the earlier books of the Bible.
One example must suffice. Chapter 8:12-21 presents wisdom as introducing herself and claiming to possess in her own right all the gifts a
young man requires, for successful living and even ruling others. The
attributes of wisdom are the same as those which are found in the
description of the messianic king of Israel (Is 11:1-9). The personification of the term 'wisdom' used here and elsewhere in the book and
indeed through the wisdom literature is a difficult notion. It seems to
be a personified description of the wisdom of God, the quality which is
found in its fullness in the divinity and in which man participates and
shares but never to the extent that a human being can be described as
wise in the sense that God is wise. Opposed to wisdom is dame folly
who leads the young astray. Chapter 9 ends with a picture of her
seducing activity.

*II/V. First/Second collection of Proverbs attributed to Solomon (10:1–
22:16; 25:1–29:27).* These two sections may be treated together as
they are simply lists of proverbs concerning ordinary human living. In
content, they present reflection, a certain reserve, discretion as the
fundamental attitude. Self-mastery and some asceticism are necessary

for growth. In the concrete, man must attend to himself, e.g. in his habits of eating and drinking (20:1), in his avoidance of idleness (26:14). His relationships with friends and neighbours is also a constant challenge to him where he must steer a middle course between over-familiarity and constancy with good friends. Attitudes at home are of importance, too, where parents are exhorted to discipline growing children for their own good (13:24).

The meaning of most of these proverbs is reasonably clear. The motivation is at times no higher than success in life, but Israel's specific contribution here is that it places all this worldly wisdom within the framework of the 'fear of the Lord', i.e. religion.

III. Sayings of the Wise (22:17–24:22). This section shows a heavy dependence on Eygptian wisdom, specifically on a work called the Instruction of Amenemope. I consider that the most interesting point of this collection is the witness to the fact that Israel recognised the real values of people outside its own borders. It is tangible evidence of the high regard in which Egyptian wisdom was held by the Hebrews.

VI/VIII. Words of Agur (30:1-14) and Words of Lemuel (31:1-9). In these two sections, we again have some contribution from extra-Israelite sources. The main thrust of the argument here is the inaccessibility of wisdom for man because only the deity has wisdom in its entirety. Some of the sayings of Lemuel urge young men to beware of strong drink and women, and show concern for the poor. It is worth noting that here the position of women is limited by the society of the time and place, although elsewhere in Proverbs, woman is on a par with man, especially after childbirth.

VII. Numerical Proverbs (30:15-33). A collection of comparative experiences, probably for mnemonic purposes.

IX. Poem on Ideal Wife (31:10-31). An alphabetical poem, which means that each strophe begins with the appropriate Hebrew letter. The woman here is celebrated for her domestic virtues, her common sense and her dedication to her husband. The Old Testament scholar W. Eichrodt (*Theology of the Old Testament, vol. 2, p. 339),* sees this passage as extolling woman as a person in her own right. He says ". . . by attaching more importance to her piety than to her outward attractions, and thus basing marriage on agreement in the highest matter of all, he (the author), accords her the worth of a personality in the fullest sense. If nothing like this is to be found anywhere else in the wisdom of the ancient Near East, then credit can only go to the Jewish belief in the Creator God, before whom man and woman stand in equal responsibility.'

Further Reading: D. Kidner, *The Proverbs*, Tyndale OT Commentaries, London, 1964. R. N. Whybray, *Wisdom in Proverbs*, London, 1965. R. E. Murphy, *Seven Books of Wisdom*, Milwaukee, 1969, pp. 8-27.

INTRODUCTION TO THE BOOK OF QOHELETH (ECCLESIASTES)

From Luther's time, Qoheleth (Ecclesiastes) has been translated as 'The Preacher'. This is an effort to discover the meaning of the Hebrew 'qoheleth' and later of the Greek and Latin 'ecclesiastes'. It seems that no great significance need be attributed to this as the work falls generally into the wisdom tradition and is one of the most puzzling, if at the same time, most interesting works of the Bible.

Impossible to date and recognise the name and place of the author, the book is generally held to be from the period 400–200 BC. It has been attributed to Solomon in accordance with general wisdom practice.

Commentators have wrestled with the problem of finding a logical structure and development of thought in Qoheleth but have not succeeded to any great extent. The reason for this is probably that is there is no specific development but rather a circular pattern where the subject matter is treated in a circular manner, viz., the thoughts of the author are considered again and again as if he were thinking out loud. Alonso Schokel in *The Inspired Word* (p. 231), offers this key to understanding the work. While speaking of some modern literary figures as removed from society he goes to say that 'not even the author of Ecclesiastes. . . can be classified in this category; he is thinking out loud and challenging the secure routine of the reader.'

Briefly, then, Ecclesiastes reflects on life and what it has to offer and repeatedly concludes that all is vanity, i.e., lacking in the sense that nothing on earth brings happiness and fulfillment to man. The author has himself tried pleasure, riches, toil, even wisdom itself, and is forced to admit that ultimately none of these pursuits brings man what he desires. He grants that a certain happiness can be gained by eating, drinking and being content with his work (1:24; 3:13; 5:17) but man is longing for something more.

In the human heart, there is an innate longing for meaning, the meaning of all experience and all time. Man can feel a unifying plan inherent somewhere in the world, but apparently it is not possible for him to grasp it. This is expressed well in 3:11: 'But though he (God) has permitted man to consider time in its wholeness, man cannot comprehend the work of God from beginning to end.'

There is something greater than man's intelligence. It is here perhaps that Qoheleth is at his best. His notion of God is worthy of the divinity.

God is the only one who knows, who is wise, and is the one who freely gives to man. The verb 'to give' is predicated frequently of God. Like the author of Job, Qoheleth appreciates God even though he cannot fathom the many mysteries of life like the suffering of the just, the similarity of the end of man and beasts, in a word, the limitations of life. He is aware that man's efforts at acquiring wisdom for successful living is all too limited; in fact, death limits the aspirations of man. The belief in the after-life as it is acknowledged among Christians was not clear to Qoheleth and hence the book can be seen as an implicit longing for further revelation.

Qoheleth has been, at different times, described as a hedonist, an epicurean, a sceptic, even an atheist. But while there are thoughts expressed throughout the book which seem to give credence to these opinions, they fail to grasp the mind and heart of the author. I consider Qoheleth to be a man of faith who is aware of God and his mysterious designs, but who is not afraid to reflect on the deficiencies and the frustrations of man's search for meaning and ultimate happiness. In this he is one with whom modern man can easily identify.

Further Reading: Roland E. Murphy, 'Ecclesiastes (Qoheleth)' in *Jerome Biblical Commentary*, London: Chapman, 1968, pp. 534-540. Lionel Swain, 'The Message of Ecclesiastes' in *The Clergy Review*, November 1966, pp. 862-868. M. Strange, *Job, Qoheleth*, Old Testament Reading Guide, 27. Collegeville, Minnesota.

Monday (Prov 3:27-34). *Do not refuse kindness.* A passage urging correct attitude towards one's neighbour, exhorting people not to refuse help to others, not to pick quarrels and not to emulate the men of violence.

Tuesday (21:1-6, 10-13). *The Lord sees good and evil actions.* A short collection of proverbs from Section II of the book. The religious aspect of pleasing the Lord by one's righteous attititudes and conduct is very evident.

Wednesday (30:5-9). *Sufficient for living is our prayer.* The first section of this passage concerns the word of God while the second asks for sufficient of the world's benefits to live well—too much might lead to forgetting God, too little to dishonesty.

Thursday (Ecclesiastes 1:2-11). *Life goes on and on.* The book of Qoheleth opens with the author's experience of the never-ending recurring seasons, which bring man no full happiness. Is there not a longing for further revelation here? Is our own experience like this?

Friday (3:1-11). *A right time for the right action.* From nature it is clear that there is a season for everything, sowing and reaping, mourning and dancing. The wisdom authors of Israel thought it important to know the right time for acting or keeping quiet. God alone, however, knows the full purpose of the universe and the meaning of all history. He alone is wise.

Saturday (11:9—12:8). *Death is the end.* Another meditation of man's experience. The joys and efforts of youth do not last. Man's limitations are very evident. Christ however has told us Christians that we can look forward to life forever and in abundance.

GOSPEL READINGS (Luke)

Luke 8:16—9:45. The teaching of Jesus on discipleship takes on a new dimension when it becomes outward-looking; those who have encountered Christ are expected to share what they have gained with others. The true test of belonging to Jesus is not the tie of blood but the will of the Father—it is his rule of life and must be ours as well. This is reinforced by the commission given to the disciples when they are sent out in Jesus' name; like him, they are to preach the Good News. The initial response is an ambiguous one—Luke records that the stir made by Jesus and his work began to worry Herod. The king is forced to ask the question at the centre of the gospel: 'Who is this?' The Galilean Ministry has almost run its course—and Peter is able to answer the question; Jesus is 'the Christ of God'. As in all of the gospels, Peter's confession is followed by a prediction of the passion which begins the gradual revelation of the mystery of the Son of Man.

Monday (8:16-18). *The light of the world.*
Tuesday (8:19-21). *The will of God.*
Wednesday (9:1-6). *The Twelve sent out.*
Thursday (9:7-9). *Herod begins to fear.*
Friday (9:18-22). *The confession of Peter.*
Saturday (9:43-45). *Prediction of the passion.*

The theme of discipleship which has already been initiated by Luke takes on a new dimension *(Monday, Tuesday, Wednesday).* The fact that the follower of Christ is to be like the lamp to enlighten people who see it already points in the direction of a mission for those who would belong to Christ. The heart of their mission and activity is the will of the Father—just as Jesus' life was bound up with the fulfilment of that will, the life of the disciple is to be the same. His words concerning his mother and family indicate that there is a new, deeper, way of belonging to him that goes beyond ties of blood and relationship. When the Twelve are sent out in his name, they are given an urgent message. Theirs is to be a decisive mission; those who accept them will have passed up the opportunity of a lifetime. Herod's reaction *(Thursday)* is so like that of many of the people of Jesus' own time and our time too: genuine puzzlement. Just like those who are puzzled today, he remains anxious to see Jesus. The point of this is that the world has to see Jesus today in his Church, in his followers. The fact that Jesus is at prayer *(Friday)* is already a warning that something of the greatest importance is about to happen: Peter is about to give expression to the first real recognition of Jesus. The mystery of the Son of Man is only half-revealed in the acknowledgement of the 'Christ of God'. The way of the cross has to be revealed and it is difficult to understand. On the long way to Jerusalem, there will be time to unveil the real nature of Jesus' messiahship. In the meantime *(Saturday)* we are faced with the tantalising prospect of an end to Jesus' life that does not fit our own desires and ideas. The gospel is told so that we may understand the true nature of the Son of God, and take to heart the principle that as he has gone we must go too.

TWENTY-SIXTH WEEK OF THE YEAR

FIRST READINGS, Year 1 (Zechariah, Nehemiah, Baruch)

Monday (Zech 8:1-8). *The Lord is going to gather his scattered people together.* Zechariah preached during bad times; yet in the rebuilding of the temple he saw the dawning of a new age. It was a mighty work of God and had him raise his sights beyond present hardship to the certainty of fulfilment of the promises. There will be a new Jerusalem, the children of God will be again united from the four corners of the globe. Prophetic vision bouys us up in time of trial. God's promises will come true; they must come true because God is faithful.

Tuesday (8:20-23). *Pagan peoples will be converted to the true religion of the Lord.* The prophet's vision now passes beyond Israel to the conversion of the pagan nations; cf. Is 2:2; 1 Kings 8:43. A glorious prophetic vision from the trying years of 520 BC or so.

Wednesday (Neh 2:1-8). *Permission granted to rebuild Jerusalem and its walls.* The building of the temple was completed in 515. The city of Jerusalem itself, however, and its walls still lay in ruins. The returned exiles made an attempt to rebuild the city and walls during the reign of Artaxerxes I king of Persia (465-424), but on representations by the Persian governor of Samaria (who had jurisdiction over Judea) and others, the Persian authorities had the work stopped (cf. Ezra 4:7-23). Fortunately, the Jew Nehemiah had a high place in the court of Artaxerxes, and in 445 he got the earlier order reversed, and received permission to go to Jerusalem to have it rebuilt and walled. Nehemiah recounts this in his memories, portion of which is read today. The work of reconstruction is progressing.

Thursday (8:1-12). *Another new beginning. The Law of Moses is made central to Jewish life.* Ezra came from the Persian court during the period of Nehemiah, with the mission of bringing the Jews to learn the Law of Moses, i.e. the Pentateuch; cf. Ezra 7:25-26. Today's reading tells of the solemn reading of this law. With this Judaism is born, i.e. the form of Jewish religion centered on the Law of Moses. The interpretation of the law would continue right into New Testament times, and among the Jews down to our own time.

Friday (Bar 1:15-22). *Israel confesses its guilt.* The book of Baruch is composed of a prologue (1:1-14), a psalm of penitence (1:15—3:8), a praise of wisdom, identified with the law (3:9—4:4) and a discourse of exhortation and consolation (4:5—5:9). In the body of the work we thus have three distinct literary genres: a penitential psalm, a wisdom poem and a prophetic discourse. The three sections are united by a common theme: Israel in exile. She is punished because of her sins which she confesses (1:5—3:8), because she has abandoned divine wisdom, made manifest in the Law of Moses (3:9—4:4). A personified Jerusalem addresses a message of hope to her exiled children (4:5-29) and is in turn herself consoled by a prophet (4:30—5:9). The three sections may have originally existed separately. Baruch is a deuterocanonical work, not being part of the Hebrew Bible. Although attributed to Baruch, the prophet Jeremiah's secretary (late seventh century BC), it was composed much later, possibly in the second or first century BC. In today's reading we have portion of the psalm in which Israel confesses her guilt. She has merited the sufferings she is undergoing.

Saturday (Bar 4:5-12, 27-29). *Jerusalem consoles her exiled children.* Their exile is due to their sins, but God will still not forsake them. Jerusalem calls on the neighbouring nations not to exult over her present misery.

FIRST READINGS, Year 2 (Job)

INTRODUCTION TO THE BOOK OF JOB

The Book of Job is universally accepted as one of the great masterpieces of world literature. It was written as a poetic drama within the framework of an old folk tale about the hero, Job. Like other works of Israel's wisdom literature, the author, place and date of composition are unknown to us. Most commentators would place it somewhere between 600 and 300 BC, but it is to the work itself we must apply ourselves, to appreciate its beauty and significance.

Chapters 1—2 put before us the pious Job who has been gradually deprived of his possessions and children, and has finally been laid low by a loathsome disease. Job realises that God is in charge of the whole of the world's happenings and accepts the privations and sufferings meted out to him. The Lord has given, the Lord has taken away, blessed be the Lord, is the edifying attitude portrayed by him. Not even the taunting of his wife with her exhorting him to curse the God who treated him thus can shake Job from his patience and resignation which have become proverbial. The other half of this story is of course the activity of the Court of Heaven where Yahweh is seen as allowing Satan, one of his courtiers (not the Devil here), to test Job. 'Is he God-fearing for nothing?' Has his religious practice been in his own interest up to now? The irony of the situation is of course that Job knows nothing of the heavenly debate and its decisions.

The author of the books keeps this edifying story and uses it to present his dramatic portrayal of the innocent sufferer in dialogue with his friends. It is obvious that the Job who opens the poetry section in chapter 3 is not the resigned, patient and accepting man of the previous two chapters. In fact, it is in passionate revolt that Job utters his first soliloquy. He curses the day of his birth and wishes for death, which he sees as the only possible release from his pain. He ends the chapter by questioning: 'Why make this gift of light to a man who does not see his way, whom God baulks on every side?' (3:23). The chapter ends with the question 'Why?' and a cry of despair.

Chapter 4 opens with what appears to be a dialogue, but which becomes more and more a series of monologues. Job's friends have come to offer him sympathy and consolation (2:11) but in fact, fail to do this. The elder, Eliphaz, speaks first and gives Job his answer: You are suffering because of your sins, repent and confess your sins and perhaps God will forgive you and restore you to your former happiness. 'Can you recall a guiltless man that perished, or have you ever seen good men brought to nothing?' (4:7).

Both the Wisdom tradition and the Deuteronomist school held that God rewards the just and punishes the sinner in this life. While there is truth in this saying, there is also the danger that God is considered to act automatically in this manner and thus is not allowed to exercise his freedom in other ways. The freedom of God is taken from him. He is not allowed to have any other purpose for individual man except that of punishment and reward. It is clear that the author of Job is fighting against such a thesis and Job, the just one, is presented as the exception to this apparent rule. Each of the three friends expound the Deutero-nomic thesis and there is little development of thought as their speeches unfold.

Neither is there any great development in Job's thought. We see him rise and fall as he contemplates and muses on his sufferings and their cause. He is convinced of his innocence; so sin cannot have brought about his present state. He believes in a just God who controls the world, so he must be responsible. 'The arrows of Shaddai stick fast in me, my spirit absorbs their poison, God's terrors stand against me in array' (6:4).

It becomes clear now that while the subject matter of the book is certainly the suffering of the innocent, a second and probably more important question emerges, viz., the credibility of a just God. Job now experiences God in a different manner than heretofore. He still believes in the existence of the deity but feels that God is present, looking at Job, doing nothing and remaining dreadfully silent. There is no contact between Job and his God: 'There is no arbiter between us, to lay his hand on both, to stay his rod from me or keep away his daunting terrors' (9:33).

Job wants to encounter God but realises that God will always have the upper hand in any argument or lawsuit. 'Suppose I am in the right, what use in my defence? For he whom I must sue is judge as well' (9:15).

Job never completely loses faith in God, even though at times he comes close to despair. At other times, the author presents his hero as less disturbed and it is in a context such as this that Job can make his famous act of faith: 'This I know: that my Avenger lives, and he, the Last, will take his stand on earth' (19:25).

This passage opens in 19:23 and continues to the end of chapter 19. Unfortunately, the text of the passage is very difficult and apparently corrupt. Most commentators hold that Job is certainly placing his trust in God whom he describes as his redeemer, his avenger, his next-of-kin. They also see Job as confident that his name will be vindicated. It is the manner of vindication that is not clear. It would appear that personal happiness in the next life as a reward for virtue here has not yet become part of God's revelation so Job's restoration will have to take place in this world, either in the reinstatement of his good name after his death or after his present suffering.

It is only in chapter 38 that Yahweh gives Job his answer. In fact, when Yahweh speaks it is to ask a series of questions of his servant. Does Job know all the mysteries inherent in creation? 'Where were you when I laid the earth's foundations? Tell me, since you are so well-informed?' (38:4).

Struck by the powerful speeches of Yahweh, Yahweh Job is forced to acknowledge that God is all-powerful, self-sufficient and not responsible to man, that his ways are not Job's, nor his thoughts those of man. Job repents for 'holding forth on matters I cannot understand' (42:3). However, he has experienced something new. 'I knew you then only by hearsay; but now, having seen you with my own eyes, I retract all I have said' (42:5). Job's knowledge and appreciation of God have increased as a result of his sufferings. While he has been given no adequate explanation of the question of his suffering and the suffering of the innocent, nevertheless, his real appreciation and knowledge of God have increased.

The prose framework resumes in 42:7, when Job is rewarded by God for his fidelity despite his sufferings.

Mention should be made of the speeches of Elihu (32–37). It is very probable that these were added by a later hand. They bear the mark of a writer who was perhaps scandalised by Job's questionings and even apparent blasphemy. He proposes Elihu with his stress on the disciplinary value of suffering and some hints on the all-powerful God, but, by and large, his contribution adds little to the real drama of the original work.

The author of Job has presented us with a masterpiece which is perennially relevant. His appreciation of pain, especially the internal stuggle of the just man, of the freedom of the Godhead, of the rejection of any formula to completely describe the activity of God towards individual men show us how well he understood the human mind in its searching for an understanding of the mysterious ways of God.

Further Reading: R. A. F. McKenzie, 'Job' in *Jerome Biblical Commentary*, London, 1968, pp. 511-533. H. W. Robinson, *The Cross in the Old Testament*, London, 1955, pp. 9-54. M. Strange, *Job,Qoheleth*, Old Testament Reading Guide, 27, Collegeville, Minnesota.

Monday (Job 1:6-22). *Job accepts misfortune with patience.* Unaware of God's deciding to test him, Job reacts magnificently to the various misfortunes which befall him. He is prepared to serve God for his own sake.

Tuesday (3:1-3, 11-17, 20-23). *The questioning of Job.* Job gives vent to his feelings in his painful condition and asks why God should treat him thus. An honest declaration of how he feels.

Wednesday (9:1-12, 14-16). *Job's inability to force and answer from God.* The major part of this passage is taken up with a description of God's majesty as manifest in creation. It is this very greatness that overwhelms Job as he strives to understand his situation.

Thursday (19:21-27). *Job's act of faith.* Job begs his friends for sympathy and rises to his act of faith in God. Despite all his sufferings, he is able to declare that God is his redeemer, his closest ally, indeed, his next-of-kin.

Friday (38:1, 12-21; 40:3-5). *God's answer to Job.* Man has gradually to learn that he does not know all the mysteries of God's universe and allow God to be God. Job has learnt this lesson well.

Saturday (42:1-3, 5-6, 12-17). *The ultimate happiness of Job.* Job acknowledges that he has learnt to know God from his experience. God for his part rewards Job with happiness beyond that which he had lost.

GOSPEL READINGS (Luke)

Luke 9:46—10:24. The most difficult lesson of all is the centre of the Lord's teaching—to receive the kingdom of God it is necessary to have the simplicity of the child. *The Journey begins:* Jesus sets his face to go to Jerusalem where death and suffering await him, but also the glory of the resurrection and return to the Father. At the very outset, we are confronted with the idea of vocation—we are to follow on this road. To be with Christ is also to be responsible for others in his name; we are to carry his peace, his good news with us wherever we go. Those who reject this peace and this good news are faced with the prospect of having lost their opportunity to form part of God's kingdom. Our Lord turns in joy to his Father, because there are those who are simple enough to receive the message of the kingdom. Through Jesus they will come to the Father himself.

Monday (9:46-50. *True greatness.*
Tuesday (9:51-56). *The journey to Jerusalem begins.*
Wednesday (9:57-62). *Three vocations.*
Thursday (10:1-12). *The mission of the seventy-two.*
Friday (10:13-16). *Jesus identified with his followers.*
Saturday (10:17-24). *Jesus thanks his Father.*

The lesson spelt out for the disciples *(Monday)* is one that runs through the whole of the gospel tradition; we can take comfort from the fact that even towards the end, they never seem to have mastered it. Like ourselves, they found the simplicity of the child hard to accept; yet, they were none the less aware that it is necessary. With the beginning of the journey to Jerusalem *(Tuesday)* the gospel of Luke moves into a new key: we are to travel this journey together, Christ, the disciples, the evangelist and his readers. The story of the vocations at the very start of the journey is instructive—each one of the three episodes highlights a characteristic which is essential for the true follower of Christ *(Wednesday)*. Like those men, we are to be conscious of what we taken on, we have to be filled with the sense of urgency, and above all, we have to be persevering. Against this background the sending out of the seventy-two *(Thursday)* takes on a further importance—they are the first expression of something that Luke sees as essential to the life of the whole Church and of every Christian: the missionary spirit. The real foundation for this is in the identification between Christ and his disciples *(Friday)* and the ultimate identification between Christ and the Father. In a very real sense, therefore, those who bear the name of Jesus are brought into the very life of God himself. When they return full of joy and flished with success *(Saturday)* the reaction of the Lord is a caution; in the midst of our work for the kingdom, we have to be constantly assuring ourselves that our purposes and motives are correct. Then, we can be sure that the revelation of the Father which is the ultimate purpose of Christ himself will be ours.

TWENTY-SEVENTH WEEK OF THE YEAR

FIRST READINGS, Year 1 (Jonah, Malachi, Joel)

Monday (Jonah 1:1–2:1, 11). *The prophet Jonah seeks to run away from his mission.* Though classed among the prophets, the book of Jonah is really not a prophetical work. Rather is it a story with a message and this probably a development of Jer 18:7-9: if a nation against which the Lord had pronounced sentence (through a prophet) abandon its wickedness, the Lord will repent and pardon it. The work is not to be taken as recounting past history; nor should we be surprised at geographical or historical inaccuracies, or such grotesque elements as the great fish swallowing up Jonah. The work was probably composed after the exile, in the fifth century BC perhaps, although some would assign it to the sixth century BC. It appears to be directed against a narrow Jewish attitude which could not conceive of the God of Israel pardoning pagans, especially the detested oppressors of Israel (the king of Nineveh–a later capital of Assyria). Today's reading gives the well known story of Jonah being swallowed by a big fish. Tarshish was probably Tartessos in Spain, but for a Jew it denoted merely a distant city (like Timbuckto for us). Note how sympathetically the pagan sailors are presented. The most unlovable character is Jonah the Hebrew. The New Testament uses the figure of Jonah as a type of Christ, but interprets it in different ways; Mt 12:40; Lk 11:29, 32 (conversion of the Ninevites), Mt 12:40 (Jonah inside the great fish). The *responsorial psalm* (Jonah 2) is really a psalm of petition of a person in distress. The 'belly of Sheol', 'the abyss' are symbols for distress. The psalm was probably not originally part of the book of Jonah.

Tuesday (3:1-10). *God pardons the repentant pagan Ninevites.* Stress is laid on the genuine nature of the repentance. Even brute creation is obliged to participate. Other examples involving beasts in penitential rites are known from Persian, biblical, Irish and Breton sources.

Wednesday (4:1-11). *God's mercy and compassion are beyond comprehension.* This final chapter highlights the message of the book. The God of Israel proves too much for Jonah. He could not bear to see God show mercy towards the hated enemy of his people. By gentle irony God drives his message home. He caters for Jonah's sullen tantrums and expresses understanding for his pity for the withered plant. But if

Jonah can pity a plant, surely he creator is permitted to show concern
for animal creation and for the population of Nineveh. The book is a
preparation for the Gospel which shows that God's loving care extends
to all his creation.

Thursday (Malachi 3:13-20). *The Lord will reward the good and punish
the wicked.* We do not know who wrote the book that goes under the
name of Malachi. 'Malachi' in Hebrew means 'my messenger' and it was
apparently placed in the title (1:1) by an editor who seems to have
taken the occurrence of the same word in 3:1 as the author's name. The
work was written in the Persian period, some time after the construct-
ion of the second temple (515 BC) but apparently before Nehemiah
and Ezra (445 BC). The morale of the people was once more at a low
ebb; the enthusiasm which the return had generated seemed to have
died away. The small Jewish community was poor and losing their
wealth (2:11). Drought and locusts were ruining the agricultural
economy (3:10-11). Family life was disintegrating through divorce (2:
16) and adultery (3:5). The rich oppressed the poor (3:5) and dishonesty seemed the key to business success (3:15). It appeared that
God favoured the lawless and 'What's the use in trying' (1:13) was the
prevailing mood. In these tragic circumstances the priests were negligent
both with regard to sacrifice (1:8), tithes (3:8) and instruction (2:7-9).

    In today's reading God replies to those who seem to have lost heart
in the moral struggle because of the apparent futility of it all. It is the
'arrogant' (i.e. the proud, possibly those 'well in' with the priests) who
prosper. The prosperity of the wicked was an old problem in Israel.
God's reply now is that he himself, in 'the day of the Lord', will sift the
good from the wicked. The book does not tell us in what this judgement will consist. The author may have God's ordinary providence in
mind or he may be thinking of some very special divine intervention.

Friday (Joel 1:13-15; 2:1-2). *A penitential rite in time of national distress.* We know nothing of Joel, the author of this book, but we can
deduce from its evidence that he most probably wrote after the exile.
The occasion of his composition was the activity of a locust plague
which devastated the land. This he interprets as a divine visitation, the
'Day of the Lord', and calls on the people to repent (1:1–2:17). Joel
sees that the people's prayer is answered; the Lord will bless them (2:
18-27). This leads on to oracles of welfare for God's people in the days
to come: the outpouring of God's Spirit (3:1-5, 29-32), a final victory
over the pagan nations (4:1-14) the manifestation of the great Day of
the Lord (4[3]:15-17), and a glorious future for Israel (vv. 18-21).

Today's reading is a call to repentance during the plague of locusts.

Saturday (4:12-21). *God will destroy the enemies of his people.* The pagan nations are invited by God to advance against Jerusalem, but only to be destroyed before the city in the valley of Jehoshaphat—destroyed by Yahweh who resides in his holy temple. The theme is already found in Ezekiel 38–39; (cf. Zech 14) and is taken up in a new perspective in the Apocalypse of John (16:13ff; 14:19ff). After the destruction of her enemies a glorious future is predicted for Zion. It is apocalyptic imagery recurring from time to time from Ezekiel onwards and is applied to the enemies of the new people of God in the Apocalypse. The central message is the final triumph of God's cause.

FIRST READINGS, Year 2 (Galatians)

INTRODUCTION TO THE LETTER TO THE GALATIANS

The letter to the Galatians is the most impassioned of all Paul's letters. He is disconcerted that the Galatians—a Celtic people living in the north-central part of modern Turkey—had so quickly abandoned his teaching for 'another gospel'. Not only that, at the instigation of 'Judaisers' they had questioned Paul's authority, and said he was not really an apostle as he did not belong to the original twelve.

Paul vindicates himself by saying his mandate is from Christ himself (1:12), that he did not even bother going to the other apostles to authenticate his 'gospel', but that when they did hear about it, they gave it their full support.

However, his main contention is against the teaching of the Judaisers —who were advocating the observance of the Jewish Law as well as faith in Christ. Paul says that he who depends on the Law, cuts himself off from Christ (5:4). That is, not only is our faith in Christ (cf. Introduction to Romans) the source of our justification, it is also the only valid principle of Christian living. Only Christ—not the Law—can give us true freedom (5:1). It is not however freedom to do evil, but the freedom that comes from the Spirit (5:18-19). In Christ we are in fact a new creation (6:15).

Further Reading: Joseph A. Fitzmyer, 'Galatians' in *Jerome Biblical Commentary*, London: Chapman, 1968. Barnabas M. Ahern, *New Testament Reading Guide*, 7. Collegeville, Minnesota.

Monday (Gal 1:6-12). *The Good News is God's News.* Having briefly introduced himself and greeted the Galatians, Paul, in today's reading, expresses his amazement that they should have so quickly deserted the gospel. And, since his authority as an apostle had been questioned, his first concern is to re-establish this (chs 1—2): Paul's mission and gospel are not from any merely human agent, but from Christ himself (1:12). So anyone preaching a different gospel—even an angel—is to be 'accursed'.

Tuesday (1:13-24). *Paul uninfluenced by others.* In order to show that he is not merely a messenger of the other apostles—like Silas or Barnabas—Paul now asserts that he was uninfluenced by anyone (except Christ himself) before, during, or after this conversion. Before—because as a zealous Jew, he persecuted the Church; during—in that he had a personal revelation of Christ (1:16); and after—in that he did not consult the other apostles (1:17). Christ is his only mentor. Nor is he dispensing from legal observance just to curry favour with the Galatians (as some had claimed), but because that is an integral part of the gospel of Christ (1:10).

Wednesday (2:1-2, 7-14). *The other apostles accept Paul's teaching.* Far from finding fault with Paul, Peter and the other apostles accept his gospel without change. So Paul is an apostle by the same title as they are—he was called by Christ himself. That being settled, he now states his 'gospel': that we are not justified by works of the Law, but by faith in Jesus Christ (2:16). And paradoxically, this justification through faith is taught by the (Old) Law itself (chs 3—4).

Thursday (3:1-5). *By faith we receive the Spirit.* The Galatians did not receive the Spirit through observing the Law—as they well knew—but through their faith in Jesus Christ. If justification is through the Law, then Christ died in vain (2:21). By accepting circumcision, and so depending on their observance of the Law, the Galatians were *ipso facto* excluding dependence on Christ (5:4) which is the very kernal of the Gospel.

Friday (3:7-14). *Abraham was justified by his faith.* As in Romans (ch. 4) Paul here turns to the Old Testament—the Scriptures—and to Abraham in particular to show that justification is through faith—not works of Law (the Law only came later anyway—cf. 3:17). In fact he goes even further: 'all who rely on works of the Law are under a curse'—because they are of themselves unable to fulfil it. We must rely not on our own observances, but on God. Faith, according to Paul, is the absolutely necessary attitude on our relations with God.

Saturday (3:22-29). *The Law was only a temporary guide or guardian.*
The effect of the Law then, is to increase transgressions (3:19)—that
man, becoming more completely aware of his own inadequacy (cf.
Romans 7), learns to have faith in God. The Law was a guardian—a
pedagogue—leading us towards faith in Christ, 'for Christ is the end of
the Law' (Rom 10:4). He enables us to fulfil the Law through the Spirit
(Rom 5:5; 8:4), particularly by loving one another (Gal 5:13; Rom 13:
8-10).

GOSPEL READINGS (Luke)

Luke 10:25—11:28. The great parable of the good Samaritan makes a
start on the qualities that Jesus demands of those who would come
with on his journey—an all-embracing love is necessary. It is also really
necessary to have a clear perspective: the one that Mary had; while we
are caught up in many things we have to keep a clear head. Prayer is to
be the quality of life of the disciple, just as it features at the centre of
the life of Jesus himself. The Lord's Prayer is a pattern, and the essential
characteristic of the disciple's prayer is that it should be persevering.
The controversy stirred by Jesus' activity rages afresh: the facts are
there for all to see; in him we can recognise the work of God, if we have
the clarity of vision which such an insight demands. The praise of Mary
is wonderful—the same praise is ours by doing what she did: following
the will of God.

Monday (10:25-37). *The Good Samaritan.*
Tuesday (10:38-42). *Martha and Mary.*
Wednesday (11:1-4). *The Lord's Prayer.*
Thursday (11:5-13). *Perseverance in prayer.*
Friday (11:15-26). *Controversy over an exorcism.*
Saturday (11:27-28). *The will of God.*

The parable of the good Samaritan *(Monday)* depends for its full
effect on the context—it is the answer to a very specific question. Every
man is my neighbour; there are to be no exceptions. The Samaritan
grasped this with clarity while those who should have known better
were unable to see it. Jesus' disciple must share that clarity of vision.
This is what comes out even more clearly in the very happy domestic
scene with Martha and Mary *(Tuesday)*. There is no condemnation in
what Jesus says to Martha; it is simply that he praises Mary for having

grasped the important side of life as his follower. The clarity of vision he demands of us will enable us to see through our worries and concerns to the true direction of life. The version of the Lord's Prayer given by Luke *(Wednesday)* responds to a very specific question too—it is the request of the disciples to be taught how to pray that sparks off Luke's 'catechism on prayer'. The prayer of Jesus himself is followed *(Thursday)* by an equally important lesson: to be the true prayer of the disciple, our prayer has to be persevering and it has to be trusting. It is, therefore, essentially an expression of faith in the goodness and faithfulness of God the Father revealed in Jesus. The controversy concerning the casting out of demons *(Friday)* is an important one, in that it points to the true nature of Jesus' ministry. The work of God is to be discerned; once it has been clearly identified, then it demands total loyalty—to be with Jesus and never against him. The woman in the crowd gives expression to a lovely sentiment of praise for Jesus and for his mother; he does not reject the sentiment expressed *(Saturday)*. Rather, he makes it the starting-point for something even more profound—by doing the will of God like Jesus and Mary, we are made happy in the same way as they are happy.

TWENTY-EIGHTH WEEK OF THE YEAR

FIRST READINGS, Year 1 (Romans)

INTRODUCTION TO THE LETTER TO THE ROMANS

The letter to the Romans is permeated with St Paul's total love and commitment to the Father of mercies, who has sent his Son to redeem us from our sins, and restore us to the intimacy of his love. The main theme of the letter is nothing less than this divine plan for man's salvation—both gentile and Jew alike. For Paul salvation means eschatological or definitive salvation—the salvation of man, body and soul, in glory.

The first step towards this is justification through faith in Jesus Christ (chs 1–4)—man's reception into God's grace, for this is what justification means. The faith that Paul speaks of is of course biblical faith—a total personal commitment to Christ—a living faith which includes love and trust in Christ, as well as an acceptance of the truth of his revelation.

Through this justification we are reconciled to God, we are at peace with him (5:1). So sin—that malevolent power which came into the world at the beginning, and which Paul personalises in 5:12—that power has been overcome by Jesus Christ, and we are imbued with God's Spirit (5:5), enabling us to live and love as Christians. For this Spirit is an internal vital principle, guiding and inclining us to do God's will. In this sense the Spirit is contrasted with the Old Law, which is only an external guide, and does not deliver us from the power of sin (cf. chs 5–7).

However, the Law of the Spirit (8:2) does deliver us from sin—it frees us, as St Paul says 'from the Law of sin and death', so that we are no longer in a state of subservience to the Law, but are rather 'in-spired' to do the will of God, in which consists our happiness.

Further Reading: Joseph A Fitzmyer, 'Romans' in *Jerome Biblical Commentary*, London: Chapman, 1968. Barnabas M. Ahern, *New Testament Reading Guide*, 7. Collegeville, Minnesota.

Monday (Rom 1:1-7). *The writer and his message.* St Paul begins his letter to the Christians at Rome with this marvellous opening sentence (comprising seven verses in Greek!), in which he touches on the main themes of the letter as a whole. He introduces himself—a servant of Jesus Christ; his mission—apostle to the gentiles; his 'gospel'—about Jesus Christ, Messiah and Saviour, Son of God, Son of Man, risen from the dead, and promised in the Old Testament; condition of acceptance —the obedience of faith. Thus the opening is a kind of brief resume of the whole letter.

Tuesday (1:16-25). *Salvation for all who believe.* Paul now states (1:16) the main theme of the letter: the Gospel is 'the power of God saving all who have faith', both Jews and Greeks (cf. chs 5–11). But first, he develops the theme of chapters 1–4: 'the just man lives by faith' (1:17). And he begins by showing that without this faith all mankind languishes in sin—both gentile (1:18-32), and Jew (2:1–3:20).

Wednesday (2:1-11). *Even the Jews have fallen.* In the previous section Paul showed the depravity of the gentile world (arguments the Jews were familiar with—cf. Wis 12:23—14:31—and with which they whole-heartedly agreed); now he turns his attention to the Jews themselves. Taking each of their privileges separately (Election, 2:1-11; the Law, 2:12-24; Circumcision, 2:25-29; the Promises, 3:1-8), he shows that far from being a blessing to the Jews, these have only served to increase their responsibility and guilt (2:24), because they did not live up to them.

Thursday (3:21-30). *God's justice is revealed in Christ.* For Paul, and the Old Testament in general, God's justice or righteousness (*sedeq* in Hebrew), means his salvific justice—i.e. his faithfulness to his promises to save his people. This justice (corresponding perhaps, more to our idea of mercy than of justice), is revealed in Jesus Christ. God sent Christ as an expiation for our sins, and the sins of all mankind (3:25), and those who have faith in him—a living faith involving a total personal commitment to him (cf. Introduction)—are justified, are reconciled to God; they are at peace with God (5:1).

Friday (4:1-8). *Abraham's faith.* Many people will be surprised at Paul bringing in Abraham at this stage. After all, he has been talking about faith in Jesus Christ, so what is the sense of going back to the Old Testament? However, his point is that the attitude of faith required of Christians is exactly the attitude required of Abraham—total trust and commitment to God. Obviously, God has revealed himself much more completely in the New Testament, but the basic response required is the same—faith.

Saturday (4:13, 16-18). *Abraham's children.* Abraham's faith that he would be the 'father of many nations' had no natural basis, since he was a hundred years old (Gen 17:17). He trusted in God—who is able to do what he promises (4:21). Consequently, the true children of Abraham are those who, like him, trust in God, not those he had by natural descent. This seems rather to exclude the Jewish people, but Paul comes back to this theme in chapters 9—11.

FIRST READINGS, Year 2 (Galatians, Ephesians)

INTRODUCTION TO THE LETTER TO THE EPHESIANS

This letter lacks the more personal touches of its companion letter to the Colossians. It would seem to have been a theological development of the latter. The author can now move from the more polemic atmosphere of an insistence on the unique redemptive role of Christ to an analysis of the unity of the Church and its universality. Controversy on its Pauline authorship has been with us a long time. Perhaps, the usually adduced differences in language and style can be explained in terms of a secretary given a freedom of writing, while keeping Paul's more developed thought after Colossians in view.

The theology is markedly trinitarian. The Father redeems us through Jesus, whose saving work we receive in the Spirit. The writing falls clearly into two divisions in which the first three chapters are of a prayerful and doctrinal nature, and the last three are clearly exhortatory. It is a statement about a Church in which all divisions have been broken down, and which expects a moral and unifying way of life from its people. A three-fold imagery expresses the nature of that community, that of head-body, of cornerstone-temple, and of husband-wife. A considerable similarity of thought with First Peter has often been noted.

Monday (Gal 4:22-24, 26-27, 31–5:1). *Born to be free.* Abraham's two sons are typical of the Jewish and Christian communities. The Galatians must expect persectuion from those who are not 'of the Spirit', just as Abraham's son Ismael, born according the the flesh, persecuted Isaac, born according to the Spirit; the elder, born of a slave-woman, persecuted the younger, because he was free, born of a free woman. So the Christians of Galatia—born to be free, must not be surprised if they are persecuted by the Jews (cf. the elder son in Luke 15).

Tuesday (5:1-6). *Christ has set us free.* Chapters 5–6 are an exhortation to the Galatians to exercise their new-found freedom wisely. The must not return to legal observances—particularly circumcision, as that would exclude dependence on Christ. Their freedom is a freedom in the Spirit, particularly the freedom to love—which is the fulfillment (*pleroma*) of the Law. '. . . through love be servants of one another' (5:13).

Wednesday (5:18-25). *Walk in the Spirit.* The Spirit is the source of all Christian life; let us then live our lives according to the Spirit, not according to the flesh. These two are opposed and antagonistic to one another—the 'flesh' being man insofar as he is weak and prone to sin, deprived of God's help, whereas the 'Spirit' means man as subject to and guided by the Holy Spirit—i.e. a new creature (6:15; 2 Cor 3:17-18).

Thursday (Eph 1:1, 3-10). *Thanks be to God who has chosen us in Christ from all eternity to serve him.* We have received the gift of the Father to become brothers in Christ (we should not neglect to mention also our sisters!). We praise the glory of such a generous God. We have been freed by sin through his blood. We know his saving plan which he initiated in Christ from the beginning to the end of this world, that in due course he would bring everything in heaven and earth under the headship of Christ. The cosmic dimension of Christ characterises this letter.

Friday (1:11-14). *We, the Gentiles, have now also been called as God's chosen people.* All choice lies in the eternal will of God. The Jewish people were first chosen to praise him in their worship, to serve him in their work, and to act as his sign before the nations. Their hope in a Christ has now been fulfilled in us who have believed in his Son, and been sealed through baptism by the Holy Spirit. This is a pledge of our eternal salvation, and the truth we have received gives us the freedom to praise the glory of God.

Saturday (1:15-23). *A prayer for the readers that they may understand their redemptive calling ever more clearly.* As in Colossians, our author thanks God for the belief and love displayed by this community, and continues to make intercession for them. He makes his prayer that they may come to a fuller knowledge of the meaning of their hope, and an understanding of his power which especially raised Christ triumphant over the dead and superior to every other being. Christ is the head of the Church, which shows forth to all creation the fulness of his exaltation.

GOSPEL READINGS (Luke)

Luke 11:29–12:12. As Jesus' journey gathered momentum, the crowds once more came round. At times he had for them words of comfort and light; at other times, he corrected their errors. The search for a sign was one of his main targets. But even that did not arouse his ire as hypocrisy did. That is why he took the Pharisees and the lawyers to task; the search for sincerity and honesty in religion is one of the themes of the gospel. Jesus flayed without mercy those who used their position of trust among the people for their own advantage, and those who misrepresented the will of his Father. It is no wonder that these people were furious with him and ultimately came to the point where they plotted his death. The defence of the common people, however, was of supreme importance to Jesus. Those who follow Jesus will encounter the same opposition as he did; then they will really experience the strength of the Holy Spirit.

Monday (11:29-32). *The sign of Jonah.*
Tuesday (11:37-41). *Condemnation of the Pharisees (1).*
Wednesday (11:42-46). *Condemnation of the Pharisees (2).*
Thursday (11:47-54). *Condemnation of the Lawyers.*
Friday (12:1-7). *The Father's providence.*
Saturday (12:8-12). *The Spirit's guidance.*

The demand for a sign which Jesus so roundly condemned *(Monday)* was a particularly deep attack on himself and on his mission. Ultimately, it expresses a lack of faith; it wants God to respond to our ways of thinking, and in a certain sense wants him to force us into an assent that we cannot refuse. That is not his way with us, and that is why Jesus so steadfastly refused to consider it. The sign which is given is Jesus himself—an he is the object of our faith. The attack on the Pharisees and the lawyers *(Tuesday, Wednesday, Thursday)* is both extensive and comprehensive. It points to this kind of controversy as typical of the ministry of Jesus; time and time again, there was a head-on collision between Jesus and the religious leaders of his time. The essence of the controversy was this: the sincerity of the religion which was being practised and being advised for the people of Israel. The problem was an ancient one: the prophets had had to face up to it themselves. Nor is it only a problem of the past; it is something that affects the life of the Church every bit as much as it affected the life of Israel in Jesus' time. Jesus himself is the very embodiment of that direction of the true religion which searches for the heart of man. After this outburst, Jesus sets about getting the lesson through to his own disciples *(Friday)*. On the one hand, they must expect to run up against the same kind of opposition as Jesus did; on the other hand, they are to be as fearless as their Master. Hence, they are to have complete trust in God their Father. When that occasion arises *(Saturday)* they will experience the power and guidance of the Holy Spirit. Witnessing to Christ can be a dangerous business; but it is also attended with the consoling presence of God's Spirit for our comfort and strength.

TWENTY-NINTH WEEK OF THE YEAR

FIRST READINGS, Year 1 (Romans)

Monday (Rom 4:20-25). *We must believe in him who raised Jesus from the dead.* Abraham's unhesitating faith in God's promise is an example for all Christians. We must likewise have faith in him who raised Jesus from the dead.

In these first four chapters Paul has been speaking about justification or reconciliation with God; from chapter 5 onwards he begins to speak about salvation—i.e. final salvation, including the resurrection of the body. This for Christians is still in the future (5:9, 10), whereas justification is already achieved by faith (justified, 5:1, 9; reconciled, 5:10). So justification is the first step on the road to salvation (5:6-11).

Tuesday (5:12, 15, 17-21). *The victory of Christ.* The Christian experience of reconciliation means that we have peace with God (5:1), have access to him (5:2), and that his love has been poured into our hearts by the Holy Spirit (5:5). This has been accomplished for us by Jesus Christ (5:1, 11). And this means, concludes Paul (5:12—'therefore'), that the relentless and all-pervading power of sin has finally been broken—by one man—Jesus Christ (5:15, 17, 21). Where sin once reigned, grace is now superabundant (5:20).

Wednesday (6:12-18). *True freedom means serving God.* The fact that Christ has conquered the power of sin does not mean we can sit back and do nothing—or worse, even continue to sin. As free creatures our salvation depends also on our free co-operation. God won't force us. We must use our new-found freedom to become servants of God (6:18, 22).

Thursday (6:19-23). *Eternal life is a free gift.* The wages of sin, on the other hand, is death. Eternal death. Sin is a gradual and ever-increasing share in death, a gradual separating of oneself from God. But justification, or sanctification, leads on to eternal life, or rather, is already a beginning of eternal life (cf. Jn 3:36—'He who believes in the Son *has* eternal life').

Friday (7:18-25). *Without the Spirit, man cannot do God's will.* In chapter 7 Paul takes on the thorny question of law. The Jews placed all their hopes of salvation on observance of the Law. For them it was one of God's greatest gifts—an instruction, a teaching, an expression of his will. Paul has already pointed out that they did not observe it (2:1-24); here he says that, although good in itself, all it served to do was to make man more conscious of his sinfulness—of his inability to fulfil God's will as expressed by law. This dilemma is highlighted in today's reading—a man knowing what to do, wanting to do it, and being unable to do so on account of the 'power of sin dwelling within him' (7:17, 20, 23). He will solve this dilemma in chapter 8 by introducing the Holy Spirit.

Saturday (8:1-11). *The Spirit gives life.* The Holy Spirit in Pauline theology is the key to all Christian living. Paul has already mentioned the Spirit in passing in 5:5; here he takes up the theme again, and shows the Spirit as God's gift to those who believe in Christ—so that the purpose of the Law is fulfilled in them (8:4; 13:10). They have life and peace, provided they live in the Spirit. He is the basis of Christian hope (5:5; 8:11).

FIRST READINGS, Year 2 (Ephesians)

Monday (Eph 2:1-10). *We who were dead through our sins have been raised to new life by the gift of God in Christ Jesus.* We are all of us human beings, and there are forces at work within us, and outside of us, which would keep us in a state of estrangement from God. The apostle insists again and again that our salvation is a free gift of God in Christ Jesus. We deserve nothing of ourselves. All we can do is to respond to him in faith by living a worth-while life (cf. 2 Cor 5:16-21, the new creation passage). We may read the Fourth Common Preface in the Roman Missal, 'It is only by your gift to us that we can give you thanks, and thereby prepare ourselves for salvation which comes to us through Christ who is our Lord'. Any movement towards good on our part is due to the favour of God.

Tuesday (2:12-22). *Jew and gentiles have been reconciled to God, and with one another, through the peace achieved by the blood of Christ.* Paul recalls the former state of the gentiles outside of Israel's privilege, worldly, despairing, without the real God. Christ has broken down the barrier-wall (probably a reference to that which separated the Court of the Jews from the gentiles in the temple area). The 'curse of the Law' (cf. Gal 3:1-3) can no longer provoke hostility. Both Jews and gentiles can find their way to the Father in the one Spirit. We are all part of a building founded on the New Testament apostles and prophets, always held together by Christ. We all of us make up the Church, the new temple of God.

Wednesday (3:2-12). *The apostle's task of proclaiming the saving design of God, fulfilled in the Church.* Paul understood the meaning of the Church in his Damascus road experience. We all receive the promise through listening to the message of salvation spoken by chosen preachers, of whom Paul is one (cf. also his humble reference to himself in 1 Cor 15:9). God's saving plan in Christ Jesus, now complete in the Church, and in which Paul believes, gives him great confidence. We might note the omission of verse 13 on the trials of the apostle (cf. Phil 3:10 and Col 1:24). These lead to glory.

Thursday (3:14-21). *The writer gives glory to God whose power at work in us can do wonderful things.* The Father causes all families to exist. He prays that through God's Spirit, in the words of the mystic 'we may know Christ more clearly, love him more dearly, follow him more nearly'. Christ's love for us will reach its fulness with the coming of the kingdom. In the meantime, we continue in each generation of the Church's existence to give glory to him whose power achieves so much in us.

Friday (4:1-6). *The apostle, from prison, appeals to Christians that, united in the Spirit, they should live harmoniously.* The unity achieved with the Father through Christ in the Spirit must be shown in real Christian love, which involves total gift. There is no place for selfishness, domineering, or angry reaction even to stupidity. The basis for our unity lies in a common Father, Lord, Spirit, faith, baptism, hope, and body. We should respond to the one Father who permeates the whole community with his peacefulness.

Saturday (4:7-16). *Each one of us receives his own gift to serve the Lord, and build up his body.* The descent of the Christ even unto death means that he is now exalted, and can bestow gifts on us. We recall paragraphs 40 and 41 of the Dogmatic Constitution on the Church: 'Each one according to his own gifts and duties must steadfastly advance along the way of a living faith, which arouses hope, and works through love'. A special emphasis is laid on the various calls to teach which leads to the maturing of the chosen people. It protects them also against false doctrine.

GOSPEL READINGS (Luke)

Luke 12:13–13:9. Another typical situation of the journey to Jerusalem arises: people ask Jesus to decide their problems for them. These occasions are turned to advantage for the revealing of the message. Servants of a Master who has confided his goods to us—that is what we are and we must never forget it; we must serve him all the time and be on our guard. This goes for those who are closest to Jesus in a special sense: the more we have given to us by him, the more our responsibili-

ties to the kingdom of God grow. This means that there will be tensions;
there will be division, for the reason that Jesus demands nothing less
than total allegiance. Hence, there is a note of stern warning running
through much of what the Lord has to say to us in these instructions.
The crowds at large are not spared either—they are warned that repentance is their only means of being prepared for what might befall.

Monday (12:13-21). *The danger of money (1).*
Tuesday (12:35-38). *Being prepared.*
Wednesday (12:39-48). *Making the best use of God's gifts.*
Thursday (12:49-53). *Not peace but division.*
Friday (12:54-59). *The signs of the times.*
Saturday (13:1-9). *Repentance.*

The question posed by the man in the crowd *(Monday)* becomes,
like everything else that Jesus encounters on this journey, an occasion
for revealing the true nature of man's relations with God. To make
ourselves rich in the sight of God: this is the first task which is set
before us—nothing else matters by comparison with that. The fact that
we are all stewards of what God has entrusted to us *(Tuesday)* is a
reminder that there is a judgment and a reckoning that we all have to
prepare for; to be ready, that is the aim. We might be very sympathetic
with Peter's question *(Wednesday)* and ask whether all of this is directed to ourselves or to everyone. Like so much of what we find in the
gospel, there is no direct answer; but we are given to understand that
the important thing is to take what Jesus says to heart, and to let others
do the same for themselves. We might reflect on how much has been
given to us and what will be demanded in return. The fact that Jesus
has come to bring division *(Thursday)* is really a fact of life: maybe the
division is not between ourselves and those we love, but it may well be
that there is a constant tension between our own will and the following
of Christ. This is something that Luke is keen to make clear to us. The
ability to read the signs of the times *(Friday)* is something that is
important in everyday living; it is even more important in the spiritual
life, Jesus tells us. The basic sign we have to interpret is Jesus himself;
to recognise in him the revelation of the Father can colour the whole of
our lives, and it should do so. The stern warning about repentance
(Saturday) brings us face to face with a basic demand of the Gospel—it
had been announced by John the Baptist; Jesus carried the message
further, and expressed it even more clearly. Yet, even in this stern
passage, we find him giving us an image of the kindness and forbearance
of God.

THIRTIETH WEEK OF THE YEAR

FIRST READINGS, Year 1 (Romans)

Monday (Rom 8:12-17). *Children of God.* Another reason for Christian hope is the fact that God has made us his children. The Spirit bears witness to our spirit that this is so. He enables us to use the personal prayer of Jesus himself as recorded in the gospels: 'Abba—Father'. This is a very intimate way of speaking to God and was not previously used by the Jews in their prayers. It is *the* Christian prayer (cf. J. Jeremias, *The Prayers of Jesus*, London: SCM).

Tuesday (8:18-25). *Expectation of glory.* For Paul salvation means eschatological or final salvation—i.e. including the glorification of our bodies (8:23). In today's reading he pictures the whole of creation eagerly ('craning their necks'), awaiting the glorious revealing of the sons of God. Like the first creation (Gen 1 & 2), this is not confined to man, but redounds to the glory of all the creation originally entrusted to man (Gen 2:15, 19-20). But not only the creation awaits it—we ourselves groan inwardly as we wait in hope.

Wednesday (8:26-30). *God turns everything to our good.* Besides our yearnings, and the yearnings of all creation, the Spirit also intercedes for us, and strengthens our weakness. And finally, God himself, through his love, had ordained that we be conformed to the image of his beloved Son (who also intercedes for us—8:34), so that he is the first-born or fore-runner of those destined for glory. So our hope, even if unseen (8:25), is nevertheless secure.

Thursday (8:31-39). *God's love accomplishes our salvation.* Having listed all the different grounds of our hope as Christians, Paul now comes, in this last section of chapter 8, to the ultimate cause of all our good: God's love for us as manifested in Jesus Christ. Our salvation, and indeed, every good we have or hope for, rests with his love. Just as, in the first part of the letter (chs 1—4), our justification manifested God's salvific justice, so now, our salvation depends on God's love for us. For our sakes he did not spare his own Son, but gave him up for us all. Since this is so, nothing, nothing at all, can separate us from the love of God in Christ Jesus.

Friday (9:1-5). *Paul's love for his own people.* Paul now expresses his concern over the lot of his own people, the Israelites. With the confluence of the gentiles to Christ, they seem to have been left out, rejected. In the next three chapters 9–11, Paul struggles with this problem. He points out that God ordains history for the good of all; that the Israelites' loss is the gentiles' gain; that this state of affairs had already been predicted in the Old Testament.

Saturday (11:1-2, 11-12, 25-29). *Israel will finally be saved.* Paul is talking of course about Israel's status as 'people of God'—not about their salvation. God has by no means rejected them—their fall from favour is but partial and temporary. When the full number of gentiles have 'come in', then *all* Israel will be saved (11:26).

FIRST READINGS, Year 2 (Ephesians, Philippians)

INTRODUCTION TO THE LETTER TO THE PHILIPPIANS

The beginnings of the Christian Way at Philippi, 'the leading city of the district of Macedonia and a Roman colony' are recounted in Acts 16:17-40. The community had sent financial aid to Paul while in prison (at Rome? cf. my commentary in NCCHS), and his reply to their sharing with him (the *koinonia*) is full of good things about the Christian life. We shall look on the epistle as a whole piece though the abrasiveness about the judaizing faction would seem to be out of harmony with the joyful and serene atmosphere of the rest of the letter and might belong to an earlier period. Of course, it could equally be said that there was still a 'bark left in the old man' as he awaited possible death.

The 'self-emptying' (*kenosis*) of Christ Jesus (2:5-11) has a parallel in Paul (3:5-10), and in those who follow his rule of life. We have been united with his passion and death, so we share in his new life (expounded with fuller emphasis in the other captivity epistles of Col 2:6-13, 3: 3-11, Eph 2:1-10; 3:14-19; 4:15-16, 22-23). As a result we hope to attain our heavenly homeland.

We note the key-ideas of partnership and joyfulness running through the entire letter (characteristics of Luke-Acts, whose author remained in the newly founded community until Paul's return in Acts 20:6).

Monday (Eph 4:32–5:8). *We are called upon to forgive one another, and behave with respect towards one another.* All of our loving follows the example of Christ who gave himself for us. While it is true that, as St Benedict says, 'let nothing be given a higher priority than the public worship of God', this must be followed through by a life good in both word and work. Our lives should be hymns of thanksgiving to God, our Father, rather than chants of idolatry as a result of promiscuity. The light-darkness imagery is found not only in the Johannine writings, but also in the Dead Sea Scrolls.

Tuesday (5:21-33). *The relationship between husband and wife should mirror the sacrificial love of Christ for his Church.* We note that a Eucharistic section precedes this passage followed by our first verse on mutual 'giving-away' in obedience to Christ. The service of one another, the give and take, builds up Christ. In the order of that day the wife was legally subject, but for Christians such an authority was given for service as Christ loved the Church even to giving up his life for her. The union of the married partners builds up the Church, images the love of Christ for his Church, causes their love to flourish, and makes Christ present to the other partner, and to every other person as a result.

Wednesday (6:1-9). *A plea for domestic harmony based on obedience to the Lord.* In this continuing 'house-table' statement, the call for obedient children and encouraging parents would still be reasonably acceptable. We notice that the secular structure of slavery is taken for granted, though readers are exhorted to experience it as Christians. The acceptance of a slave as a real brother in the Lord had already been suggested in the letter to Philemon, though it took eighteen centuries for many Christians to see the point. We must always remember that the Lord will not distinguish between the social status of people at the judgement.

Thursday (6:10-20). *A final call to rally behind the standard of the Lord against the evil powers in the world.* We recall paragraph 37 of the Pastoral Constitution of the Church in the Modern World, 'The whole of man's history has been the story of dour combat with the powers of evil, stretching, so our Lord tells us, from the very dawn of history until the last day'. All the armoury available to the messenger of salvation is to be found in the book of Isaiah. There follows an exhortation to continuing prayerfulness as in 1 Thes 5:17, and the apostle asks for prayer that he may carry out that function so well delineated in Acts of the Apostles 'to proclaim the word with courage'. The end of that book bears a remarkable similarity to this closing passage of Ephesians.

Friday (Phil 1:1-11). *Paul thanks the Philippians by praying for the maturing of their Christian work.* They have shown their partnership with him in the Gospel through their sharing in word and work. He prays that they may persevere in this kind of living. We paraphrase his intercession for them: 'It is my prayer that your love may abound more and more with a profound knowledge of every situation and a moral discrimination so that you may in a fitting manner choose what is excellent'. He prays that they may develop a conscience of always choosing the better, that which is 'more', and thus they will live for the glory of God and ready for the second coming of his Son.

Saturday (1:18-26). *Life is Christ brings good results, while death is the gate-way to eternal joy.* Paul is happy because even while he is in prison Christ is proclaimed. He will be saved by their prayers, and the help of the Spirit. He is faced by the dilemma of a life which may have to continue for the sake of helping the brethren to progress in the faith, or a death which would join him forever to the glorious Christ in heaven. We recall that in the life of St Martin of Tours, the first non-martyr to receive the cult of saint, he continued another twenty years after a death-bed scene following the entreaties of his disciples!

GOSPEL READINGS (Luke)

Luke 13:10–14:11. The healing of the woman who was bent double gives rise to a controversy; the point at issue is the old one—the Sabbath was made for man, not vice-versa. Making religious institutions absolute takes away from the true spirit. The kingdom of God, in reality, is humble and has room for everyone. The hardness of the human heart is a great mystery and Jesus fought all the way with it. In the kingdom, there will be a great reversal: those who should have known better may find themselves excluded. Jesus is conscious that the way he is going will lead to his death; but this is the role and fate of the prophet of God. So, he returns to the attack to persuade the religious leaders of their hypocrisy. To seek to exalt ourselves leads untimately to disaster: God will resist the proud.

Monday (13:10-17). *The healing of a woman.*
Tuesday (13:18-21). *The mustard seed.*
Wednesday (13:22-30). *The kingdom of God for all.*
Thursday (13:31-35). *The end of Jesus' journey.*
Friday (14:1-6). *Controversy with the Pharisees (1).*
Saturday (14:7-11). *Controversy with the Pharisees (2).*

The whole of this week centres around one basic theme: sincerity and humility as the hallmark of the true child of God our Father. The fact that there are those who are ready to criticise Jesus for healing on the Sabbath *(Monday)* may seem somewhat extreme; yet, when we analyse many of our own reactions, we may find that we are doing exactly the same thing. The vision of the kingdom of God as the mustard seed may run contrary to our own vision *(Tuesday)* but Jesus speaks with authority; this is, in fact, how it is. It points to the necessity of recognising the kingdom where it is, in people and in events. There is something of the security and righteousness of the Pharisees in the Church too *(Wednesday)*; the sense of 'belonging' is a great comfort. Yet, we have to be ready to seek for the signs of the kingdom in the unlikeliest places. If we do not, then we may find ourselves excluded, even though we were the ones who ate and drank in the company of the Lord. The Lukan theme of perseverance appears again: this time in relation to Jesus himself *(Thursday)*: he must go on and attain his end. All of this is in fulfilment of the will of the Father; if we are to follow Jesus on his journey, then we can rest assured that our end will be like his. The direct question put to the people who were at table with Jesus *(Friday)* really puts them on the spot, because it challenges them to examine their basic attitudes. This is what the Gospel does for us, too; it may well be that we can find no answer either. The situation which finds Jesus at table is by this time familiar; he uses all of these occasions to shed the clear light of revelation on human behaviour and attitudes *(Saturday)*. The jostling for position which he witnesses leads to the point with which the whole section started—in the kingdom of God human values are turned upside down; humility is the key to advancement in God's eyes.

THIRTY-FIRST WEEK OF THE YEAR

FIRST READING, Year 1 (Romans)

Monday (11:29-36). *God wants all mankind to be saved.* God never takes back his gifts or revokes his choice; so the Jews are not rejected. First the gentiles strayed, now the Jews—but only that God might have mercy on all mankind—Jew and gentile alike. Paul then ends this section of the letter with a hymn to God's wisdom: 'O the depth of the riches and wisdom and knowledge of God!' (11:33).

Tuesday (12:5-16). *We are all members of Christ.* These final chapters of Romans (vv. 12-16) are an exhortation to the Christian community to live a truly Christian life. They are developed around the basic Christian precept of charity—to love one another. We are all members of the one body of Christ, and so should love each other.

Wednesday (13:8-10). *Love fulfils the Law.* Paul here underlines the fact that the Law is fulfilled by love of one's neighbour. This is the explanation of his earlier statements—'we uphold the Law' (3:31), and 'that the just requirements of the Law might be fulfilled in us' (8:4). It is precisely by love that this is achieved. All the commandments are fulfilled in this one (as indeed Christ had said in the gospels).

Thursday (14:7-12). *We all belong to the Lord.* In this chapter he deals with some moral problems concerning fraternal love. We must not give scandal to one another; the strong must have consideration for the weak, and even sacrifice their own rights for them: 'Do not let what you eat cause the ruin of one for whom Christ died.' For the kingdom of God does not consist in these things, but in peace and joy in the Holy Spirit (cf. 5:1-5). It is the Spirit who fulfils in us the precept of love (5:5; 8:4).

Friday (15:14-21). *Apostle of the gentiles.* Finally, Paul speaks of his own personal ministry—a ministry to the gentiles scattered throughout Greece and Asia Minor, a ministry wrought through the power of the Holy Spirit. Not that Paul did not preach to the Jews; we know from Acts that he invariably addressed them first. But it was his destiny always to be rejected by them, thus becoming by circumstances as well as by vocation the apostle of the gentiles. (Cf. Gal 2:7).

Saturday (16:3-9, 16, 22-27). *Greetings in Christ.* And so with his greetings to his friends in Rome still ringing out, Paul ends his great letter to the Romans. There is probably no more beautiful piece of writing in the Scriptures; majestic in design, grand in its sweep of history, it is filled with the apostle's love and enthusiasm for Christ and his message—and his untiring zeal for the salvation of mankind.

FIRST READINGS, Year 2 (Philippians)

Monday (Phil 2:1-4). *In the midst of factions, Paul encourages them towards unity, always looking towards the interests of others.* Paul outlines for them reasons why they should try to be at one. They live together in Christ; they have experienced the Father's love; theirs is a community of the Holy Spirit; they have a sympathy for his pleas. If they are humble people i.e. open to the Spirit, then selfishness disappears, and a regard for the rights of others appears.

Tuesday (2:5-11). *The humility of Christ who was obedient even unto death, and so has been exalted over all other beings.* Jesus is not just an exemplar. We live in him, and so this has implications for our behaviour. His type of life was one of giving up all the dignity due to his divine sphere, and being born like any other man. He experienced human suffering even to the death of a slave, obedient to the saving plan of his Father. So he has been exalted, and we acclaim him as Lord, and all of this redounds to the glory of the Father, who initiates the whole work of salvation.

Wednesday (2:12-18). *Paul asks the Philippians to follow the way of God, who works in them, with reverential obedience.* The fear and trembling really means an openness to the will of God, our Creator, who 'energises' us. They will be as a light before the 'deceitful and underhand brood' of Deut 32:5, offering them the word of life. This would give great hope for the future life to Paul after all his labours, and even if his blood has to be shed would give both the Philippians and himself a cause for rejoicing.

Thursday (3:3-8). *Paul describes the honours which he has given up himself for the supreme advantage of knowing Christ Jesus.* Those who are united in the Spirit of Jesus Christ have no need of Jewish circumcision. He gave up his excellent Jewish 'qualifications' as so much rubbish because of his faith in Christ. Here we should read the next eight verses not in our daily lectionary. They describe the Christian share in the sufferings of Christ which leads to our hope in the resurrection of the dead. Such a life is a process towards perfection. It is like a race for a winning-post, the prize being our eternal possession of the risen Christ.

Friday (3:17—4:1). *Paul exhorts his brethren to follow his heavenly way of life, rather than that of worldly people, and thus ensure their transfiguration.* The apostle does not hesitate to propose himself (as any

Christian should) as a sign of belief in a heavenly homeland. His way of life is contrary to Jewish formal observances (in diet and in circumcision) and also any manner of living which places earthly things first. The Lord Jesus our Saviour will transform those who follow him and remain faithful, when he comes again.

Saturday (4:10-19). *Paul declares his ability to cope with the 'ups and downs' of life because of Christ who strengthens him.* This passage follows the beautiful section in which the apostle stresses the fact of Christian joy 'the echo of God's life in us', achieved through a carrying out of all that is truly human. We recall St Irenaeus, 'the glory of God is man fully alive'. Again he refers to their 'sharing' but declares his own ability, because of Christ's help, to be content with whatever comes his way. The Philippians will be rewarded by the ever generous God for their continuing sacrifice in help sent to himself.

GOSPEL READINGS (Luke)

Luke 14:12–16:15. The situation at table is again the starting point: this time Jesus opens up the subject of care and concern for the poor. The real return that comes from God is much more worthy of our efforts than anything we can gain here. The kingdom of God is like such a meal: only those to whom the invitation is sent must be ready to accept. The total demand made by Jesus comes across forcefully: we must give up everything to follow him. At the very centre of Luke's gospel stands the clear message of the love and forgiveness of the Father. The danger of riches and money is again brought to our attention—have it we must; but at the same time, we must make proper use of it. The basic principle is something that goes back to the very beginning of the journey—a sense of priority and a clear perspective.

Monday (14:12-14). *Controversy with the Pharisees (3).*
Tuesday (14:15-24). *The kingdom of God for all.*
Wednesday (14:25-33). *Jesus demands renunciation.*
Thursday (15:1-10). *The mercy of God our Father.*
Friday (16:1-8). *The danger of money (2).*
Saturday (16:9-15). *The danger of money (3).*

The 'social gospel' of Luke reaches its high points in this section. The care and concern of Jesus for the poor and the outcast is reflected in the lesson he teaches that our concern is to be similarly universal

(Monday). Again, the simple situation becomes the means of looking at the nature of the kingdom of God itself *(Tuesday)*. This is how God works with us: he invites all of us to his feast; there are those of us who are too caught up in other things to be bothered. We have to be careful, because if the invitation is refused, then we shall never taste of the feast prepared for us. No doubt in its original setting, this had a great impact on Jesus' hearers who could discern the kingdom passing from Israel to other peoples. The reason why it has been preserved in the gospel is so that the Church will never fall into the same trap. The total demand made by Jesus of those who would follow him *(Wednesday)* is presented with all due clarity; it represents what was set forth at the start of the journey—if we hope to follow Jesus, then we must be clear in our minds what we are taking on. The message of repentance is the centre of the gospel *(Thursday)*: Jesus came above all to teach us the way back to the Father who welcomes us in forgiveness and mercy. The major obstacle to the true following of Jesus, as far as Luke is concerned, is money. Hence the lessons on how to use it *(Friday and Saturday)*. This is one of the most acute problems of the present time when all of us are aware of the injustices and imbalances in our world. The gospel teaches us to be careful; the worst thing we could do is laugh at this. It is far too serious and each Christian community has to sort it out for itself.

THIRTY-SECOND WEEK OF THE YEAR

FIRST READINGS, Year 1 (Wisdom)

INTRODUCTION TO THE BOOK OF WISDOM

The deuterocanonical work known as the Book of Wisdom or the Wisdom of Solomon was written probably in the second century BC. It is generally held to have been composed in Alexandria which had a large Jewish population. As Alexandria was a centre for intellectual activity the purpose of the author was to encourage his co-religionists to remain faithful to their traditional values despite the challenge of Greek scientific and philosophical thought. The author is certainly open to some of the insights of Greek thought, while holding that true wisdom comes from God, is active in creation and history and is the source of all wisdom. His advance over the other wisdom books lies in his acceptance of a personal afterlife at least for the just, a life which is a reward for virtue. The book is clearly divided into three sections, viz.

(1) Chapters 1–5: this section asserts that religious belief and righteous living are necessary for true wisdom and that wise living leads to immortal life with God.

(2) Chapters 6–9: the nature of wisdom.

(3) Chapters 10–19: a sermon in poetic form on God's (i.e. Wisdom's) working on his people, from Adam to the Exodus inclusive.

Monday (Wis 1:1-7). *God is found by the just.* It is the person who lives virtuously who is open to receive God. He is not to be found by the unjust. Wisdom is identified with the Godhead in this passage and enters the soul of the righteous. The author adds that the Spirit of God fills the whole earth. There is therefore only a notional distinction in this passage between God, Wisdom and the Spirit of God.

Tuesday (2:23–3:9). *The just enjoy everlasting happiness.* It was God's will that man should be immortal. Death was brought into the world by the devil. Consequently despite all appearances to the contrary the just who have died are in peace with God. The verses from 'But the souls of the virtuous...' (3:1) are often used at Masses for the Faithful Departed.

Wednesday (6:1-11). *An invitation to strive for wisdom.* The author addresses himself to rulers, a literary device to stress the importance of his subject, viz. the acquiring of wisdom. Today's passage is largely a warning against those who in their folly neglect justice, the observance of the law and God's will.

Thursday (7:22–8:1). *The nature of wisdom.* The climax of the book of Wisdom! The author has gradually risen to this fine description of the characteristics of wisdom. He predicates twenty-one qualities of wisdom, signifying its all-perfect nature. (Twenty-one, a multiple of seven, the complete and perfect number.) He stresses its divine origin, its all pervading power, its reflection of God's goodness. It is superb because God is superb. God loves the man 'who lives with wisdom'.

Friday (13:1-9). *The universe can show God to man.* Creation should have led men to reverence God. Their failure to do so is a result of their lack of wisdom, they are 'naturally stupid'. On the one hand this is understandable as the works of the creator can be taken as the divinity because of their splendour; on the other hand, knowledge acquired as a result of investigating the world ought to have led intelligent man (the Greeks) to acknowledge the author of the universe.

Saturday (18:14-16; 19:6-9). *The word of God delivered his people.* This passage is from the final section of the book of Wisdom. It reinterprets the Exodus in the light of the author's understanding of Wisdom as the word of God. It was God's word which descended on the Egyptians and released Israel from its bondage. God in his wisdom has saved us through Jesus, his word.

FIRST READINGS, Year 2 (Titus, Philemon, 2 & 3 John)

For an Introduction to the Pastoral Letters, including Titus, confer above Week 9, Year 2, pp. 118-119.

Monday (Tit 1:1-9). *The bishop's character and task.* After an elaborate introduction upon the connection between apostolate and Christian faith and hope, Paul states his reason for leaving Titus on Crete as his delegate: namely, to organise the church on that large island, correcting moral abuses and appointing suitable ministers in each village. It is unclear whether the 'presbyters' (vv. 5f) are identical with the 'episkopos' (vv. 7ff); possibly the bishop was already a definite individual selected from among the local presbyterate. At any rate, he is required to be a man of blameless character, upright, temperate and hospitable. That his primary task was to instruct the Christian community in right doctrine is indicated by verse 9; this task naturally included as its corollary the refutation of whatever contradicted the Christian message.

Tuesday (2:1-8, 11-14). *Applying principles to people, while we await the Lord's return.* Paul here gives a practical example of pastoral instruction. Each group of people in the community requires a special application of the principles of Christian living. Thus he outlines in turn what most needs to be said to various categories: elderly men and women, young wives, youths. (Our text omits v. 9, a special message for slaves.) The underlying spirit common to these instructions is one of steadiness and responsibility. By teaching, and by personal example, Titus must try to uphold the good reputation of the Christian community. Life in the present moment is lived between two great moments established by God: the first and second comings of Jesus Christ. His first coming rendered visible God's plan for our salvation; his return will bring this plan to fulfilment. Our lives in the meantime must be lived in accordance with his teaching (hence, 'sober, upright and godly'), so as to become what he planned to make us, 'a people of his own, zealous for good deeds'. As it stands, verse 13 offers the clearest affirmation of our Lord's divinity to be found in the whole New Testament.

Wednesday (3:1-7). *A people purified and regenerated.* Still on the theme of edification, based on profound theological faith: submission to authorities, honest work, gentleness and courtesy must spring from the inner reality of Christian re-birth. From sharing in the general corruption and vice of the heathen world, the believers have now been lifted and transformed by God's grace—poured out through Christ, and applied to each individual at baptism. While emphasising the utter freedom of this gift, Paul insists that it must express itself in a renewal of conduct. Only thus is our 'regeneration' completed, and we become 'heirs in hope of eternal life'.

Thursday (Philemon 7-20). *Philemon's Problem.* This is the daily dilemma of the Christian, says the modern book called *Philemon's Problem*. It is the demanding vision of the relentless love of a Father. It is a gospel which gives no rest but offers peace. It is the memory of crucifixion and the vision of resurrection which summon him beyond what is merely just and legal, beyond its plans, desires and struggles to be a virtuous man, to possibilities of love that stretch endlessly on.

This is Paul's smallest letter, written about 60 AD from Paul's prison in Rome to Philemon a well-to-do Christian who lived at Colossae in Asia Minor (Col 4:9). One of his slaves, Onesimus had evidently stolen from his owner, run away and ended up in the same jail as Paul who converted him to Christianity. We see Paul's sense of humour as he sends Onesimus back. Onesimus has become true to his name (i.e. useful) whereas he was useless before. Paul, it is interesting to note, does not order Philemon and demand freedom for Onesimus or attack directly the practice of slavery or the idea of punishment for runaway slaves. Paul *asks* Philemon to receive him back as a beloved brother as he would receive Paul himself. The approach of the early Christians was to create such relations of brotherhood in Christ that there would no longer be 'slave and free'. (See *Philemon's Problem*, Chicago:Acta Foundation, 1973. W. Barclay, *The Daily Study Bible.*)

Friday (2 John 4-9). *The commandment of mutual love.* This short note, whose literary characteristics make it highly probable that it was written by the same hand which produced 1 John and the fourth gospel, is addressed to an unknown community, styled as 'the Elect lady' (v. 1). It is both an encouragement to the faithful to persevere in love and a warning against error. Like Jude and the author of 2 Peter, the 'Elder' v. 1) insists that his readers should walk in the 'truth' (v. 4) and warns them against the danger of error (vv. 7-10). But he also explains that the 'truth' in question is not abstract doctrine but the concrete truth of 'love' (vv. 5-6). Moreover, he suggests that there is a connection between the 'doctrine' of Christ (v. 9) and mutal love (v. 5). In fact the 'incarnation' (v. 7) is not just an important 'truth' or 'doctrine' in itself, a fact to which the believer assents with his mind. It is a revelation for all men, having profound implications for their conduct. If the 'truth' is that Jesus Christ, the Father's Son, has come in the 'flesh', that is, among men, it follows that he is now met among men. Thus to 'abide in the doctrine of Christ' means to follow God's commandment, that is, his will which he has revealed in Christ. This commandment is, quite simply, to 'love one another' (v. 5; cf. Jn 13:34). Just as God has shown his fellowship with men by loving them in Christ, so men show their fellowship with God—are really his children—in their love for one another.

Friday (3 John 5-8). *Participation in the Church's mission.* The 'Elder' commends Gaius—this letter is the only 'occasional' Johannine letter, sharing with the Pastoral letters of Paul the distinction of being addressed to an individual, Gaius who is probably the leader of a community— for the hospitality he has shown towards certain visiting 'brethren'. This hospitality is an expression of his love, which is the Christian hallmark. It would appear that these 'brethren' are missionaries who have left their homes (v. 7). From this particular case of hospitality, the 'Elder' draws a lesson which is important for all Christians. It is by the support of such men that we become 'fellow workers in the truth' . In other words, loving hospitality given to missionaries (whose role it is to communicate the 'truth') is sharing in their mission. Since, according to John, 'truth' is the revelation of love, effective love within the community must be a communication of truth.

Although not all members of the Church are called to be missionaries, in the specific sense of this term, all are called to love and to support materially and spiritually those who do leave their homes in order to witness to the truth. Providing the material means necessary for the mission is not only to make the mission possible. It is also an actual participation in the mission itself.

GOSPEL READINGS (Luke)

Luke 17:1–18:8. With a stern note of warning, the gospel spells out the message that our treatment of each other has to be like our Father's: tolerant and forgiving. There is nothing out of the ordinary in this: it will be the normal pattern of life for those who belong to the kingdom. This is what it means to be a follower of Jesus. The virtue of gratitude and faith is highlighted, is underlined in the case of the Samaritan leper; the follower of Jesus must manifest the same virtue. The signs of the coming of the kingdom of God are a common theme of the discussions between Jesus and the religious leaders: the point is that the kingdom is already present in him and his words. This leads to the discussion of the great trial which will precede the establishment of the kingdom in the revelation of the Son of Man. So, once again, Luke is able to develop his theme of perseverance; significantly, however, he ends with a question—will the Son of Man find faith?

Monday (17:1-6). *Mutual forgiveness.*
Tuesday (17:7-10). *Doing our duty as servants.*
Wednesday (17:11-19). *The ten lepers.*
Thursday (17:20-25). *The kingdom of God among us.*
Friday (17:26-37). *The Day of the Son of Man.*
Saturday (18:1-8). *Perseverance in prayer.*

The tone of the readings during this week becomes distinctly affected with the spirit of crisis; they are the forerunners of the eschatological teaching which Jesus delivered in the Holy City itself. The eye is caught by those strong phrases which refer to the life of the community in Luke's vision *(Monday)*. Scandal, forgiveness, the necessity of faith—in the space of one short passage we are confronted with three basic areas of concern to the disciple of Jesus. The lesson of the servants *(Tuesday)* in many respects is the most important one to learn—there is nothing special in our service; this is what we have to do, precisely because we are servants. The gospel of the poor and the outcast gives expression to the lesson of thankfulness and faith in the person of the leper who was a Samaritan *(Wednesday)*. The assurance of Jesus that his faith had saved him is the point at issue—faith is possible for everyone. The sequence of three readings from that point onwards *(Thursday, Friday, Saturday)* is concerned with the coming of the kingdom of God. Jesus is at pains to point out that the important element is the recognition of the kingdom already present in himself. Faith is what is required in the

time when we await the revelation of God's Son and the definitive establishment of his kingdom—but will there be faith? Will it survive? That
is the question Luke poses to the Church, just as Jesus posed it to his
disciples.

THIRTY-THIRD WEEK OF THE YEAR

FIRST READINGS, Year 1 (1 & 2 Maccabees)

Monday (1 Mac 1:10-15, 41-43, 54-57, 62-64). *Persecution of God's
people breaks out. The temple is profaned.* The book of Daniel, now
known to be written about 165 BC during the persecution of king
Antiochus Epiphanes, is to be read next week, during Week 34. In order
to set this book in its historical context, during the present week we
have select readings from the two books of Maccabees on the persecution itself and on the end of the persecutor Antiochus. Times were not
prosperous for the Jews during the Persian period, but they lived in
harmony with the Persian rulers who respected their religious customs.
Since 397 BC or possibly 458, Jewish life was governed by the Mosaic
law (see above, Thursday, Week 26, Year 1, p. 221). Palestine came
under Greek rule in 333 and had been ruled by the Ptolomies of Egypt
until 198 when control passed to the Seleucids of Syria under Antiochus
III who reaffirmed Jewish rights and the role of the Torah. Matters
changed when Antiochus IV Epiphanes (175-163) seized the Seleucid
throne. A hellenising party of priestly families wanted the introduction
of Greek ways alien to Jewish customs. Antiochus IV favoured this and
abolished the rule of the Torah. In December 167 he desecrated the
temple of Jerusalem and erected there a statue of the pagan god Zeus
Olympus. Systematic persecution followed. Some time afterwards
Jewish resistance to Antiochus was led on to open revolt by Mathathias
of Modein (of the priestly family of Hasman), father of the Maccabees.
After his death, the mass of the population rallied to his son Judas
Maccabee, who conquered Jerusalem in 164, purified and rededicated
the temple in December of that year. The feast of Dedication (Hanukkah)
mentioned in the New Testament (Jn 10:22) was instituted to com-

memorate the event. Soon afterwards (163) Antiochus IV died in an
expedition to Persia.

Today's reading tells of the beginning of the persecution. The 'abomination of desolation', mentioned by Daniel the prophet (Dan 11:31,
Mt 24:15, Mk 13:14) was the statue of Zeus Olympus. Details of the
persecution are given in 2 Mac 5:22—7:42.

Tuesday (2 Mac 6:18-31). *An old man bravely dies for his faith.* 'An
example of nobility and a record of virtue.' Pork was forbidden by
Jewish law.

Wednesday (2 Mac 7:1, 20-31). *A mother and her seven sons bravely
give their lives for their faith.* Belief in the bodily resurrection of the
just on the last day, then becoming common (cf. Dan 12:1-3), sustained
the mother's faith. An example of woman's strong faith in God who
created and sustains all things.

Thursday (1 Mac 2:15-29). *The Maccabean revolt breaks out.* See Introduction, Monday above. For the zeal of Phinehas against Zimri, see
Num 25:6-15.

Friday (1 Mac 4:36-37, 52-59). *The solemn rededication of the altar
that had been desecrated.* See Introduction, Monday above.

Saturday (1 Mac 6:1-13). *God's judgement on Antiochus the persecutor.*
The 'flood' which engulfed the king was the overwhelming of the wrath
of God.

FIRST READINGS, Year 2 (Apocalypse)

INTRODUCTION TO THE APOCALYPSE

The Apocalypse of John was written to help Christians faced with
persecution. These were handfuls of Christians in Asia Minor faced with
the might of Rome. It must have seemed to them that the world was
definitely overcoming them. In a way, the book admits as much: it
accepts that they will suffer. But it does confidently assure them that,
if they are faithful to Christ, they will share his victory. It insists that
he has indeed won the victory as he had claimed—but through suffering
and death.

The book conveys a sense of the weight pressing down on the faith
of the first-century Christian. Christ had delivered the world but the
world refused to be delivered by Christ. These Christians experienced an
almost unsurmountable contradiction between the truth of their faith

and their own daily experience. The felt the very *absence* of Jesus. John wants to show that the Jesus whom they may feel is absent is very near to his followers—even while they pass through many tribulations. They need the assurance that their response to a 'call for the endurance and faith of the saints' (Ap 14:12) will bring them a share in his resurrection after they have endured to the point of death. They need to be assured that evil can never ultimately prevail.

Monday (Ap 1:1-4; 2:1-5). *'You have abandoned the love you had at first.'* The greeting which opens the book already shows its special character and how it should be read: it is in the genre of apocalyptic literature. Chapters 2—3, however, (the letters to the seven churches) are presented as prophetic messages: through his prophet, Christ, the supreme pastor, addresses the churches in turn. Ephesus, capital of the Roman province of Asia, has pride of place. The praiseworthy works of this church are its 'toil' in resisting and overcoming false teachers and its 'patient endurance' for the sake of Christ. But orthodoxy was preserved at a price: their love had waned. Inquisitorial zeal will claim its victims.

Tuesday (3:1-6, 14-22). *'I stand at the door and knock.'* These two letters make wide use of topical references. Sardis had by then shrunk to a shadow of its former glory; and it had twice been captured by stealth. John suggests that its Christianity has fallen away from its former eagerness; and warns that it may be taken unawares by the second coming of Christ. Laodicea, under Roman rule, had become a centre of commercial activity. Yet, its Christians are 'poor, blind, and naked'—ironic allusions to the banking-business, eye-ointment and clothing industry of the city, objects of its complacency. They are 'neither cold nor hot': like the water, lukewarm when it reached the town, from adjacent hot springs. The letter concludes with a reference to the Eucharist, where Christ pressingly invites all his faithful to fellowship with himself.

Wednesday (4:1-11). *Holy is the Lord God Almighty who was, and is, and is to come.* The apocalyptic part of the book opens with a vision of God: the 'one seated on the throne'. The 'twenty-four elders' are, most likely, the saints of the Old Testament. The 'four living creatures' are the angels responsible for directing the physical world (their identification with the four evangelists is wholly fanciful).

Thursday (5:1-10). *The root of David has conquered.* Reference is to the death and resurrection of Christ: he, the Lamb, was slain, but is up-right and standing because he has risen from the dead. 'Horn', in the Old Testament, is a symbol of power; the number seven means fulness—therefore fulness of power. The seven eyes stand for fulness of know-ledge, and for the fulness of the Spirit which he gives. The 'sealed scroll' is, likely, Old Testament warnings against unfaithful Israel. The point that only the Lamb can break the seal fits in very well with the early Christian view that only Christ can give its full meaning to the Old Testament.

Friday (10:8-11). *A new prophetic investiture.* A not unreasonable interpretation of the Apocalypse presents the author as from chapter 12 concerned with the Church and pagan Rome, while in chapters 4–11 he is preoccupied with the Church's relation to the chosen people. The verse 10:11 marks a fresh prophetic investiture: John must 'again' prophesy and this time about 'many peoples and nations and tongues and kings'. Significantly, the magnificent angel of chapter 10 stands on sea and land, because his message is for all mankind. This message is bitter-sweet (cf. Ezek 3:1-3): sweet because it proclaims the triumph of the Church; bitter because it must include the sufferings of Christians.

Saturday (11:4-12). *The new Israel bears witness to the old.* The two witnesses are modelled on Elijah (power to bring about drought: v. 6) and Moses (power to turn water into blood and to smite the earth with many plagues: v. 6). It appears that the witnesses are the incarnation of the testimony—from the Law and the Prophets—which the Church bears to Christ in the Jewish world. The survivors 'give glory to God': this typically Jewish expression signifies the conversion of Israel at the end of the 'times of the gentiles'.

GOSPEL READINGS (Luke)

Luke 18:35–20:40. The healing of the blind man near Jericho gives us a further insight into the nature of Jesus' work—to give sight to the blind, not just in the physical sense, but spiritually as well. Zacchaeus was outcast and despised, and yet out of the whole crowd, it was him Jesus chose, for he recognises in this man the true humble faith he seeks. The putting off of the manifestation of the kingdom is a hard lesson for people to learn; Jesus explains it patiently but also forcefully. As he weeps over Jerusalem, Jesus' emotion is a genuine expression of sorrow that he has not been recognised. Going into the temple, he tackles those who have deformed the true spirit of prayer and worship which ought to pervade the people of God. The dispute concerning the resurrection started as an argument between two parties, Sadducees and Pharisees, and ended with an authoritative statement from Jesus on the nature of God.

Monday (18:35-43). *The blind man of Jericho.*
Tuesday (19:1-10). *Zacchaeus.*
Wednesday (19:11-28). *Stewards of God's gifts.*
Thursday (19:41-44). *Jerusalem's fate.*
Friday (19:45-48). *The clearing of the temple.*
Saturday (20:27-40). *Controversy with the Sadducees.*

The recognition of Jesus by the blind man at the gates of Jericho *(Monday)* is an important aspect of Luke's story: he consistently calls the Lord 'Son of David'. This is a fulfilment of the image of Jesus that Luke presents at the outset of the public ministry: the Spirit is upon him, and so his task is to give sight to the blind. But, those who are even witnesses of the event are caught up in something that goes far beyond their expectations; in the same way, we have to have the eyes of faith to see behind what is happening to what is really taking place. The story of Zacchaeus sums up what Luke's gospel is about; this man has manifested the faith and repentance that Jesus is looking for. This is the only criterion for entry into the kingdom. Those who say that Jesus has gone to a 'sinner's house' have missed the point *(Tuesday)*. The parable of the kingdom's delay is a warning *(Wednesday)*; the servants are expected to make the most of what their master has given them. We are expected to make the most of what God has given us in Christ. The fact that so many people have failed to recognise what Jesus is really saying *(Thursday)* comes to a head when he looks upon the Holy City itself. The city has not recognised the opportunity given it by God; again, there is a message there for the Church and for the Christian. God is again and again providing us with such opportunities. The somewhat vehement reaction of our Lord in the temple is understandable; the behaviour of those who had turned the place into a robbers' den had deformed the spirit of true religion so much that there was no other reaction possible *(Friday)*. While those who had been attacked resisted, the people listened. The famous case of the woman with seven husbands *(Saturday)* was supposed to be unaswerable; Jesus takes the discussion onto another plane altogether, because he can speak with authority. Not only does he answer the problem of the Sadducees, he reveals the true nature of the resurrection.

THIRTY-FOURTH WEEK OF THE YEAR

FIRST READINGS, Year 1 (Daniel)

Monday (Dan 1:1-6, 8-20). *Fidelity to God's law is rewarded.* This week we have a series of readings from the book of Daniel. As noted already, this book was written about 165 BC during the persecution of Antiochus (see Monday, Week 33). The purpose of the work was to give encouragement to the faithful Jews suffering for their faith and to remind them that the persecution would not succeed; Antiochus' fate was already predetermined by God; God protects those faithful to him. Naturally, the tyrant is not mentioned by name. To make his point, the author takes up some old Jewish traditions from the period of the exile and slightly recasts them. The message of these stories is that God's providence towards his people is very real indeed. In the second part (chapters 7–12; chs 13–14 are not in the Hebrew text) the author adopts another device; that of Apocalyptic in which he recounts past and contemporary history as if it were the future revealed long since in vision. Each of these chapters ends with detailed but veiled references to Antiochus Epiphanes' persecution and carries the clear message that defeat by God was imminent. After the end of the persecution a new reign of God would be introduced. Not being a historical account the articifical framework of four kingdoms (not precisely historical) and other historical inaccuracies should not surprise us. See further 'Daniel' in NCCHS.

In today's reading the stage is set. Daniel and his companions are taken into exile, remain faithful to the Jewish dietary laws, complete their period of training and are found to be more learned than their fellow students. The opening verses speaking of a siege of Jerusalem in the third year of Jehoiakim (606 BC) is most probably inaccurate. The siege in question took place in 597, the first year (or the beginning of the reign) of king Jehoiachin, Jehoiakim's successor (cf. 2 Kings 24:10-16). The same error is found in 2 Chron 36:5-7.

Tuesday (2:31-45). *God will set up a kingdom which shall never be destroyed; it will absorb all kingdoms.* The same message is given in another form in chapter 7 (read Friday, Saturday). The four kingdoms, represented by the four metals in descending order of value, were Babylong (represented by Nebuchadnezzar), Media, Persia and Greece (represented in the author's day by the detested Antiochus). The harsh character of this kingdom is stressed. These four kingdoms are really a symbol of all earthly power. The fifth kingdom, introduced directly by God himself, is the universal kingdom of God, a kingdom destined to embrace all nations. We have here a clear preparation of the kingdom of heaven proclaimed by Christ.

Wednesday (5:1-6, 13-14, 16-17, 23-28). *The kingdom of Babylon is given to the Medes and Persians.* This well-known passage is based on legend, not history. Nebuchadnezzar of the text is the Nabonidus of history, the last monarch of the Babylonian kingdom. Nabonidus' son Belshazzar was crown-prince, not king, although he ruled Babylon while his father withdrew into the desert oasis of Taima. Babylon opened its gates peacefully to Cyrus, king of Persia in 539. Cyrus had previously conquered Persia. The message of the passage is that God punishes the desecration of the vessels of his temple in Jerusalem. Antiochus, let us recall, had perpetrated a similar offence just before the book of Daniel was published.

Thursday (6:12-28). *Daniel is saved from the lions' den.* A further example of divine protection.

Friday (7:2-14). *Eternal sovereignty is conferred on one like a son of man.* The message is similar to that of chapter 2 (read Tuesday). The four beasts (in descending order of ferocity) represent four kingdoms: Babylon, Media, Persia and Greece. The fourth beast, to which the author pays particular attention, was Greece. The ten horns of this kingdom were ten kings which cannot be identified with certainty. The little horn is the upstart and blasphemous Antiochus Epiphanes who was then persecuting the Jews. He ousted others to seize the throne. The great sea from which the beast emerged is a symbol of the forces withstanding God. The kingdom of God comes from heaven. The 'one like a son of man' is a symbol for the faithful Jews, 'the saints of the most high' who will inherit the kingdom. In the New Testament the Son of Man is Jesus who will receive all power from the Father and inaugurate the kingdom of God on earth.

Saturday (7:15-27). *The kingdom of God will be given to the holy ones of the Most High.* The vision is explained. The powers opposing God will be destroyed and the eternal kingdom of God given to his faithful one. The author expected the prophecy to be fulfilled after the downfall of Antiochus. Christians know that it was fulfilled partially in the death and resurrection of Christ, whose work will be completed at the end of time when Christ returns and hands his kingdom over to the Father.

FIRST READINGS, Year 2 (Apocalypse)

Monday (Ap 14:1-5). *The elect bear the name of Christ and the Father.* The Lamb and his followers stand in sharp contrast to the beast and his followers (ch. 13). The 144,000, who bear on their foreheads the name of the Lamb and his Father, are the faithful remnant of the new Israel —the martyrs. The designation 'virgins' should be understood metaphorically. The 144,000 are contrasted with the followers of the beast precisely because they have not adored the beast but have remained faithful to the Lamb—they have remained virgins because they have not given themselves to the idolatrous cult of the beast.

Tuesday (14:14-19). *'Now is the judgment of this world.'* This vision of harvest and vintage is based on Joel 3:13—the extermination of the pagan nations. It is a vision of retribution: God's judgment on the evil and unredeemed element in the world.

Wednesday (15:1-4). *'All nations shall come and worship thee.'* The seven plagues (or bowls) are explicitly called 'the last', thus marking them off from the previous two series (of seals and trumpets); they are the last because 'with them the wrath of God is ended'. Unlike the original song of Moses (Ex 15:1) the marytrs' song is not one of triumph over their enemies—while it does praise God for their victory. The song holds out hope that the nations, in view of the righteous deeds of the Lord, will fear him and render him homage and worship.

Thursday (18:1-2, 21-23; 19:1-3, 9). *The victory of God.* The historical background of the Apocalypse from chapter 12 onwards is the persecution of the Church by Rome, and the precise occasion of the persecution is the Church's refusal to countenance Caesar-worship. For the first readers of the book this description of the destruction of Rome would be a guarantee of eventual triumph. This reading is a reminder that every achievement of human greatness is provisional and is marked by its own contingency or non-necessity.

Friday (20:1-4; 11-21:2). *The triumph of the martyrs.* Throughout the book John has showed his preoccupation with the fate of the martyrs— understandable in a persecution situation. He insists that they are in blessedness with the Lord. It would seem that his 'reign of a thousand years' fits into the same pattern: it signifies the reign of the martyrs with Christ, who has won the final victory for them. The conquest of all the powers hostile to God is followed by the general resurrection of the dead and the last judgment. The final part of the Apocalypse opens with the vision of a new heaven and a new earth, the setting of the new Jerusalem.

Saturday (22:1-7). *Night shall be no more: for the light of God will be the light of the saints.* In the new Jerusalem there is no temple, nor any need of one: God himself dwells there, and the Lamb (21:22). The association of God and Lamb, noted elsewhere, is here expressed more forcefully—it is the mystery of the equality and onenes of Father and Lamb.

GOSPEL READINGS (Luke)

Luke 21:1–36. The gospel of the poor manifests itself again in the story of the poor widow, whose contribution is valued more than anything else. The temple is the scene of Jesus' activity, and yet it must soon come to an end; there is a new way of God's presence. However, there will be a great travail before God's kingdom is able to establish itself. For the disciples of Christ, there will be real persecution; but there will also be for them the care and protection of God their Father. The signs of the coming trial are expressed with great clarity and colour. But the point is that the Father will see us through it all. The value of the word of Jesus is that it is true, and because it is true it is lasting. What he has told us of God is the pattern for our lives. The last note in the gospel is a note of warning: to be prepared and ready for the coming of our master, so that we can stand with confidence at the judgement.

Monday (21:1-4). *The widow's mite.*
Tuesday (21:5-11). *The coming destruction.*
Wednesday (21:12-19). *The coming distress.*
Thursday (21:20-28). *The Day of the Son of Man.*
Friday (21:29-33). *Jesus' words last forever.*
Saturday (21:34-36). *Call to prayer.*

The lesson of the poor widow *(Monday)* is profound; what Jesus recognises in her is the giving of self. What Jesus has been trying to teach his disciples all along the way to Jerusalem is the same kind of self-giving. The theme of the destruction of Jerusalem and the temple is a painful one in the gospels *(Tuesday)*. The first aspect is that it represents the end of many things that Israel regarded as irreplaceable. the second is that it gives rise to the discussion of the coming of the kingdom of God which will be prefaced by trial and upheaval for everyone. Hence, the disciples have to be clear in their minds *(Wednesday)* that they will be hounded and persecuted for the sake of Jesus. Here, the Lukan theme of perseverance reaches its summit—it is through perseverance that the follower of Jesus will emerge victorious. In the midst of the great trial and all the upheavals that have to be faced *(Thursday)* the thought of the coming of the Son of Man emerges as a sign of hope; those who have been faithful can look forward with their heads held high. Liberation, the freedom that Jesus set out to bring to the captives, is dearly won; the gospel's challenge is for us to ask ourselves whether we really want it badly enough. Hence, the conclusion that when all of this happens *(Friday)* we will know that the kingdom of God is in process of establishing itself. The gospel sequence ends with a clear directive to all of us: to stay awake *(Saturday)*. Luke, however, has spelt out what this means in detail—praying at all times for strength to survive and to stand with confidence. The Gospel is our way to that confidence. Luke has left us with a complete guide to the Christian life, where the accent falls on the important things; at no point has he cut corners or minced his words. We should be grateful for that alone.

ARRANGEMENT FOR FIRST READINGS
FOR THE WEEKDAYS OF THE YEAR

Week	Year 1	Year 2
1	Hebrews	1 Samuel
2	Hebrews	1 Samuel
3	Hebrews	2 Samuel
4	Hebrews	2 Samuel, 1 Kings 1–16
5	Genesis 1–11	1 Kings 1–16
6	Genesis 1–11	James
7	Ecclesiasticus	James
8	Ecclesiasticus	1 Peter, Jude
9	Tobit	2 Peter, 2 Timothy
10	2 Corinthians	1 Kings 17–22
11	2 Corinthians	1 Kings 17–22, 2 Kings
12	Genesis 12–50	2 Kings, Lamentations
13	Genesis 12–50	Amos
14	Genesis 12–50	Hosea, Isaiah
15	Exodus	Isaiah, Micah
16	Exodus	Micah, Jeremiah
17	Exodus, Leviticus	Jeremiah
18	Numbers, Deuteronomy	Jeremiah, Nahum, Habakkuk
19	Deuteronomy, Joshua	Ezekiel
20	Judges, Ruth	Ezekiel
21	1 Thessalonians	2 Thessalonians, 1 Corinthians
22	1 Thessalonians, Colossians	1 Corinthians
23	Colossians, 1 Timothy	1 Corinthians
24	1 Timothy	1 Corinthians
25	Ezra, Haggai, Zechariah	Proverbs, Ecclesiastes
26	Zech., Nehemiah, Baruch	Job
27	Jonah, Malachy, Joel	Galatians
28	Romans	Galatians, Ephesians
29	Romans	Ephesians
30	Romans	Ephesians
31	Romans	Ephesians, Philippians
32	Wisdom	Titus, Philemon, 2 & 3 John
33	1 & 2 Maccabees	Apocalypse
34	Daniel	Apocalypse

CONTRIBUTORS

Martin Brennan teaches scripture at St Kieran's College, Kilkenney.

Charles Conroy, M.S.C., teaches scripture at the Gregorian University and at the Biblical Institute, Rome.

Jeremiah Creedon, C.S.Sp., who taught scripture in the Holy Ghost Missionary College, Kimmage, Dublin, is now on missionary work in Brazil.

John H. Fitzsimmons teaches scripture at St Peter's College, Cardross, Scotland.

James Foley teaches scripture at St Peter's College, Cardross.

John Greehy teaches scripture at Holy Cross College, Clonliffe, Dublin.

Wilfrid Harrington, O.P., teaches scripture at St Mary's Priory, Tallaght, Co. Dublin, and at the Milltown Institute of Theology and Philosophy, Dublin.

Seán Kealy, C.S.Sp., teaches scripture at Kenyatta University College, Nairobi, Kenya.

Sister Carmel McCarthy, Sister of Mercy, Carysfort Park, Blackrock, Co. Dublin, teaches in the Department of Semitic Languages, University College, Dublin.

Martin McNamara, M.S.C., teaches scripture at the Milltown Insitute of Theology and Philosophy, Dublin.

James McPolin, S.J., teaches scripture at the Milltown Institute of Theology and Philosophy, and lectures in New Testament Greek at University College, Dublin.

Michael Maher, M.S.C., teaches scripture at the Mater Dei Institute, Dublin.

William Maher, C.S.Sp., teaches scripture at St Patrick's College, Maynooth, Co. Kildare.

Edward J. Mally, S.J., who has commented on Mark's Gospel in the *Jerome Biblical Commentary*, resides at Loyola University Medical Center, 2160 South First Avenue, Maywood, Illinois, 60153 U.S.A.

John Quinlan, S.M.A., who has taught scripture at St Patrick's College, Maynooth, is now doing further study in missiology.

Patrick Rogers, C.P., teaches scripture at the Milltown Institute of Theology and Philosophy, Dublin.

Thomas Stone, O.D.C., teaches scripture at the Milltown Institute of Theology and Philosophy, Dublin.

Lionel Swain, 57 Sarratt Avenue, Woodhall Farm, Hemel Hempstead, Herts, England, lectures in scripture at the University of London.

Henry Wansbrough, O.S.B., teaches at Ampleforth Abbey, York England.